# BUILDING BETTER ENGLISH LANGUAGE PROGRAMS

## PERSPECTIVES ON EVALUATION IN ESL
### EDITED BY MARTHA C. PENNINGTON

NAFSA: ASSOCIATION OF INTERNATIONAL EDUCATORS

NAFSA: Association of International Educators is a nonprofit membership association that provides training, information, and other educational services to professionals in the field of international educational exchange. Its 6,500 members—from every state in the United States and more than 50 other countries—make it the largest professional membership association in the world concerned with the advancement of effective international educational exchange. Members represent primarily colleges and universities but also elementary and secondary schools, public and private educational associations, exchange organizations, national and international corporations and foundations, and community organizations. Through its publications, workshops, consultations with institutions, and conferences, the association serves as a source of professional training, a reference for standards of performance, and an advocate for the most effective operation of international educational exchange.

Support for this publication was provided by the Advising, Teaching, and Specialized Programs Divisions of the U.S. Information Agency.

Copies of this publication may be ordered from the Publications Order Desk, NAFSA: Association of International Educators, 1860 19th Street, N.W., Washington, D.C. 20009.

**Library of Congress Cataloging-in-Publication Data**

Building better English language programs : perspectives on evaluation in ESL / edited by Martha C. Pennington.
     p.   cm.
    Includes bibliographical references.
    ISBN 0-912207-57-4
    1. English language—Study and teaching—Foreign speakers—Evaluation. I. Pennington, Martha Carswell. II. National Association for Foreign Student Affairs.
PE1128.A2B77   1991
428'.007—dc20                     90-28560
                                  CIP

# Dedication

*This book is dedicated to all those dedicated ESL administrators who made it the hard way and who built up successful programs using a combination of sweat, savvy, and seat-of-the-pants management.*

# Contents

# Preface

Until recently, the profession of teaching English as a Second Language (ESL) was considered to be exclusively a field for teachers and researchers. In the last decade, however, the field has developed a constituency of individuals who regard themselves as primarily ESL program administrators. Until this decade, the focus of training in ESL has been exclusively on teaching and research, and even today, only a few programs at the M.A. or Ph.D. level have begun to include specialized courses for ESL administrators.

As a result of a lack of attention until now on the administrative aspect of ESL, many program administrators—some of whom administer budgets that run well into the millions and service hundreds or even thousands of students every year—have come to their positions with little or no specialized background or training outside of ESL teaching. Of necessity, these individuals have had to be absolutely dedicated to their goals, creating programs almost from scratch through their own drive and initiative, learning decision making and other necessary skills in the "Trial-and-Error School of Management."

As we seek to raise the degree of professionalism in the ESL field, we should strive to increase the competence not only of the classroom teacher, but also of the administrator who heads an ESL unit, program, or team of faculty at any level—whether that person holds the title of department chair, program director, academic coordinator, teacher supervisor, educational specialist, or professor. One way of increasing the competence of administrators in our field is to provide them with specialized publications that address their job-related concerns.

This volume was developed in response to the expression of a need by members of the ATESL (Administrators and Teachers in English as a Second Language) section of NAFSA: Association of International Educators for a book on program evaluation. In attempting to meet that need, I have drawn on the resources of a wide range of professionals in the field of ESL and designed the book to address a variety of concerns within a broadly conceived notion of ESL program evaluation. The articles incorporate the available sources of theory and published literature in each area, while presenting a practical focus intended for the working administrator. It is hoped that the experience of the authors and the topics selected will provide useful information for a variety of readers who might be looking for practical advice in the different areas that are subsumed here under the comprehensive heading of "evaluation."

The book took approximately a year and a half to produce from the time the "Call for Papers" was issued until the time the manuscript was submitted to NAFSA. This has been a relatively short time in my experience for an edited collection, thanks to the diligence and enthusiasm of the authors, who responded to my (often extensive) editorial suggestions quickly and efficiently. As editor, I have worked hard to try to ensure that the articles will be accessible and enjoyable to read and that they will represent a consistent style and tone. I have also requested that authors provide figures, charts, and appendices to elucidate and extend the text. I enjoyed reading each article myself, and I hope that all of you who take the time to read the book will find something of interest and value in it.

MARTHA C. PENNINGTON
Honolulu, Hawaii
December 1989

# Introduction

*Martha C. Pennington*

This book is intended to provide broad-ranging coverage of the topic of evaluation in the field of English as a Second Language (ESL). Among the concerns addressed are issues of the design of the evaluation system, the conduct of the evaluation process, self-study, the use of computerized records in evaluation, the assessment of curricular concerns as well as the noninstructional aspects of the program, and the evaluation of personnel—in particular, the faculty and the program administrator. The articles are theoretically grounded and include references to published literature that may be of value to those who wish to explore the topics addressed here in greater depth. At the same time, the volume presents a practical focus on the concerns of ESL professionals in the many different aspects of evaluation that are relevant to English language programs. To make the material as useful as possible, authors have included figures and checklists that can be copied or adapted for use in the evaluation process of individual programs.

The collection is divided into four parts, each of which contains three articles. Part One, "Approaches to ESL Program Evaluation," provides general background on program evaluation from three different perspectives. The first of these perspectives (James D. Brown and Martha C. Pennington, "Developing Effective Evaluation Systems for Language Programs") characterizes language program evaluation as a comprehensive, ongoing, and cooperative process of review and change. The second perspective on evaluation (Patricia Byrd and Janet C. Constantinides, "Self-Study and Self-Regulation for ESL Programs: Issues Arising from the Associational Approach") is that of self-regulation through an internally directed evaluation process. From the third perspective (David E. Eskey, Richard Lacy, and Cheryl A. Kraft, "A Novel Approach to ESL Program Evaluation"), evaluation is viewed as a way of promoting the program's effectiveness to an audience outside of ESL.

Part Two, "Evaluating Curriculum Process and Content," begins with an article outlining a systematic curriculum process (Martha C. Pennington and James D. Brown, "Unifying Curriculum Process and Curriculum Outcomes: The Key to Excellence in Language Education") and showing how the process leads to a striving for excellence in a language program. This article is followed by one that examines ESL testing procedures (Louis J. Spaventa and Janis S. Williamson, "Participatory Placement: A Case Study") based on a case study of the evolution of an effective and efficient system for placement testing in one particular program. The final article of this section (Christine Winskowski-Jackson, "Evaluation of Culture Components in ESL Programs") offers a comprehensive system for assessment of the ESL program in its cultural dimensions.

Part Three, "Assessing Noninstructional Aspects of the Program," includes a variety of articles on evaluation of noncurricular, administrative aspects of a language program. The first of these (Geoffrey C. Middlebrook, "Evaluation of Student Services in ESL Programs") presents guidelines for the examination of the student services component of an ESL program. The next article (Roger Ponder and Bill Powell, "Creating and Operating a Statistical Database for Evaluation in an English Language Program") outlines the available resources and procedures for setting up and using a computerized database for ESL program evaluation. The third article in Part Three (Frederick L. Jenks, "Designing and Assessing the Efficacy of ESL Promotional Materials") offers suggestions for evaluating brochures and other types of promotional materials that an ESL program might develop to attract favorable attention and enrollments.

In the final section of the book, Part Four, "Reviewing the Performance of Teachers and Administrators," the focus shifts to the evaluation of personnel in ESL programs. The first article (Martha C. Pennington and Aileen L. Young, "Procedures and Instruments for Faculty Evaluation in ESL") describes approaches to faculty evaluation and provides a number of sample forms for this purpose. The next two articles develop approaches to the evaluation of the ESL program director or administrative head, through assessment by an outside evaluator (Robert P. Fox, "Evaluating the ESL Program Director") or through self-evaluation (Barbara F. Matthies, "Administrative Evaluation in ESL Programs: How'm I Doin'?").

Individually, the 12 articles that comprise this collection present a picture of evaluation in the ESL context as a highly diversified set of administrative functions. Taken together, this group of articles indicates that evaluation must be a continuous activity and a central part of the management of any ESL program. Evaluation in some form or other is at the heart of the design, the implementation, and the revision of every aspect of an ESL program.

As a group, these articles also stand as a collective statement of detailed and comprehensive standards for the products, processes, and personnel associated with ESL programs. This includes not only those that make up the instructional program, but also such noninstructional products as promotional materials, computerized records, and processes such as the many student and administrative services that might be offered by personnel whose specific training may not be in ESL.

Once it is understood how pervasive the topic of evaluation is in relation to an ESL program, it becomes clear that an examination of evaluation such as that provided in the present volume is an excellent general focus for a program's activities. Moreover, a focus on evaluation—and the resultant attention to standards—may help the field of ESL to define its purposes and to evolve its own unique goals and approaches to education.

Evaluation is thus a timely subject for ESL as the field seeks to clarify its status as a profession and to gain credibility with the general public and within academia. It is hoped that the present book will be only the first of many volumes to appear on this very important subject in our field.

# PART ONE
# Approaches to ESL Program Evaluation

DEVELOPING EFFECTIVE EVALUATION SYSTEMS FOR LANGUAGE PROGRAMS
*James D. Brown and Martha C. Pennington*

SELF-STUDY AND SELF-REGULATION FOR ESL PROGRAMS:
ISSUES ARISING FROM THE ASSOCIATIONAL APPROACH
*Patricia Byrd and Janet C. Constantinides*

A NOVEL APPROACH TO PROGRAM EVALUATION
*David E. Eskey, Richard Lacy, and Cheryl A. Kraft*

# 1

# Developing Effective Evaluation Systems for Language Programs

*James D. Brown and Martha C. Pennington*

## Introduction

Richards, Pratt, and Weber (1985, 98) define evaluation as "in general, the systematic gathering of information for purposes of decision making." Within this broad definition, many specific views of evaluation are possible. The ESL (English as a Second Language) literature contains a wide variety of philosophies of language program evaluation highlighting formative and summative approaches, product and process approaches, and quantitative and qualitative approaches (see Bachman 1981; Brown 1989; Long 1984; Nunan 1985; Tucker and Cziko 1978). Additionally, a large number of different types of evaluation procedures are available (e.g., questionnaires, tests, and observational data), and individual researchers have favored certain procedures over others. For some researchers, the focus of evaluation is primarily on measuring learning, frequently with an emphasis on the outcomes of instruction through comparison of pretest and posttest measures (e.g., Beretta and Davies 1985). Or the emphasis may be on the interactional process between teacher and students in the classroom (Long 1984). In other cases, evaluation focuses on assessment of teaching performance through student questionnaires or on the fiscal health of the organization through examination of budgeting and accounting procedures. In our view, an evaluator can benefit by considering the merits of a variety of evaluation procedures, of which more than 20 have been described in the literature.

Given this variety, it is important for administrators to know the options available to them when determining the best mechanisms for evaluation in a particular program. The purpose of this article is to offer

3

an overview of mechanisms for program evaluation relevant to departments or proprietary programs in foreign languages, bilingual education, language arts, and ESL at all levels. A view of evaluation is described that offers a broad array of options. The goal is to provide the evaluator with a range of choices as well as a basis for choosing among the options in a principled manner. The procedures are described and classified in terms that allow the evaluator to gather comprehensive information across six categories without having to use all of the more than 20 available procedures. The language program administrator's role in evaluation, particularly in relation to the faculty, is also examined. Throughout the discussion, we argue for an evaluation process that reaches beyond the program administrator to include faculty, students, and others in development and implementation. The concluding section outlines conditions for conducting program review in an effective and fair manner.

## Redefining Evaluation

In contrast to Richards, Pratt, and Weber (1985, 98), we wish to focus on evaluation as a process of determining the value of the individual aspects of an organization, as a basis for ongoing change and development within that organization. Organizational evaluations take place for a variety of purposes and under a variety of circumstances. Evaluation may occur as a response to internal or external pressures for improvement or change, or the administrator may initiate a change process through evaluation in the absence of any external pressure. As an example of a response to external pressures, a review process may be set into motion by political factors, such as a change in administration or a new legal requirement imposed on a school district. Evaluation is often a response to budgetary pressures—either from inside the organization or from a higher administrative authority. In contrast, evaluation may be self-imposed by an administrator wishing to know how well the organization is achieving its current goals. A thoroughgoing examination of the workings of an organization at a particular time provides valuable information for making cost reductions or routine fiscal decisions as well as for setting organizational goals for the future.

Language program evaluation is not an exact science and requires subjective judgments at many points. It is a multifaceted, long-term process in which many people will be involved. In evaluating the worth or success of a language program, value must be defined relative to the needs and desires of all of the groups who make up or interact with the program. These groups include the administration of the school or other body in which the program is housed; the program's own administration; its faculty; its students; and the parents, sponsors, and external agencies that are concerned with the success of the program and its students. The point of view of each group will vary on three criteria: *academic criteria*, which have to do with the conduct and character of instruction; *administrative criteria*, which encompass the bureaucratic and organizational aspects of the program; and *fiscal criteria*, which relate to budgetary matters. That is, the success of the program will be measured relative to the needs and preferences in these three categories of different groups and individuals (Saltzer 1982). Although there are certain program features (such as an effective testing and placement system, a balanced budget, good working relationships, and student satisfaction) that most language educators would find desirable, each interest group will assign different weights to the academic, administrative, and fiscal aspects of the program's structure and functioning.

## Procedures for Language Program Evaluation

**Evaluation Categories.** In Table 1, the right-hand column contains 24 different procedures (from Brown 1989, 233) for gathering information about the functioning of a program and the needs and wishes of those who have an interest in its success. This array is not as complex as it may at first appear. For instance, although there are four ways to test, each of which is considered a separate procedure in the table, these forms of testing are related and can be considered as one category of evaluation procedure. Through such analysis, the 24 instruments listed in Table 1 are classified into six categories—as shown in the second column—with which program evaluators need to be concerned.

Furthermore, the categories themselves can be grouped according to the role that the evaluator has when applying them. Existing records, tests, and observations are similar in that they put the evaluator in the position of being "an outsider looking in." As a consequence, the evaluator may tend to be more objective, even detached, when using these types of procedures. In contrast, the other three—interviews, meetings, and questionnaires—draw the evaluator into the process of gathering information from the participants within the program. The evaluator becomes involved in the process and so may influence the resulting information. This difference can affect the way in which the procedures and the results based on them will ultimately be viewed by both the target group members and the evaluator. The remainder of this section offers a more detailed discussion of each of these instruments or classes of procedures. This discussion provides a basis for further elaboration of potential interactions between the procedures and the program participants.

## TABLE 1

### CATEGORIES OF PROCEDURES FOR EVALUATION

| Evaluator's Role | Categories | Procedures |
|---|---|---|
| Outsider looking in | Existing records | Records analysis<br>Systems analysis<br>Literature review<br>Letter writing |
| | Tests | Proficiency testing<br>Placement testing<br>Diagnostic testing<br>Achievement testing |
| | Observations | Case studies<br>Diary studies<br>Behavior observation<br>Interactional analyses<br>Inventories |
| Facilitator drawing<br>out information | Interviews | Individual<br>Group |
| | Meetings | Delphi technique<br>Advisory<br>Interest group<br>Review |
| | Questionnaires | Biodata surveys<br>Opinion surveys<br>Self-ratings<br>Judgmental ratings<br>Q sort |

(Brown 1989)

**Existing Records.** Existing records is the easiest category of procedures to describe. It includes any program files or records that may be on hand when the evaluation begins, including records on new and past students, financial records, teacher evaluations, and others. Such records can turn out to be quite useful in evaluation. A straightforward *records analysis*, for instance, might examine trends in individual program components, such as enrollments, profits, materials selection, or students' evaluations of facilities and instruction. A more complex *systems analysis* is similar but is conducted on a larger scale. In a systems analysis, components

6

such as facilities and instruction are defined and their mutual interactions examined. For example, an evaluator might examine past assessments by students of teaching quality and physical facilities to determine whether they were related to levels of enrollment and profit.

The category of existing records might include a review of the literature *(literature review)* published in a certain area of program development (e.g., curriculum) or by a particular faculty member as part of a review process. It might also include the solicitation of letters to colleagues in the field *(letter writing)* to obtain information about already functioning programs that can be applied in a program development effort or to obtain assessments of the qualifications of a faculty member in a performance review process. There are many ways in which existing records can be used, and they should not be overlooked as a valuable source of information.

**Tests.** Tests are an indispensable source of information in the evaluation process, in addition to being an integral part of the curriculum that is being evaluated. *Proficiency tests* are measures of how much of a given language a person has learned, without reference to a particular program or its objectives and materials. An example is the TOEFL (Test of English as a Foreign Language), which was designed as a general purpose proficiency measure. It is correctly used when employed to indicate a student's relative position in the distribution of scores produced by all students who sat for the examination. *Placement tests,* on the other hand, though still general in purpose, are designed to help decide what each student's appropriate level will be within a specific program or course. That is, a placement test is designed with a specific program in mind or, at least, is checked for its appropriateness to a given program. *Achievement tests* are measures of how much language a person has learned, but with specific reference to a particular program or set of skills or objectives. Such tests are typically given at the end of a course of study to determine the degree to which students have mastered the subject matter. Finally, *diagnostic tests* are essentially the same as achievement tests but are administered to determine individual strengths and weaknesses. Such tests are usually administered at the beginning of a program—or in the middle of a course—to help students and their teachers focus their efforts where they will be most effective.

**Observations.** Procedures within this category all involve watching an individual (whether it be oneself or others), or a number of individuals or members of a group, and recording the behaviors that occur. The observations, which normally include both linguistic and nonlinguistic behavior, might be recorded in informal notes or more formally, as in an ethnographic study. Such a study is termed a *case study* if the linguistic characteristics or behaviors of a selected individual (or perhaps several individuals) are recorded in detail as a basis for drawing conclusions about a certain phenomenon. The observer might, for example, wish to study the classroom language of one instructor, or several, to determine how effectively error correction strategies are employed or to examine the style of speech in interactions between the instructor and students in different situations. If the individual being observed is also the observer, this would be termed self-observation, which may take the form of a *diary study* (see Bailey and Ochsner 1983 for an overview). This kind of observation occurs, for example, when linguists record their feelings and thoughts as they go through the process of learning a language (see, e.g., Schmidt and Frota 1986). It might be revealing if the students in a language program were asked to do the same kind of self-conscious observation. Reflective observations on the part of students could provide important insights about the degree of fit between the program curriculum and the values and preferences of those who are the intended beneficiaries of instruction.

*Behavior observation* is a more formal procedure in which a checklist or data sheet is used to investigate specific verbal and nonverbal behaviors occurring in a classroom. Such a procedure can be used to observe the frequencies of certain language forms or functions in the speech of native speakers to other speakers, such as second language learners. If a checklist or other recording procedure is applied to the study of behaviors that occur between people during a specific kind of interaction, the study is termed an *interactional analysis*. For example, one might study the effect of error correction in classroom interactions between teacher and students by using a checklist to determine the frequency of different types of correction, coupled with notes on how students reacted to each instance of correction.

Finally and most simply, *inventories* are used to record a count of objects (as in determining how many of each textbook a language program has) or to describe the fit of resources to instructional requirements of the program. Minimum conditions for a language program might be defined for the purposes of evaluation as including, for example: (1) one classroom per twenty students; (2) one administrator per ten teachers; (3) two textbooks per student; (4) one janitor per one hundred students, and so on. While the instructional aspects of a program are central in evaluation, the administrative and fiscal aspects should not be overlooked. A "simple" inventory can often be of considerable value in an evaluation because it provides quantifiable information about the allocation and use of equipment, materials, space, human resources, and other administrative and fiscal aspects of a program. This information can in turn provide the basis for a comparison of the patterns of resource allocation and use in a particular language program as against some other specific or ideal program. In this sense, different types of inventories can be the basis for a variety of evaluative measures of the program's attributes.

**Interviews.** Interview procedures are often a relatively open-ended category of procedures. *Individual interviews* allow for gathering personal responses and views privately. This confidentiality can, in turn, lead to insights into the true opinions of the participants involved, whereas other types of procedures such as questionnaires filled out during class time might fail to gather candid views. Because interviews are time-consuming, they are often not used in evaluations. This is unfortunate because they can be useful for discovering appropriate questions or issues that can then be investigated through more structured procedures such as questionnaires and behavior observations. Group interviews might seem at first to be one way around this problem, but it is important to remember that the information collected under such procedures is not confidential. As a result, what is learned may reflect the "public" opinions of the participants, that is, the views that they are ready to express in front of others. Contrasts in the opinions of the same person when interviewed as an individual versus the opinions of that person as part of a group can also be illuminating.

**Meetings.** Meetings differ from group interviews in that the latter are designed to help an evaluator gather information from the group, whereas meetings are structured to accomplish certain tasks. However, the process of trying to accomplish a task may bring to light unexpected information about the program in question as a by-product. The *delphi technique* is a meeting (or a series of meetings) in which the task to be performed is the reaching of a consensus. For instance, the delphi technique might be used to get the faculty to agree on an overall philosophy for the evaluation or for the program as a whole. It might be designed to build consensus on the goals or objectives of the curriculum and/or any other elements of the organization. As part of the delphi technique, *interest group meetings* are convened to air the views and ideas of selected individuals or groups. For instance, teams can be convened to argue the relative merits of different program philosophies, different views of students' needs, different ideas about how much detail must be written into objectives, and so on. *Review meetings* are conducted to draw participants into the process of sifting through and analyzing the information gathered using other procedures. Unlike the delphi technique, these meetings do not have a predefined goal. In review meetings, the consensus that must be built is still central to the group process, perhaps on issues such as what information to gather, what relative weights to give different types of information, and how to deal with conflicting information.

**Questionnaires.** Sometimes interviews and meetings provide insights into questions on a variety of topics that might usefully be asked on a broader scale, perhaps of all participants in a program. A helpful type of instrument in this case is the formal questionnaire. The type of questions posed with this procedure can be broached in a wide variety of ways, from the very open-ended, as in "What do you think about the ABC Language Program?" to much more structured five-point likert scale question types, such as the following example.

Indicate your degree of agreement or disagreement with the following statements (circle one):

|  | Strongly Disagree | Disagree | Neutral | Agree | Strongly Agree |
|---|---|---|---|---|---|
| 1. I think foreign language study is important. | 1 | 2 | 3 | 4 | 5 |
| 2. I now understand what a likert scale question is. | 1 | 2 | 3 | 4 | 5 |

There are a number of other possible types of questions that might be asked, and questionnaires are useful for gathering information on a larger scale than is possible with many other instruments. Questionnaires may be designed for a variety of purposes, or to gather information with a combination of purposes. The more clearly the questions are structured, the more precise the results will be (see Bailey 1982). *Biodata surveys* are used to elicit facts about the background of the students or teachers. Such information might include student age, place of birth, sex, marital status, number of years of language study, and so on. *Opinion surveys* are often considerably more complex because they are designed to uncover more subjective information about participants' opinions and attitudes. For example, a series of questions might be developed to determine what teachers think about the existing program, its objectives, its materials, its tests, and other aspects.

Another useful sort of information can be gathered using *self-ratings*. This procedure requires individuals to rate their own abilities, interest levels, motivations, and so on. It can give a perspective on the self-image of the individuals, even if the ratings themselves are not always accurate.

10

tion can supplement other sources of information on student abilities and instructional needs. Participants might also be asked to do *judgmental ratings* in which they give their evaluation of various aspects of the program. For instance, students might be asked to judge the effectiveness of the different materials that they are required to use, both from a pedagogical perspective and from the standpoint of interest level.

The last procedure to be mentioned here is the *Q sort*. This procedure combines several of those defined above in asking individuals to rate their own attitudes. The Q sort is designed so that subjects first give their opinions on a set of questions and then rank-order the relative importance of those views.

**Choosing Appropriate Instruments.** The purpose of an evaluation in large part determines the types of instruments that will be appropriate. For example, if the purpose is to explore student satisfaction with the curriculum, then the evaluation process might focus on instruments such as interviews, meetings, and questionnaires. If the scope of the evaluation were expanded to include examination of the relationship between student satisfaction and effectiveness of instruction, then instruments such as tests, classroom observations, and perhaps existing records might also be relevant.

## The Role of the Program Administrator

The functions of selecting procedures and of focusing and directing the evaluation process may be the most demanding of the administrator's many roles within a language program. This section discusses the degree to which the administrator ought to be involved in the process, the need for experience and skill, and the desirability of establishing a team effort in performing the evaluation.

Extensive data gathered from a variety of sources will provide the most useful and unbiased evaluation results and will help to ensure that those results will not hinge on the program administrator's individual abilities, perceptions, tastes, and judgments. Still, the program administrator—whether a dean, a director, or a department chair—ought to be a central figure in the whole review process, in the data-gathering phase as well as in the interpretation of the results. In cases where teachers or students resist the evaluation process, react negatively to it, or do not perform well according to the established criteria, the administrator will probably have to be the final arbitrator. If the evaluation is imposed by an authority outside the program, the program administrator may still have the responsibility for determining the evaluation format and the procedures to be used. Thus, the program administrator may ultimately be responsible for decisions made about such aspects of the evaluation process as the amount of data to be gathered, the types of data to be gathered, the procedures to be used for gathering data, the people to be involved in the evaluation, the relative weightings to be assigned to different types of information, and the actions to be taken on the basis of that information. Even when the administrator does not have freedom of choice in the evaluation format or procedures, and even when outside evaluators are brought in to conduct the evaluation, the program's own administrator should still take an active role in the process. In fact, we believe that evaluation is an essential part of the curriculum process that provides for ongoing maintenance of a language program (see Chapter Four, this volume), whether or not there is outside pressure to evaluate.

While there are situations in which an evaluation is externally imposed and conducted entirely by outsiders, it can be seen as part of administrators' responsibility to periodically initiate evaluations of their own programs. In this way, administrators gather data that can help them manage resources and continually upgrade program components to meet the needs of the students, the faculty, and others who interact with the program. The data gathered through periodic evaluation also provide a basis for promoting the program to those within and outside of the program, including higher authorities who may be responsible for their own evaluations of the program. In this way, the administrator prepares the program for an externally imposed evaluation, for which the data gathered internally can furnish a helpful starting point or balance.

The effectiveness of an evaluation—and its potential for contributing to the making of a successful program—relates directly to the language program administrator's experience and skill. Three types of administrative skills will be required in the evaluation process: technical, human, and conceptual (Katz 1974). The administrator will need to be technically skilled in testing and other administrative procedures relating to evaluation, as well as in the methods and materials of language teaching, to carry out the whole evaluation process in a competent manner. Conceptual and human skill are of particular importance in language programs, which tend to be less structured and more "humanistic" than some other types of organizations. The "loose coupling" (Weick 1976) of parties and interests in a language program demands strong conceptual skills enabling the administrator to see how all parts of the operation fit together and then to make plans for the future that will promote the welfare of the overall organization as well as of the individuals within it. Most importantly, the administrator will need the conceptual skill to be able to decide on the procedures for the evaluation, to interpret its results, and to make decisions based on those results.

The loose coupling of interests within educational organizations necessitates a mature leadership capability and highly developed human skill on the part of the administrator to build a cooperative spirit. It also requires a strong sense of purpose and the ability to persuade others to function in terms of a common purpose, which must be articulated to staff members "with eloquence, persistence, and detail" (Weick 1982, 675). In the evaluation process, the administrator will need human skill for data-gathering, team-building, conducting meetings, and dealing tactfully with complaints or other negative aspects of the evaluation process. In an educational organization, morale-building to keep instructors' confidence up and perceptions of their professional efficacy high becomes a central activity of the administrator, especially during an evaluation process. Thus the administrator must be careful to avoid hypercritical comments and to give positive and constructive feedback in the review process, particularly in the performance review of instructors (Pennington 1989).

It is highly unlikely that a language program administrator—or any individual administrator—will be equally skilled in all three areas: technical, human, and conceptual. One way of compensating for any weaknesses or shortcomings that are manifested in individual administrators is to work through teams of individuals with complementary skills (Katz 1974; Pennington 1985). It is therefore advisable for program evaluation to be a team effort involving many different personalities and varied input into the review process from others, both within and outside the program. One way of accomplishing these goals is by a curriculum development focus in which evaluation is tied to the development of curricular objectives and testing mechanisms (see Chapter Four, this volume).

## Developing and Implementing the Evaluation Process

The establishment of an effective team effort requires consideration of a number of factors. For an evaluation to be most effective, a participatory approach with a focus on professional development for the staff and faculty should be considered. Cooperation and input from all parties ensure that the evaluation will result in improvements to the program and that change will occur with minimal disruption. The elaboration of these points forms the basis in this section for the description of evaluation guidelines in the final section.

Different notions about the process of evaluation and the purposes for which it is to be conducted will result in different systems of evaluation. Moreover, the level at which the evaluation takes place and the organizational context and climate in which the evaluation system is implemented are significant variables in determining both its form and results. An evaluation system that is accountable exclusively or primarily to those within the organization is more likely to further the goals of that organization than one that is designed according to external criteria. For example, summative evaluations of teaching performance based on external criteria may be at odds with formative evaluations aimed at modifying teaching behavior according to the goals of a particular program:

> It is one thing to define and measure teacher competence in a standardized fashion; it is quite another to change teacher performance. Research on individual and organizational behavior suggests that first-order solutions are unlikely to effect change, and, further, that successful approaches involve processes that may be inconsistent with those used to derive summative evaluation judgments. That is, the context-free generalization necessary for implementing a uniform evaluation system may counteract the context-specific processes needed to effect change in individual or organizational behaviors. (Darling-Hammond, Wise, and Pease 1983, 288)

Hence, it is desirable for the procedures that make up the evaluation system to be designed or modified on the basis of input by faculty members and others who have an interest in the success of the particular language program under review.

The core of a successful organization is development according to academic, administrative, and fiscal criteria that are relevant to that organization. For the administrator, development is often tied to growth and innovation. For the faculty member, development is often linked to professional growth and evolution in one's field of specialization (Pennington 1989). Ideally, the goals of individuals affect and are affected by the goals of the program. The evaluation system, accordingly, should be tied to a professional development plan through which individuals further the goals of the program by furthering their own professional growth. Motivation is a natural by-product of such an evaluation system, which offers faculty members an array of opportunities for professional development.

Hence, it is essential that an evaluation system be seen as providing opportunities for change and evolution of the program as a whole, as well as for the individuals who make up the organization. Individualized, cooperative evaluation in which the faculty is involved in determining evaluation criteria and procedures and in which self-evaluation plays a major role provides developmental opportunities in both the general and individual cases. Evaluation models that are built around

14

teacher input at various stages of the evaluation—for example, through periodic interviews and meetings with the administrator—foster the teacher's sense of self-determination and professionalism (see Chapter Ten, this volume). This in turn contributes to a positive concept of self and of the program, which ultimately furthers the goals of the organization. The program as a whole benefits by cooperative evaluation, which allows for criteria defined in relation to that particular organization to evolve and to shape future policy and innovation.

Rodgers (1979), in his discussion of implementation of the Hawaii English Program curriculum at individual schools, stresses the importance of faculty involvement in the early and ongoing stages of curriculum implementation. According to Rodgers (p.90ff.), the greater the degree of faculty involvement in the Hawaii English Program curriculum development effort, the greater the teachers' enthusiasm toward the curriculum and their motivation to actually implement it in the classroom. Analogously, when faculty members help to determine the criteria and processes by which curricular effectiveness and teaching performance will be assessed, they are more likely than faculty members not involved in this way to support and to benefit from the review process.

The degree of involvement in the evaluation process of parties affected by the evaluation will in large measure determine the success of the evaluation system:

> Research on individual and organizational change indicates that the degree of control and autonomy characterizing participants' roles in the implementation process is critical to success of a planned change effort. (Darling-Hammond, Wise, and Pease 1983, 313)

Autonomy and self-determination are appropriate and indeed inevitable in the kind of participatory organization that most educational enterprises exemplify.

Instructors and other staff members in educational programs will likely have a strong voice in the conduct of affairs of the organization, and many different views and tastes will likely be integrated into the structure and operation of the program. Moreover, the evaluation system must have an inherent flexibility, to be able to respond to changing conditions within and outside the organization. A view of a language program evaluation system as inherently flexible is consistent with a "natural systems" model of the organization of educational enterprises (Corwin 1974). According to this model, structure in educational organizations is not imposed in a bureaucratic, hierarchical, "top-down" fashion. Rather, systems and relationships among parts of the organization evolve in direct response to local, context-specific variables.

According to this line of reasoning, all parties who have an interest in the results of the evaluation should be involved in the design, the implementation, and the interpretation of results. That is, evaluation, if it is intended to effect change, should have a strong "bottom-up" impetus (Johnson 1980) in which all phases involve participation by students, faculty, and other staff members. Evaluation based on "local" factors will be more responsive to the perceived problems and needs of a particular organization and so will be more effective in helping that organization to evolve in a positive direction. As the evaluation is based on more input from a larger number of individuals, personal standards will begin to evolve toward organizational standards, and organizational standards will evolve toward the personal standards of those who make up the organization. Ultimately, if this type of procedure in the process of evaluation is followed, the system that results will incorporate the combined perspectives of all parties who have an interest in the program. The evaluation then becomes a vehicle for development and effective change in the organization:

> Effective change requires a process of mutual adaptation in which [participants] at all levels can shape policies to meet their needs—one in which both the participants and the policy are transformed by the convergence of internal and external reference points. (Darling-Hammond, Wise, and Pease 1983, 17)

## Conclusion: Conditions for Effective Evaluation

Different notions about the purposes of evaluation and the role that the evaluation process is to play in the organization determine the type of system that evolves. Just as different notions of evaluation will determine the type of system that is developed, different philosophies and theories about language, about education (both teaching and learning), and about the practice of language education will determine different types of evaluation systems. These different notions will come in part from the history of the field but will also be determined by the particular views of those who are involved in the review process. Thus, an exclusively top-down system of evaluation—both in terms of criteria and in terms of implementation—will not be as effective as one that includes strong bottom-up elements in the design and conduct of the evaluation. Adapting and synthesizing from discussions of evaluation in Darling-Hammond, Wise, and Pease (1983, 320), Weick (1982, 674), and Nunan (1987, 99), we suggest that fair and effective evaluation will occur under the following conditions:

- Information for program evaluation is drawn from a variety of sources.

16

- Different types of instruments are used for collecting data on the program's effectiveness.
- All parties understand that evaluation is an ongoing process.
- All parties to the evaluation share the same understanding of the criteria and processes involved in the evaluation system.
- All parties to the evaluation understand the relationship of these criteria and processes to the educational philosophy and goals of the program.
- Instructors believe that the evaluation system both enables and motivates them to improve their performance and to grow as professionals.
- Administrators believe that the evaluation system enables them to interact productively with instructors and to provide educational leadership.
- All parties see the evaluation system as achieving a balance between administrative control and individual autonomy, a balance "between adaptation and adaptability, between stability to handle present demands and flexibility to handle unanticipated demands" (Weick 1982, 674).

# References

Bachman, L. F. 1981. Formative evaluation in specific purpose program development. In Mackay, R. and J. D. Palmer, eds., *Languages for specific purposes: Program design and evaluation*, 106–116. Rowley, MA: Newbury House.

Bailey, D. B. 1982. *Methods of social research.* 2d ed. New York: Free Press.

Bailey, K. M. and R. Ochsner. 1983. A methodological review of the diary studies: Windmill tilting or social science? In Bailey, K. M., M. H. Long, and S. Peck, eds., *Second language acquisition studies*, 188–198. Rowley, MA: Newbury House.

Beretta, A. and A. Davies. 1985. Evaluation of the Bangalore project. *ELT Journal* 39:121–127.

Brown, J. D. 1989. Language program evaluation: A synthesis of existing possibilities. In Johnson, R. K., ed., *The second language curriculum*, 222–241. Cambridge: Cambridge University Press.

Corwin, R. G. 1974. Models of educational organizations. In Kerlinger, F. N., ed., *Review of Research in Education*, vol. 2. Itasca, IL: F. E. Peacock.

Darling-Hammond, L., A. E. Wise, and S. R. Pease. 1983. Teacher evaluation in the organizational context: A review of the literature. *Review of Educational Research* 53:285–328.

Johnson, S. M. 1980. Performance-based staff layoffs in the public schools: Implementation and outcomes. *Harvard Educational Review* 50:214–233.

Katz, R. L. 1974. Skills of an effective administrator. *Harvard Business Review* 52:90–102, September-October 1974.

Long, M. H. 1984. Process and product in ESL program evaluation. *TESOL Quarterly* 18:409–425.

Nunan, D. 1985. *Language teaching course design: Trends and issues.* Adelaide, South Australia: National Curriculum Resource Centre.

_____. 1987. *Learner-centred language curriculum in theory and practice.* Adelaide, South Australia: National Curriculum Resource Centre.

Pennington, M. C. 1985. Effective administration of an ESL program. In Judd E., D. Messerschmitt, and P. Larsen, eds., *On TESOL '84*, 301–316. Washington, D.C.: Association of Teachers of English to Speakers of Other Languages.

_____. 1989. Faculty development for language programs. In Johnson, R. K., ed., *The second language curriculum*, 91–110. Cambridge: Cambridge University Press.

Richards, J. C., J. Pratt, and H. Weber. 1985. *Longman dictionary of applied linguistics.* London: Longman.

Rodgers, T. 1979. Teacher training: In progress. ELT Documents, *Developments in the training of teachers of English.* ETIC Publications, 84–98. London: British Council.

Saltzer, M. G. 1982. The evaluation of an intensive English program. In Barrett, R. P., ed., *The administration of intensive English language programs*, 89–97. Washington, D.C.: National Association for Foreign Student Affairs.

Schmidt, R. W. and S. N. Frota. 1986. Developing basic conversational ability in a second language: A case study of an adult learner of Portuguese. In Day, R. R., ed., *Talking to learn: Conversation in second language acquisition*, 237–326. Rowley, MA: Newbury House.

Tucker, G. R. and G. A. Cziko. 1978. The role of evaluation in bilingual education. In Alatis, J. E., ed., *International dimensions of bilingual education*, 423–426. Washington, D.C.: Georgetown University Press.

Weick, K. E. 1976. Educational organizations as loosely coupled systems. Administrative Science Quarterly 21:1–19.

_____. 1982. Administering education in loosely coupled schools. *Phi Delta Kappa* 63:673–676.

# 2

# Self-Study and Self-Regulation for ESL Programs: Issues Arising from the Associational Approach

*Patricia Byrd and Janet C. Constantinides*

## Introduction

In the late 1970s, two different but related trends in international education exchange led first NAFSA (National Association for Foreign Student Affairs) and then TESOL (Teachers of English to Speakers of Other Languages) to study the feasibility of becoming accrediting agencies. An explosion had occurred in the numbers of foreign students coming to the United States to study in intensive ESL (English as a Second Language) programs and in degree programs. This great increase in numbers tempted some individuals and institutions to act in less-than-ethical ways, for example, by selling I-20 forms and making false promises to potential students about their academic future. At the same time, ESL professionals became increasingly disturbed that ESL programs (those at nonprofit institutions as well as proprietary programs) were enhancing their profits at the expense of classroom teachers, many (if not most) of whom were hired on term-to-term contracts as part-time teachers and were paid little above minimum wage, without fringe benefits.

NAFSA took the first step in 1980 by appointing a Task Force on Standards and Responsibilities to study alternatives and to make recommendations to eliminate unethical practices, and to do so without government intervention (NAFSA Task Force on Standards and Responsibilities

1981, 1983a; Peterson 1984). This task force initially considered having NAFSA become an accreditation agency on the model of regional and professional accreditation agencies in the United States. To be members of these agencies or to have their seal of approval, institutions must conform to standards established by the member groups making up the agency.[1] For example, to be accredited by the Southern Association of Colleges and Schools (SACS), an institution must be investigated (with self-study as the first stage of that investigation, followed by an inspection by a team made up of administrators and faculty members from other institutions) and shown to meet the standards set by the institutions in SACS. The NAFSA task force soon realized that such a change in the association's purpose was not realistic for two reasons: the great cost of developing such a program, which was beyond NAFSA's resources;[2] and the sense of the task force that U.S. institutions were unlikely to welcome yet another accreditation group (NAFSA Task Force on Standards and Responsibilities 1981, 1983a). That is, NAFSA had neither the money nor the power to force institutions to behave ethically.

At the same time that the NAFSA task force faced the realities of attempting to control institutional behavior from outside the institution, the task force members did not want to limit their work to the production of a document on standards that would in all likelihood hardly live beyond its initial publication (NAFSA Task Force on Standards and Responsibilities 1983a). Out of their discussions of the need for an approach that could realistically be expected to influence institutional behavior came the current NAFSA program in self-study and self-regulation. The basic characteristics of the program are that the institution (1) endorses the NAFSA Principles (and advises NAFSA formally of that endorsement); (2) conducts a self-study that focuses on some aspect(s) of its international education programs (including ESL); and (3) files a report of that study with NAFSA.

TESOL's self-study program has a similar history that began with a strong desire to control the behavior of institutions and ended with an understanding that the association had a better chance of creating change through internal influence than through external force (Kreidler 1983, 1988; Larson 1986). Thus, by the mid-1980s both NAFSA and TESOL had developed similar approaches to influencing the institutions within which their members functioned, differing primarily in that NAFSA focuses on higher education while TESOL provides for self-study at all of the levels of education and types of institutions represented by its membership, from K-12 to college and university ESL and bilingual programs. Both NAFSA and TESOL have prepared detailed explanations of the procedures required by their self-study programs (see the *NAFSA Self-Study Guide* 1983b, and TESOL's various publications on its standards and self-study questions listed in the references to this article). What follows is therefore not a guide to conducting a self-study but rather a discussion of issues that have arisen as institutions (through their administrations and faculty members) have attempted to understand the implications for ESL programs of these new associational approaches to self-study and self-regulation.

## Process vs. Product in Self-Study

While NAFSA and TESOL are enthusiastic about self-study, seeing it as a possible solution to a set of difficult problems, most of the rest of the academic world has already experienced self-study in its least attractive form: the accreditation review. Self-study has been for most departments and programs a tedious, unproductive task of answering in detail a list of questions handed down from above. A report is produced and handed back up. Little if any change results; little if any reward is given for the effort. This type of self-study is not what NAFSA and TESOL intend. In terms familiar to our profession, the process is supposed to be as important as (if not more important than) the product.

A great danger in the NAFSA and TESOL systems is the potential for overrewarding the report and not insisting on a valuable process of self-study. In 1988, a major agency in international educational exchange announced that it intended to indicate in one of its publications the ESL programs that had completed the NAFSA or TESOL process as a method for signaling to overseas advisers that these were high-quality programs. After discussion with leaders of NAFSA and TESOL, the organization decided to provide information on both NAFSA's and TESOL's self-study programs without indicating the individual programs that had participated in a self-study. There is genuine cause to fear that this use of only the reporting portion of the NAFSA and TESOL self-study could easily lead to a rush to prepare self-study documents of doubtful worth, as program administrators seek special mention or commendation of their programs in publications that list ESL programs.

The desire to reward report-makers harks back to the very beginning of NAFSA's and TESOL's efforts, returning again to the desire to create an accreditation system within the two associations. The push for such a simplistic reward system seems no better an idea now than it was then, for neither association is in a significantly richer or more powerful position now than it was in 1980. More importantly, a system of recognition must not be allowed to undermine the process aspect of the self-study programs. Kells (1983, 17) describes the features of successful self-studies, putting the report (the self-study product) into the overall context of a self-analysis and self-improvement process:

21

1. The process should be internally motivated.
2. The top leadership must be committed to the process.
3. The design of the self-study must be appropriate to the circumstances of the institution.
4. The process should contain an informed attempt to clarify organizational goals and to assess achievement of the goals (to study outcomes) for purposes of improvement.
5. There should be representative, appropriate, and useful participation by members of the various segments of the larger community.
6. The process must be well led.
7. The ability of the organization to function effectively should be studied and enhanced.
8. Some improvement should occur both during and as a result of the process.
9. A readable report, potentially useful to several audiences, should result from the process.
10. A better system of ongoing institutional research, self-analysis, and self-improvement should be a major product of the process.

To Kells's list of features of successful self-studies, we would add an eleventh factor:

11. The study should encompass both the strengths and the weaknesses of the program.

The description of the program's characteristics must be complete and objective. Focusing only on weaknesses is demoralizing; that kind of self-study leads to a reluctance on the part of the participants to involve themselves in any further cycle of self-study. Focusing on strengths and not only on weaknesses or areas in need of improvement is one way of building rapport and confidence among the participants in the self-study and the other members of the program.

When planning a self-study for an ESL program, the commitment should not come just from inside the ESL program itself or only from NAFSA or TESOL outside the program. Ideally, strong support for the ESL self-study should come from as high in the organization as possible—for example, the director of the ESL program, the person to whom the director reports, the provost, the president, or the trustees. The higher in the organization the commitment resides, the more likely it is that any suggested changes resulting from the self-study will be implemented. In the case of a self-study conducted by an ESL program, not only the ESL program staff but also members of the larger academic or organizational community should have roles in the self-study. Besides increasing the number of participants and the sense of ownership for the self-study process, widespread participation can also increase the visibility of the ESL program within the institution.

Though the final written report is not the focus of a self-study, it still is important, in part as it furnishes a historical document for future administrators, faculty, and staff. Therefore, the report should be written with that audience as well as the immediate audience in mind. The immediate audience will have been defined by the purpose and the design for the self-study. Is this primarily an internal document to be used by the ESL program itself? Is it to be part of a larger self-study that views the entire institution as its audience, or will part of the audience be from the outside, for example, an accreditation agency team with only limited prior knowledge about the program and the institution? Carefully identifying the audience for the report and then writing for that audience will help ensure that the report is useful. The report should be of a length that invites reading, not a tome to be filed on a shelf or used as a doorstop. The effectiveness of a report is not measured in pounds.

Ultimately, the process itself is the most valuable result of a successful self-study. By creating in the ESL program an ongoing commitment to self-knowledge and to adapt to changing circumstances, self-study can help ESL programs become more effective in meeting the needs of students, faculty, administrators, and institutions.

### Focused vs. General Self-Study

For many ESL programs, an effective approach to self-study will be to focus on a single aspect of the program rather than to attempt a full-scale study of all its aspects. For example, the faculty and administration could choose to focus on the goals and purposes of the program, on analysis of the students' needs, on curricular revision, or on other topics of immediate concern. In these times of rapid change in the status and purpose of academic-based ESL programs (Byrd and Fox 1988), many ESL programs might benefit from a thorough study of the program's goals and purposes in light of the goals and purposes of the academic institution where it resides. That is, study of goals and purposes is not necessarily a matter exclusively internal to the ESL program, but could very well extend to matters of articulation of the ESL program (and its courses) with the larger institution.

These focused self-studies can be conducted in an ongoing pattern of evaluation and change that can prepare the program for an eventual full-scale study. A possible pattern of study would be to take on some limited project every year while building to a more general review every three to five years. The smaller studies will build the skill of the faculty and administration at data collection and analysis and will lead to a collection of information that can be a useful base for the larger self-study.

A major disadvantage of the full-scale, general self-study is that it demands significant reallocation of resources, including faculty and administrative time. These general studies cannot be carried out successfully if they are merely added to the regular assignments of faculty and administrators. A general self-study needs to be well led, carefully planned, and adequately funded (see Kells 1983). The danger for NAFSA and TESOL of the poorly led, hastily planned, and underfunded self-study is that the membership of both associations will find the process an unproductive burden. In these initial stages of learning to use the process, the goals of NAFSA and TESOL will be better served in many contexts by the smaller-scale, focused self-study.

A major advantage of the focused self-study is that it will not require a large expenditure of resources (in terms of materials or staff time), nor will it demand much reallocation of faculty time away from the fundamental academic triad of teaching, service, and scholarship. Through the process of giving attention to one important aspect of the ESL program at a time, the faculty and administration can build skill at self-study and self-regulation. As importantly, most programs (and faculty members and administrators) find needed changes to be more manageable when they handle them in small chunks rather than attempting to make adjustments in many different areas of the program within a limited period of time. A useful result of the focused self-study is to have such self-analysis become part of the routine service responsibilities of the faculty and administration.

### Benefits of Self-Study

Why, given the difficulties outlined above, should an institution or a program undertake a self-study? The benefits of self-study (suggested by both NAFSA and TESOL in their self-study documents) for a program, its faculty, and its administration can be divided into two categories: internal benefits for the program and benefits to the institution. On each of these levels, the benefits are numerous, as detailed in the sections that follow.

**Program Benefits.** A self-study can benefit a particular program by (1) clarifying the goals of the program; (2) identifying any problems that may exist; (3) reviewing programs, procedures, and resources in a systematic, nonthreatening fashion; and (4) identifying and producing needed changes. Each of these benefits will be discussed in turn.

*Clarifying goals.* The self-study process itself should result in clarification of the goals of the ESL program and its ability to achieve those goals. Goals clarification must be an integral part of any self-study so that by the end of the process everyone involved is clear about the purposes of not only the self-study, but of the program and of the larger institution or organization to which the ESL program belongs.

Too often, ESL programs, like Topsy, just grow. The original motivation becomes lost in the demand for the program to meet continually changing needs. In fact, in some cases, the original goals may have been completely obscured by later needs to provide services, to adapt to a variety of crises, and, in some cases, to take care of problems that other parts of the institution have refused to handle. An ESL program originally intended to prepare students for academic work may find itself teaching survival skills to spouses or doing special contract work for groups of tourists. A careful, objective look at the program may find that the goals have shifted, that new goals have been acted upon though never clearly articulated, or—in the worst cases—that no goals were ever set.

*Identifying problems.* Often, faculty members and administrators are so busy carrying out their daily work routine that they do not have time to stop and look at exactly what is happening to the program. Although faculty and administrators may feel that everything is not going as well as it might, in many cases no specific problems will be noticed that demand immediate attention. The time necessary to identify the source of any uneasiness that exists in the minds of faculty members or administrators and to pinpoint the areas of the program that need revision is used instead in carrying on the everyday work of the program. Allocating time to look at the program systematically is one way of identifying the location and causes of problems.

*Reviewing programs, procedures, and resources.* Programs may have continued and procedures may have been kept in place simply because they are there rather than because they are effective. The process of resource allocation and the ability to capture additional resources need to be reviewed periodically to see if the unit is benefiting from a clearly articulated plan. A self-study can be of particular value for a new director or chair of an ESL program: the self-study process offers many opportunities for learning more about the program, for building relationships with faculty and students, and for demonstrating commitment to enhanced functioning of the program.

*Identifying and producing needed changes.* As a result of the previous three benefits, a self-study helps to identify and to introduce needed changes. Self-study is not just about the identification of problems but also about planning for change, in order to build on strengths and eliminate weaknesses. As it becomes apparent that there are some problems that have relatively short-term and simple solutions, those solutions should be instituted immediately, rather than waiting to undertake them until the end of the process and the filing of the summary report. In addition to making the program or institution more effective, making such changes also provides immediate positive feedback to all involved.

A self-study can result in ongoing useful research and self-analysis. The self-study process, if it is carried out correctly, is not limited to a few weeks or months. It should be the beginning of a series of increasingly useful and, at the same time, less stressful processes of review and change.

Often the first self-study cycle undertaken by a program or institution must, of necessity, devote a great deal of time to research and self-analysis, asking such questions as: Who are we? What are we doing? Who are our clients? What services do we provide? How many of our clients complete a certain course and go on to a certain other course or situation? Many programs and institutions lack the necessary data to make relevant judgments or evaluations about their strengths and weaknesses; one of the benefits arising from self-study can be the establishment of research and data-gathering procedures and mechanisms for self-analysis. Once it becomes apparent that the needed self-study information is useful on an ongoing basis, the initial self-study may result in the program or institution putting into place review procedures and record-keeping systems that make ongoing operations and any subsequent self-study cycle easier to accomplish.

Perhaps most important, self-study can be used for team building. In ESL programs, where faculty and staff members may be so involved with their own students that they lose sight of the larger program, and where many of them may have part-time or temporary positions, there can be few opportunities for faculty and staff to interact in a coherent fashion. A self-study can provide an occasion for needed interaction and result in individuals having a better sense of the overall nature and structure of the program and a better understanding of their own roles in the program.

**Context Benefits.** A self-study can benefit an institution in at least four ways as the ESL program grows in self-knowledge and as the institution learns to understand the contribution of the ESL program to institutional goals. These context benefits are described below.

*Orientation for new administrators.* The self-study process can be used as an effective orientation for new administrators of the units to which the ESL program reports. The self-study report, the product of the self-study, can function as a document for introducing and explaining the program to those unfamiliar with it. Moreover, if administrators as well as other faculty and staff members in the institution are included, the self-study process can provide an orientation for the rest of the institution to the goals, courses, services, and successes of the program, a benefit discussed in more detail in the following section.

*Portraying the program to a larger institution.* The self-study process can provide an opportunity for the ESL program to become better known and understood within the institution. Although carrying out the general self-study usually required for an accreditation review can strain program resources, participation in such a process offers ESL programs invaluable opportunities. At most U.S. colleges and universities, ESL programs have in the past been isolated from the regular academic system of the institution. For example, ESL teachers have not had faculty status nor have they participated in the institution's governance activities, and the courses in the ESL program have not been reviewed through the institution's curriculum committees. Participating in the institution's accreditation review can provide the ESL program with insights into the ways in which the larger institution governs itself, as ESL faculty members serve on committees with faculty from other departments. At the same time, the participation can lead the larger institution to better understand the characteristics of the ESL program—the contribution it is making to the institution as well as any need it might have for better institutional support.

*Data collection and analysis for external reviews.* The self-study can provide useful information for evaluation teams, departments of education, accrediting agencies—all of the outside agencies that in some way assess the overall effectiveness of the institution. A cycle of self-study keyed to the need to present information to such external evaluation agencies can be useful to the program in that the information requested is available ahead of time and does not have to be collected under last-minute deadline pressure.

*Portraying the larger institution to the ESL program staff.* A self-study provides an opportunity for the ESL administrators, faculty, and staff to better understand the parent institution. Just as the ESL program may not be well understood by those outside the program, it may also not fully understand the host environment. A program-specific self-study, or a self-study that is part of an institution-wide process, should include exploration of the links between the program and the larger institution. The flow of information and the opportunity for interaction are both beneficial to the ESL program in that they provide the program with an understanding of how the institution works and so should result in the program's being more effective in clarifying and achieving its goals.

## Self-Study as an Ongoing Process

When a self-study is completed and the final report has been written, the process should not have ended. As emphasized earlier, the report (the product) is not the most important part of the self-study—although, if done well, it can be useful as a basis for further planning, as an orientation document, and as a historical document. However, if the self-study process has worked correctly, there should now be within the unit an openness to self-analysis and to change that may not have been present before. If that openness has been achieved, then the process will be much easier the next time a self-study is undertaken. It will no longer be necessary to dispel the myths that self-study is an exercise in futility or that any data collected will be used only in a negative manner.

**Changing the Focus.** If the original self-study focused primarily on the collection of data and the clarification of goals (as many first self-studies do), the next cycle in the process might focus on evaluation of outcomes or further clarification of goals and revision of the curriculum. Each cycle of the self-study should have a slightly different emphasis. It is counterproductive to have each cycle simply replicate the previous one. Such a repetitive approach to ongoing cycles of the review process is what often introduces the negative reactions to self-study: "We've already done this." Refocusing on another part of the process will revitalize the self-study process and reenergize the participants.

**Continued Data Collection.** Once a decision has been made about the types of data needed for analysis of the ESL program, there should be continuous collection of that data between cycles of self-study. (For additional discussion of the ongoing and cyclical nature of evaluation, see Chapter One, this volume.) This data collection should result in increased program or institutional research that is then available for making appropriate decisions. Later cycles of self-study can then begin with the necessary data, rather than having to devote time and resources to its collection. (See Chapter Eight, this volume, for further discussion of storage and analysis of the data collected.)

**Adjustment to Outside Influences.** The self-study process must take into account any changes in the surrounding environment that affect the program. For example, changes in the economy (e.g., the downturn in the economic well-being of energy-producing states in the mid-1980s) or in institutional goals that may affect program responsibilities (e.g., change in admissions policies for the larger institution, expansions in international programs in a certain subject area such as agriculture or business, or the decision to include a larger international component in the general education requirements for undergraduates) will have an effect on the ESL program. Such changes can result in increases in the number of its students, alterations in the composition of the student body, or additional competition for the available limited resources. Likewise, changes in accreditation standards and requirements of outside agencies may place different demands on the institution and the ESL program. One example is the requirement recently proposed by ABET (Accrediting Board for Engineering and Technology) that all engineering faculty must provide evidence of their ability to read and write English. This would obviously result in added responsibilities for ESL programs, specifically those that currently test and train foreign teaching assistants and faculty members.

**Review and Evaluation as a Part of Planning.** All projected modifications of a program should include review and evaluation of current and previous program or institutional performance. If, as suggested above, continued data collection is one of the results of a self-study, then the information on which review and evaluation are based will be available, thus increasing the probability that review and evaluation will be undertaken as part of the planning process. This in turn helps create an expectation within the institution or the program that all subsequent planning will benefit from the review and evaluation of current performance.

**Time Lines.** Time lines for ongoing self-study may be keyed (1) to accreditation cycles, either institution-wide (such as those conducted by the regional accrediting agencies) or program-specific (e.g., in a particular college or program); (2) to funding cycles (e.g., legislative budget sessions or major fund drives within the host institution); or (3) to internal review cycles, an option that has become increasingly popular in American colleges and universities. If the ESL program can time its self-study to be a part of the regional accrediting agency's cycle, the program can also request a member of the visitation team to be a specialist in ESL, thus increasing the visibility and importance of the program.

## Choosing a Design for a Self-Study

The size of the program or institution, the amount of time that can be committed to the self-study, and the resources available for carrying it out will determine the exact design of the ESL self-study, which must be tailored in each case to fit the situation. An elaborate design that involves a large steering committee and clearly defined multiple sub-committees is not appropriate to a self-study at the program level, especially in a small ESL program in which there may be fewer than a dozen faculty and staff members.

The choice of a design for organization of the activities included in a self-study will largely determine the success of the self-study process. Consequently, it is important that the design reflect the reality of the program's ability to analyze itself and to conduct a thorough analysis of the forces within the program and the surrounding institution operating upon it. One useful way to accomplish this is by doing a force field analysis. Figure 1 illustrates what is meant by a force field. Once each of the factors legislating for and against the self-study has been analyzed, effective decisions can be made about design and implementation of the self-study.

FIGURE 1. DIAGRAM FOR FORCE FIELD ANALYSIS

| Older faculty with non-TESL degrees who fear new education requirements | New director with support of higher administration |
|---|---|
| Poor time: end of year and everyone is tired | Research report on recruiting that shows that potential students want faculty with TESL degrees |
| | Faculty involved in NAFSA/TESOL professional development work |

On the left side of the force field are listed all of the forces that can be identified as opposing the self-study, change, or modification of the current program, or that would inhibit the process. On the right side of the force field those forces favorable to self-study and/or change are enumerated. They can be categorized according to the the four groupings described below.

**Forces for or against Self-Study and Change: Who.** Which individuals within the program and the surrounding institution or larger environment are firmly ensconced, have territory to protect, probably will not react positively to any suggestion for change, have expressed opinions that self-studies are exercises in futility, or in any other way can be identified as having negative reactions to the possibility of a self-study? The names of those individuals go on the left-hand side of the diagram. On the right-hand side are placed the names of those who appear receptive to change, are concerned about the current situation, and are supportive of the program and its growth. It is also important to list what positions these people occupy within the program, the surrounding institution, or the larger environment and to evaluate their strength within either the formal or informal power structure and networks.

A positive force in this area is the NAFSA Consultation Service. NAFSA has trained its Field Service Consultants in the self-study process so that they can advise on self-study as part of their work within particular subareas of international education. That is, a consultant who specializes in ESL is also trained to help carry out self-study within ESL programs and within other academic departments or divisions that include ESL as a subspecialty.[3]

**Forces for or against Self-Study and Change: When.** Self-studies can, of course, begin at just about any time in the life span of an ESL program. Two traditional times for self-studies are at the beginning of the tenure of a new chief administrative officer and as part of the accreditation review of the larger institution.

While self-study can be a valuable process, there seem to be at least three situations in which delay or avoidance of self-study might be a wise decision. In NAFSA workshops on self-study, H. R. Kells has emphasized the importance for success in the self-study of the first three factors listed above: (1) internal motivation for the study; (2) support from the highest administrative levels; and (3) appropriate design to fit the particular program. Self-study might be unwise, therefore, in situations such as the following:

1. If the sole or driving motive for the self-study is to gain recognition by filing a report with either NAFSA or TESOL, delay might be wise until such time as self-study can be accepted as a change-oriented process.

2. When strong support from the chief administrative officer(s) is not given, self-study will probably be a frustrating waste of time for faculty; only with administrative support for necessary changes can self-study live up to its potential. Delay might be considered until such commitment can be assured.

3. Delay is a wise choice when faculty and administration cannot agree on the purposes and organization of a self-study. Self-study can be successful only when faculty members and the administration agree on a design that uses resources well, that focuses on significant aspects of the program, and that promises to deliver changes (and not just to produce another report).

The person designing the self-study should consider other questions about timing of the effort: What other activities or commitments influence the selection of a favorable time for a self-study? That is, is summer rapidly approaching, or some major holiday, when many of the faculty will be away? What about particularly busy times during the year, such as registration and final exams? Or, on the positive side, are there some breaks in the schedule that would allow the faculty and staff to devote more time to the activities that the self-study will require?

**Forces for or against Self-Study and Change: How.** How will the self-study be undertaken? This question involves two areas for consideration. The first is the organization of the self-study steering committee or task force. Is it better to have individual assignments for parts of the self-study, or would it be better to have people work in groups? This decision will depend on how many people need to be involved. The answers to these questions can usefully be lined up as positive and negative forces in the force field diagram.

The second part of this "how" question relates to available resources, for example, personnel. Are there so few people within the program to carry out the self-study that only a limited number of activities can be undertaken? Or, is it a large program from which selection of participants can be made or subcommittees organized so that many different activities can be undertaken simultaneously without unduly infringing upon the time of any one participant? What kind of support services are available to the self-study group, such as clerical services, computerized data storage and statistical analysis, and duplicating and wordprocessing facilities? Does the institution or program have adequate resources in terms of staff and money to collect the kind of data that is envisioned? How much of the data may already be available, and how much is going to have to be not only collected but ferreted out from existing data or, worse yet, generated for the first time? Again, the answers to such questions will define positive and negative forces for the force field analysis.

**Forces for or against Self-Study and Change: Why.** Why should a given design for the organization of the self-study be chosen? A design should be selected depending on the answers to the other questions. For example, answers to the other questions might indicate that only a short time period, a small group of people, and limited resources are available. In that case, the best design choice would be a focused self-study with assignments to individuals to do relatively small or focused projects. If there is a long time period available, a large number of people to be involved, and adequate resources to draw on, then it would be reasonable to spread the process out over a long time, to organize subcommittees,

32

and to rely on staff support for some of the data-gathering activities.

## Conclusion

In conclusion, the following factors, as described at the beginning of the paper, are essential to the successful self-study:

- Internal motivation
- Commitment of top leadership
- Appropriate design
- Goals clarification
- Participation by representatives of many different groups
- Good leadership of the self-study process itself
- Effective functioning of the program to be studied
- Improvements to occur during as well as after the process
- A readable report
- Development of a system of ongoing self-study
- Description of the strengths and weaknesses of the program

The administrators and faculty members responsible for a self-study in an ESL program can benefit by studying these factors thoughtfully. If the evaluation process does not include these features, the NAFSA or TESOL self-study process will not achieve the high goals both associations have set of improving U.S. institutions so that they are better places in which to study and to teach. If the self-study process occurs in a context of internal motivation, commitment by the appropriate leadership, and the other features outlined above, then we can expect it to have great benefits for the individual programs that undertake the process and, eventually, for the field of ESL and for international education at large.

# Notes

1. For readers outside the United States, additional information about the accreditation system might be useful. The accreditation system is a voluntary, nongovernmental self-regulation program. That is, institutions or professions organize themselves into associations; membership in an association depends upon meeting the standards established by that association. State-financed colleges and universities have established regional accreditation associations for all regions of the United States; private colleges and universities also have accreditation associations; many professions (such as law, medicine, business, speech, and others) have also established accreditation associations. Membership is voluntary, but the status of being a member has become so important that

institutions and programs submit to the changes required by the accreditation associations. It is culturally interesting to note the nongovernmental status of these associations: state institutions that belong to state governments regulate themselves to a great extent through a nongovernmental system. NAFSA's early desire to develop a method for controlling institutional behavior without involving governmental action was consistent with this U.S. approach to education.

2. These costs include an astonishing sum for insurance for the association and for any members of review teams to pay for legal counsel, especially for coverage in case of suit by institutions that might lose their accreditation.

3. The NAFSA Field Service Consultant Program is partially supported through a grant from the United States Information Agency, so that NAFSA is able to offer professional consultants to educational institutions on a cost-sharing basis. For information on the consultant service, contact NAFSA's central office in Washington, D.C.

# References

Byrd, P. and L. Fox. 1988. Survey on college ESL credit: A report from a subcommittee of the Committee on Professional Standards. *TESOL Newsletter* 22(2):11–12.

Kells, H. R. 1983. *Self-study processes: A guide for postsecondary institutions.* 2d ed. New York: American Council on Education and MacMillan Publishing Company.

Kreidler, C. J. 1983. Standards, accreditation, certification: Defining terms. *TESOL Newsletter* 17(4):30.

_____. 1988. Program standards and evaluation. *TESOL Newsletter* 22(3):25–26.

Larson, D. 1986. Program self-study. *TESOL Newsletter* 20(5):15.

National Association for Foreign Student Affairs. 1983b. *NAFSA self-study guide: A guide for the self-assessment of programs and services with international educational exchange at postsecondary institutions.* Washington, D.C.: NAFSA.

_____. 1989. NAFSA code of ethics. Washington, D.C.: NAFSA.

National Association for Foreign Student Affairs Task Force on Standards and Responsibilities. 1981, 1983a. *NAFSA principles for international educational exchange.* Washington, D.C.: NAFSA.

Peterson, M. 1984. NAFSA's program of self-regulation. *TESOL Newsletter* 18(6):7–8.

Teachers of English to Speakers of Other Languages. Undated. *Standards and self-study questions for postsecondary programs.* Washington, D.C.: TESOL.

Teachers of English to Speakers of Other Languages Committee on Professional Standards. 1984. *Statement of core standards for language and professional preparation programs.* Washington, D.C.: TESOL.

# 3

# A Novel Approach to ESL Program Evaluation

*David E. Eskey, Richard Lacy, and Cheryl A. Kraft*

## Introduction

Program evaluation is an area that has attracted considerable interest within the fields of ESL (English as a Second Language) and SLA (Second Language Acquisition) in the last few years. While some authors (e.g., Beretta and Davies 1985; Perkins and Angelis 1985) see language program evaluation as primarily a matter of the testing of student achievement, others (e.g., Long 1984) have broadened the scope of program evaluation to include assessment of the effectiveness of classroom processes. Still others (e.g., Brown and Pennington, this volume; Jarvis and Adams 1979) have recognized that the evaluation of a language program may go well beyond assessments of classroom teaching and language learning. Indeed, Pennington and Brown (this volume) have made a first attempt to develop a broad range of descriptive criteria for evaluating program success that goes considerably beyond tests and classroom process measures. Yet there are very few studies of the application of such measures in the evaluation of actual programs. This paper, a description of several evaluations of a large program in relation to what the authors believe are both valid and novel criteria, constitutes one such study.

While most second language programs have some justifiable means of assessing and validating student progress, very few such programs have strong and compelling means of demonstrating *program* effectiveness—that is, means that are both inclusive enough and objective enough to be convincing to all the parties that have an interest in the issue. This is especially regrettable because in today's cost-conscious and competitive market for language teaching services, validating program effectiveness has become an increasingly critical component of program evaluation for those who will decide which programs will survive and in what form. A major problem for language programs is that many of the commonly used approaches to validating program effectiveness simply do not provide compelling results in relation to the real objectives of these programs. For purposes of discussion, these approaches can be divided into *subjective* and *objective* categories. The differences between the two categories is explored below.

Typical of the subjective approaches are user-based procedures that depend on measures of user satisfaction with the program. Prototypical among these are approaches that focus on the student as user and purport to measure student satisfaction. The implicit assumption is that if the student is satisfied, this is *prima facie* evidence of program adequacy. Such evaluations are clearly too subjective. While a student's attitude toward his or her experience is certainly important to measure, it cannot reasonably be taken as a sufficient measure of adequacy, any more than a patient's attitude toward his or her gallbladder operation can be taken as the final measure of its success. The problem here is not that the student is a poor judge of his or her own training; the student may be a good judge, and in fact has an important role to play in any evaluation, as stressed in Chapter Four of this volume. The problem, we shall argue, is that the concept of the user here is too narrow, and, moreover, that the criteria by which the student is asked to judge are not in themselves objective enough to be convincing to other kinds of users.

In contrast to the subjectivity of many user-based evaluations, there are a number of so-called "objective" approaches (for discussion, see Beretta 1986). In these approaches, effectiveness is measured in terms of performance on either a broadly standardized test instrument (such as the Test of English as a Foreign Language [TOEFL]) or a locally developed and standardized one (such as the University of Southern California's International Student English [ISE] Exam). The student's success is measured either relativistically, in terms of his or her change in scores on the test instrument (e.g., pretest versus posttest), or absolutely, in terms of his or her ability to meet some predetermined criterion of performance (e.g., a given TOEFL score or intelligibility to native speakers).

While these measures—when reliable—provide a certain appearance of objectivity, they do not necessarily provide better measures of program adequacy. Although they may be considered objective measures within testing theory, they may in fact be irrelevant to the real goals of the program, and in that sense are invalid (for further discussion of the invalidity of some tests, see Chapter Ten). On the one hand, some may simply be measuring the wrong things, such as formal grammatical skills in a context that calls for spontaneous spoken fluency. On the other hand, even if the right data are being obtained, the results may be useless or irrelevant because they are not tied closely enough to user goals and needs; for example, a given TOEFL score is meaningless unless the level of language skill achieved is sufficient for performing the communicative tasks that the user will in fact be required to perform when he or she has completed the program.

The two approaches that have been identified establish student satisfaction and standardized test scores, respectively, as measures of program effectiveness. We would argue that both are important but that alone or in combination neither can provide a thoroughgoing demonstration of program adequacy. We will argue here for a different approach that integrates elements of both: the emphasis on the user in the first and the search for objective measures in the other.

Specifically, we will argue for an approach that recognizes the need to develop a broader concept of the user—one that not only widens the concept of student as user but also extends the concept of user itself to include other individuals and institutions that are also affected parties. For example, in the case of a program such as the American Language Institute (ALI) at the University of Southern California (USC), which has formal ties to an academic institution, the users are not just the students in the program. Arguably, the users also include, at least: (1) the university at large; (2) counselors of international students; (3) administrators and office staff who work with international students; (4) specific academic departments (e.g., business and engineering) that have heavy enrollments of international students; and (5) other departments (e.g., the Freshman Writing Program) that have special curricular and pedagogical responsibilities for the education of international students. While not all language institutes have explicit, formal ties with these units and individuals as does ALI, we would argue that most of them do in fact have identifiable ties—either explicit or implicit—and that most of them act as "feeders" to other institutions (academic, governmental, commercial, etc.). In this important sense, ALI is typical of other language institutes.

Accordingly, we present the following case study as an example of a different approach to measuring program effectiveness for such institutions. The approach includes first developing a broadened concept of the user—in our case, the faculty and staff, as well as the students, of the university—and within this broadened framework searching for the most objective measures that the various users will accept as valid. In our case, these are formal measures of academic success, which can in turn be correlated with the institute's own formal measures of performance. In the case study, these correlations provided solid evidence that the students who met ALI's standards were also academically competitive with other student groups. In our opinion, this is a much more compelling demonstration of general program effectiveness than positive student evaluations or gains on standardized tests.

## Defining the Users of ALI at USC

During the period within which our data was gathered (1975–1985), USC enrolled the largest number of international students of any four-year institution of higher learning in the United States. Typical enrollments at any given time during the period ran to about 3,500 undergraduate and graduate students, representing more than 100 countries, especially those of the Far East and Middle East. The American Language Institute, the ESL program at USC, functioned mainly as a service program for regularly matriculated students, both undergraduate and graduate, who were pursuing degrees at the university.[1] The program also offered limited admission for students pursuing full-time ESL study only, but such students made up less than five percent of the total student body. Students were placed in, or released from, the program on the basis of their performance on a five-part program-specific examination (the ISE), which included a short composition and a personal interview.

The program offered four basic levels of instruction, from beginner/ false beginner[2] (intensive) through low intermediate (also intensive) and high intermediate (12 hours per week), to advanced (4 hours per week), supplemented by a number of remedial courses and electives. During the relevant years, enrollments for fall and spring semesters typically ranged from 500 to 600 students per term (with smaller summer enrollments). Instruction was provided by a faculty that included 6 full-time teacher-supervisors (M.A.-level professionals), 40 to 50 teaching assistants (most of them experienced, some very experienced, and nearly all enrolled in graduate programs leading to a career in second language teaching), and 10 to 20 part-time lecturers (experienced M.A.-level professionals).

The ALI curriculum could best be characterized as a vehicle for instruction in English for Academic Purposes delivered in a heavily content-oriented mode. For the average student moving up through the various levels of the program, the percentage of time absorbed by ESL classes systematically decreased (from 100 percent at the intensive levels to no more than a one-third program at the advanced level), such classes being gradually replaced by courses in the student's major field of study. In complementary fashion, the ESL courses themselves became increasingly content-specific as the student moved up from the intensive levels (strong skills emphasis) to the intermediate levels (emphasis on the use of English for general academic purposes with limited attention to specific fields) to the advanced level (strong specific field emphasis). At both the advanced and intermediate levels, graduate students were separated from undergraduates to accommodate their differing academic needs. Thus the program was for its most obvious users— the students enrolled—very much a preparation for successful participation in the academic life of the university.

As this description of ALI course structure suggests, a second major group of users were the university's schools and departments. Advanced classes were, in fact, so closely tailored to the needs of particular academic units that these units themselves often played a major role in determining the content and format of the instruction delivered. There were, for example, special sections reserved for undergraduate and graduate students majoring in scientific fields and in business, and additional sections reserved for graduate students in the fields of education and public administration. Thus, in trying to meet the needs of its students, the program was, simultaneously, trying to meet the needs of the academic units into which these students gradually moved in pursuit of degrees in their various fields. Since both ALI and the academic units in which its students would eventually major were, by definition, involved in the evaluation of these students, the administration of the ALI program reasoned that some means should be found for combining and comparing these two kinds of evaluation. Evaluation according to both of these measures would then provide a way of validating program performance in relation to the ultimate goal of both the ESL and major field programs: the successful completion of academic study at the university.

## Methods of Evaluation at ALI

During the period in question, ALI employed a nine-point stanine system for the evaluation of its students, both on the ISE and within the program itself. Of the nine possible scores, three (scores of 7, 8, or 9) represented levels of performance higher than those of students requiring course work in ALI; students achieving scores at these levels on the ISE were released from any ALI requirement, thus providing us with a group of international students who had never attended ALI courses with whom we might compare those who had. The remaining six scores correlated roughly with the ALI levels to which students were assigned. The major advantage of such a system is that it frees instructors from the problem of having to redefine for each level such traditional scales as A to F or percentages (an exercise that may also be misleading to students) or of having to invent ad hoc systems of their own (e.g., using "+" marks or "–" marks).

Since this system was designed for the evaluation of student performance across the full range of skills, some sense of the actual proficiency levels represented by scores of 4 to 6 (those most relevant to the subject of this paper) may be obtained by a reading of the six samples of student writing reprinted in the appendix. For our purposes here, the system may be further simplified by focusing only on minimum scores for exit from each level, as in Table 1.

## TABLE 1
### THE STANINE SYSTEM

| Proficiency | Level | Amount of Interaction | Minimum All-Skills Exit Stanine |
|---|---|---|---|
| Zero to low intermediate | 090/200 | 24–28 hrs/wk | 3+ |
| High intermediate | 201 | 12 hrs/wk | 5– |
| Advanced | 202 | 4 hrs/wk | 5+ |

It should be noted, however, that the exit scores recorded here represent the system that ALI had adopted by 1981, the year that the first of these studies was conducted. In previous years, from which some of our data were taken, students had occasionally been released from the program (on the recommendation of faculty) with scores lower than those accepted after 1981, thus providing us with still another group for comparison.

The few students who, despite repeated attempts in ALI courses, never managed to achieve a level of proficiency in English equal to ALI's minimum standard for release were simply "dropped" by the institute, that is, they were denied permission to reenroll in ALI classes. For those students who had been admitted to full academic programs (as opposed to those studying English only, who had to leave USC if dropped), ALI, at the time of such action, sent formal written notification to the academic department in which the student was majoring that the student had in fact been dropped from the ALI program. The underlying notion here was that the admitting department should have the final say, in these circumstances, as to whether the student should be permitted to continue pursuing a degree at USC. In a small but significant number of cases, such students continued in their academic programs, thus providing us with a group of students who had "failed" at ALI yet continued on at USC, a group we were therefore able to compare with those who had "passed" out of ALI and into other USC classes at various levels of proficiency.

### The First Study Group: Students Released by ALI

Since ALI had determined that to validate program effectiveness the critical context was in fact the university at large, the critical measure was identified as the subsequent academic performance of its students—both those released and those dropped from the program—within that larger context. The question thus became: How did these two groups (released students and dropped students) perform in the university?

If ALI training had been efficacious and its evaluation of students' proficiencies correct, then these two groups of students should have performed rather differently in the university; specifically, those dropped from the program should have performed relatively more poorly than those released. Above all, the released students as a group, in contrast to the dropped students, should have performed up to some recognizable standard of success, since the program had trained and certified these students as being ready for and capable of full-time university work.

We began our attempts to answer this general question by focusing on the ALI-releasees, reserving the detailed analysis of the fate of the dropped students for later. Moreover, our studies of the releasees themselves divided into two logically sequential phases: a first effort, which compared the releasees to each other, and a second effort, which compared them to other students in the university.

**The First Effort: ALI-Students Compared to Each Other (FWP Pilot).**
In the pilot study to our first effort—comparing ALI-released students to each other—we did not look at student performance in the university at large. Rather, we chose a narrower academic domain, the university's Freshman Writing Program (FWP). FWP became a testing ground for our overall approach and our basic working assumption that some subset of valid academic measures would successfully correlate with our own (ALI) measures, thus allowing us to statistically assess our program's effectiveness.

The FWP was a good pilot testing ground for several reasons:

1. Since all university undergraduates—both international and domestic—are required to take the FWP courses, performance in these courses provided a common measure for comparisons among the members of any undergraduate group we set up.

2. The value of such measures was enhanced by the fact that FWP administers a program-wide final exam that is holistically scored following an ETS (Educational Testing Service) model of administration that ensures high levels of reliability. Since this test instrument plays an important role in determining semester grades and the passing of the university's writing skill level requirement, there was reason to expect that one or more FWP measures of performance could be usefully compared to ALI measures.

3. Since students typically take writing courses in the freshman or sophomore year, we were able to make our comparisons relatively quickly following students' release from the ALI.

The FWP pilot thus allowed us to test our general approach and assumptions in a promising environment, one that also obviated the need for the longer lead times of the longitudinal studies we were ultimately considering. However, the pilot was more than a mere test of performance, because in a narrower context it directly addressed the problem of validating the effectiveness of the ALI program. In releasing students, the ALI not only certifies that these students are ready for the university at large, but also that they are ready to take the regular FWP writing curriculum (which they are not permitted to do prior to release). The pilot proposed to evaluate that claim. Specifically, it proposed to do so by following a group of ALI students who were released during a period of more lenient stanine standards, in which students with scores below the present minimum of 5+ were sometimes released.

Thus we followed a group of 274 ALI undergraduate students who were released from the ALI between fall 1979 and fall 1981. Their writing skill as holistically measured (by the ALI) at the time of their release was compared with their writing skill as later holistically measured by the FWP at the end of the normal composition sequence. We found a significant correlation between the two measures of writing skill (Pearson $r = 0.35$, significant at .0001 level). Furthermore, we found a discrete ALI writing skill level—6— on the 1–9 scale—that corresponded to a significant increase in the percentage of released students who passed the FWP requirement at the end of the normal composition sequence (see Table 2). Students at this skill level had about an 85 percent chance of passing; students below this level had only slightly better than a 50 percent chance of passing.

## TABLE 2
### Success in Passing FWP by ALI Written Skill

| ALI Written Skill | No. of Students | Passing FWP (%) |
| --- | --- | --- |
| 4+ or lower | 10 | 60 |
| 5– | 17 | 53 |
| 5 | 41 | 61 |
| 5+ | 49 | 47 |
| 6– | 50 | 88 |
| 6 | 67 | 81 |
| 6+ | 25 | 92 |
| 7– or above | 15 | 87 |

These results had a number of interesting implications, as follows:

1. There was, within the ALI grading system, a surprisingly discrete measurable level of skill that seemed to insure higher levels of success in the FWP.

2. This discrete level roughly coincided with the new minimum level of proficiency in *all* skills required for release from ALI (an average of 5+), in part validating the ALI's program and its release procedures.

3. The data suggested that standard measures of academic performance—such as course grades or grade-point average (GPA)—could be usefully studied; this was especially important since measures such as GPA are relatively objective measures that all users recognize and accept.

**The First Effort Continued: ALI Students Compared to Each Other (University at Large).** From the original group of 274 ALI undergraduate students, we then took all those students who were released in fall 1979 ($N = 110$) and followed their progress in the university at large. We chose cumulative GPA as our main measure of success in the university, adopting the university's own minimum acceptable standard—a cumulative GPA of 2.00; thus "GPA success" meant a GPA of 2.00 or better. The sample group achieved a reasonably high overall "GPA success rate" of 85 percent; the mean GPA for the group was 2.46 (about a "C+").

In addition to GPA, we considered a number of other university and ALI variables, including number of withdrawals from university courses, number of semesters on academic probation, graduation and completion of a university degree program, university major, ALI measures of student affect (attitudes and motivation), and a calculated rate of progress in ALI. These variables—by themselves or in combination with GPA—provided potential alternative ways of measuring "success" in the university, should GPA by itself have proved to be problematic. However, GPA did not in fact prove to be so, and these variables did not in the end provide much additional information. On the contrary, there was a close relationship between ALI measures and GPA. Table 3 provides a clear and interesting example of this. It compares the writing scores of released students with "student GPA success" rates—that is, the percentage of students who maintained a 2.00 GPA or higher. The results reveal that here, as in the pilot study, there is a distinct skill level that assures that those students who have attained it will achieve higher levels of GPA success (92–96 percent versus 57–73 percent).

TABLE 3
GPA SUCCESS BY ALI WRITTEN SKILL (N=110)

| ALI Written Skill | GPA Success Rate (%) |
|---|---|
| 4/4+ | 57 |
| 5–/5 | 73 |
| 5+/6– | 96 |
| 6/6+ | 92 |
| 7–/7 | 92 |

Perhaps most importantly, when students who did not meet ALI's minimum skill level criteria were removed from the database, the university performance of the fall '79 released students was substantially improved. The "GPA success rate" for this group was 93 percent and their actual mean GPA was 2.62 (about a "B–").

The results that we obtained have the following implications:

1. They show that we can in fact validate program effectiveness in terms of an academic measure such as GPA that is broadly validated by user acceptance (i.e., it has high *face validity* as a measure of academic success).

2. They provide a base level validation of the effectiveness of the ALI program, showing that its successful students clearly meet, and in fact exceed, the university's minimum requirements.

Universities, however, want their students to surpass minimum criteria—in fact, to do as well as possible. While it is clear from the data that ALI's students did exceed the minimum, and might be said to have done reasonably well, it is not clear from the data exactly how well they did. Hence, there was really no precise measure of how effective the program had been.

**The Second Effort: ALI Students Compared to Other Students at USC.** Based on the implications of our first study of ALI-released students, our second research effort with this group focused on GPA as the measure of academic success. More importantly, this second effort sought to overcome the obvious limitations of the first study by broadening the scope of the comparisons. First, both graduate and undergraduate populations among ALI students were considered. Furthermore, both of these groups were compared to their counterparts in other significant student populations: U.S. citizens, permanent residents, and international students as a group, including those who did not attend ALI (i.e., those deemed not in need of ESL instruction by virtue of their scores on the ISE exam).

In the case of undergraduates, the ALI population of the first study was used, but only (of course) those who met the current minimum release standard. As before, GPA success was defined as a cumulative GPA of 2.00 or more. As Table 4 reveals, ALI undergraduates compared favorably with the other undergraduate groups, both with respect to GPA success rate and overall GPA. In the case of the graduate students, ALI-released students from the spring and fall of 1981 were followed through the university, and their GPAs were compared to those of other groups of graduate students as of fall 1984. GPA success was again defined in terms of the university's own minimum standard—in this case, a cumulative GPA of 3.00 or more. ALI graduate students compared favorably with the other graduate student groups (see Table 5).

TABLE 4
COMPARISON OF ALI AND OTHER UNDERGRADUATES

|  | N | GPA | GPA Success Rate (%) |
|---|---|---|---|
| All Students | 10,819 | 2.77 | 91 |
| U.S. Citizens | 8,679 | 2.78 | 91 |
| Permanent Residents | 833 | 2.76 | 89 |
| All International Students | 1,307 | 2.74 | 88 |
| ALI Student Sample | 84 | 2.62 | 93 |

## TABLE 5
### COMPARISON OF ALI AND OTHER GRADUATE STUDENTS

|  | N | GPA | GPA Success Rate (%) |
|---|---|---|---|
| All Students | 4,653 | 3.51 | 93 |
| U.S. Citizens | 3,600 | 3.53 | 93 |
| Permanent Residents | 261 | 3.44 | 87 |
| All International Students | 792 | 3.50 | 93 |
| ALI Student Sample | 150 | 3.38 | 91 |
| ALI Sample of Students Waived by Departments | 95 | 3.42 | 86 |

The GPA results in Tables 4 and 5 argue forcefully that students who succeeded in ALI were competitive academically with all other major groups of students, thus providing a strong and compelling validation of the effectiveness of the program.

## The Second Study Group: Students Dropped by ALI

Our studies of ALI-released students ultimately had shown that ALI's program was certainly not overly liberal in releasing students, that is, it was not releasing students who were underprepared. However, these studies did not directly show whether or not ALI was too conservative, perhaps retaining for too long in the program students who were in fact ready for successful university careers. To be sure, the noticeably poorer performance of those students who had been released with stanines below the current 5+ standard (see Table 3) suggested that this was not in fact a problem. Nevertheless, a closer investigation of this group was called for. Thus, in the summer of 1985, we undertook a study of those students ($N$ = 55) who had been dropped from the program without successfully completing their ESL requirements from fall semester 1981 through spring semester 1985. These students were dropped because they failed to succeed at some level of ALI instruction after two (sometimes three) attempts. Forty-one were undergraduates, five were graduate students, and nine were enrolled in ESL classes only.

The results were revealing. Of the 55 students dropped from the program, 22 (40 percent of the total) left USC the same semester as they were dropped (this included those who were taking only ESL classes), and 12 (21 percent) left USC without attaining their degrees in subsequent semesters; thus, a total of 34 (62 percent) had left USC after being dropped. As of spring 1985, 16 (29 percent) were still attending USC;

of these, 14 were undergraduates, 2 graduates, and 5 (9 percent) had received their degrees (4 undergraduate, 1 graduate); thus, a total of 21 (38 percent) did not leave USC after being dropped. Of the 14 undergraduates remaining, 11 had so far not even completed their basic freshman writing requirement.

In this small but telling study, the academic histories of the 55 students dropped from ALI but retained by their major departments were developed. Of these, only 5 had successfully completed their academic programs. These dramatic facts argue that ALI was not only correct in recognizing its successes, but equally correct in recognizing its failures. It had neither undershot nor overshot the mark; it had in fact hit the mark.

## Studies of this Type Are Both Desirable and Feasible

For all of the reasons discussed above, we believe that our more broadly user-based approach to program evaluation is preferable to those now more commonly employed for ESL program evaluation. Furthermore, we would like to argue that such an approach is not only desirable but also quite feasible. Neither the collection nor the analysis of data posed any special problems.

With respect to the collection of data, the university proved a very willing and collaborative user. The FWP, for example, maintains extensive records of its exam results and made these available for analysis. Moreover, the university administration, once it was assured that we had a specific and viable proposal and a commitment to maintaining student anonymity, readily provided the information we needed. To some extent this goodwill and largesse may be attributed to the regular liaison that is maintained between ALI and many of the university units with which it interacts. However, it reflects to an even greater extent the self-interest of the users themselves. In our approach, it is generally to the user's clear advantage to cooperate in the collection of data.

During the process of the studies, data collection itself became increasingly simplified in two ways. In our earlier work we tracked a variety of variables; this was in part due to uncertainty about how well a variable such as GPA alone would serve as a criterion measure. As analysis revealed that GPA alone would suffice as a reliable measure, data collection became simpler and simpler. Further, toward the end of our study, analysis also revealed that we did not need four years' worth of data on a student to evaluate GPA performance. Analysis showed that we could learn as much about our students' GPA performance after one year as we could after four. The long-term significance of this is that we do not have to wait four years to find out what happened to this year's class; we could replicate our work on a yearly basis if we wanted to.

As for data analysis, "high-tech," high-expense machinery is not required. While we did in fact do much of our earlier work on a university mainframe computer using one of its statistical packages, this was more a matter of personal convenience than necessity, since we already had the mainframe accounts and skills. The same work, however, could have just as easily been done, perhaps even more efficiently, on a personal microcomputer. An IBM AT machine with a hard disk or an Apple Macintosh with a hard disk would have been adequate. As for software, most of the important table results in this study could have been routinely handled through one of the conventional database packages. Or, if more sophisticated statistics are needed, there is a variety of statistical packages for the microcomputer available (see Chapter Eight for suggestions).

Finally, analysis did not require daunting amounts of statistical expertise. While it was clearly important for some of us to have such expertise or access to it, many of those in the institute who made substantial contributions to the project had none. They either needed none or acquired what they needed along the way. In a project like this, much of the work requires accuracy, persistence, and patience—not statistical genius.

### Conclusion

In sum, we believe that we have developed a method of program evaluation that is valid, feasible, and, above all, convincing. For all who are interested, we can now provide statistical evidence that students who succeed in the ALI program also tend to succeed in their academic work. For faculty critics who sometimes complain that our students have not acquired the language skills they need for success in university courses, we can now retort, "Then why are you giving them passing grades in your courses?" By combining the reliability and face validity of the numerical measure of student GPA with the equally obvious validity of equating program effectiveness with academic performance at the user institution, anyone can evaluate a program of instruction in second-language skills in a way that is both objective and meaningful in relation to the real purposes of second-language programs.

# Notes

1. Our use of the past tense here should not be taken to imply that the current situation is radically different. In most respects, the situation described has continued, but it should be noted that in the past

three years ALI has made some changes, such as the formal revision of the scoring system described here.

2. By "false beginner" we mean students who have studied English formally in school and have thereby acquired some knowledge of its grammar and vocabulary (at least in written form) but who have not acquired any real ability to communicate orally in the language. Despite their passive knowledge, such students cannot participate successfully in a class where some oral proficiency is assumed (where, for example, directions are given in English and students are expected to understand—and be able to respond to—simple questions in English).

# References

Beretta, A. 1986. Program-fair language teaching evaluation. *TESOL Quarterly* 20:431–444.

Beretta, A. and A. Davies. 1985. Evaluation of the Bangalore project. *ELT Journal* 39:121–127.

Jarvis, G. A. and S. J. Adams. 1979. Evaluating a second language program. *Language in Education: Theory and Practice 19.* Arlington, VA: Center for Applied Linguistics.

Long, M. H. 1984. Process and product in ESL program evaluation. *TESOL Quarterly* 18:409–425.

Perkins, K. and P. J. Angelis. 1985. Some considerations for ESL program evaluation. *RELC Journal* 15:72–92.

# Appendix

## Samples of ALI Writing Stanines

### 4 / 4 +

Most students is studying very hard during the Exams, but unfortunately they cannot achieve high grade each of them. Of course, they tried studying hard as much. The reason is that their capability were not on same levels, their idea were different. Even if some students did not have a good grade in final exams, they might not give up their studying continue, because anybody know that they will have a good grade in a next Exams. One thing to say is "Do your best" and "Don't give up to do"

Did you have any stress on your final Exams? In my case, I was pressing on excessive stress during final Exams. I have never taken to a final Exams without nervousness, extremely stress in my head.

### 5 –

I'm so lonely here. I don't know English very well and I don't have best friends. So I miss my country very much. And I have to study very much, but that's a so hard. I have a very hard time of my life. So, I have a homesick, but nobody help me. Sometimes I couldn't study and couldn't play the piano. I have a very strong pressure. How am I conquer myself? But I am trying. If I have a hard time, I was listen to the music and go to beach. And I think about my situation and my lifestyle. I don't like too much talk with someone. But if you have some problems, talk to your friend, that might be help you. We have to take out our pressure. That's bad your mental condition.

### 5

Why students occur their stress? They want to make high grades. However they do not prepare too much. They use improper management of time. That's why they get nervous and high pressure. Excessive stress lead to like excessive smoking, drinking, lack of exercises, overeating, a lot of drinking coffee and etc. Therefore they get more stress final exams than routines.

In order to avoid excessive stress during final examination there are six things. The first thing is that students do not have afraid of examination and eliminate their anxiety or boredom and unhappiness. The second...

## 5 +

The good lifestyle is an important factor to coping with stress efficiently and successfully. John had a very good lifestyle. He did not smoke and drink, and had a regular exercise. These physical habits helped him to reduce the great physiological stress that the deadly disease gave him, since smoking and drinking could make his health even worse. he also had good mental attitude which helped him to cope with the great psychological stresses. His good mental attitude kept him happy that was beneficial to his health. Therefore, he seemed to be getting well.

On the contrary, Smith did not have these, and he died.

From above we see that lifestyle is very important for a person to be healthy. Because John had a good lifestyle, he had overcome the stress that the disease gave him, and he was seemed to be well. And Smith failed to do that, he was collapsed by that stress, he died.

## 6 –

I think students should arrange their everyday time schedules for studying. It doesn't have to be a long period of time, just two or three hours a day. It can be night or day, whenever they have their comfortable and suitable time. They can read their lectures over and organize it, so they can remember well. They can use this time to go to library to read the assigned books. And they can use this time to make their assignments too. Day by day, after using that time, their knowledge will increase little by little and their memories will work well and be well organized. Then, I think their stress will be reduced. Because they have good preparations and don't have anything to fear of. One of my friends always does this and gets good grades. She spends every night time between 1 a.m. to 3 a.m. to study. She goes to bed at 8 p.m. while her roommates are watching T.V. She wakes up while others are sleeping. Using only two hours at night, she can finish her paper on time and be ready to take examinations. She has a good sleep at a night before the exam while her friends have a few time to sleep. Usually she gets "A" or "B" grades.

## 6

Youth is the best period in men's life. But at the same time, this is a transitional period to independent men. Thus, there are not only enthusiasm and youth which are considered as symbols of the young, but also a great deal of stress. Many factors are associated with the stress, such as school, family, friends, and so on. The proportion of school in students' whole life would be the greatest one. The most stress which is derived from school life in which students suffer from, are mostly from examinations. As an university student, especially, I would like to consider the stress of University students during finals. The stress in which we, as students, are suffering from, must be relieved. Therefore, I would like to consider the method to avoid excessive stress during finals, such as to take breaks at proper intervals, to keep doing exercise regularly, to try to be relax, and to have self-confidence.

PART TWO

# Evaluating Curriculum Process and Content

# 4

# Unifying Curriculum Process and Curriculum Outcomes: The Key to Excellence in Language Education

*Martha C. Pennington and James D. Brown*

### Introduction

In the context of language education, the term *curriculum* usually refers to an explicit design or written statement of the organization of courses offered by a school, department, or other academic unit specializing in foreign languages, bilingual education, language arts, or ESL (English as a Second Language) (for an overview, see Stern 1983, part six). However, curriculum can be defined not in the narrow sense of a structure, document, or product, but more globally as a systematic process—from needs analysis, through the more narrow sense of curriculum as the design of a structure of courses, to program evaluation (Richards 1984). Curriculum in the latter sense centrally involves people and their interaction in developing a program (see Chapter One, this volume). Active participation in the joint endeavor referred to here as *curriculum process* is the key to achieving an array of *curriculum outcomes* that are desirable for all parties involved and that are the basis for excellence in language education.

In a language program, three primary constituencies can be identified whose interests and needs are both reflected in and affected by the curriculum process: students, faculty members, and administrators. Curriculum development in all of its phases can be seen as a cooperative project involving input and participation by members of each of these groups. Cooperation helps to ensure that the curriculum will be an accurate representation of the abilities, interests, and characteristics of all three groups and so will be realistic and workable in the language program for which it is designed. Moreover, through the process of curriculum development, administrators, teachers, and students can explore their needs and discover common concerns while learning how to work more effectively to achieve mutually beneficial goals.

The administrator's responsibility to involve all parties in the process of curriculum development will be the starting point for the discussion. Following these observations on the administrator's role, a proposal is offered for a systematic approach to curriculum design and maintenance that can aid in achieving productive working relationships among the various interest groups within a program. This approach is illustrated by means of a Curriculum Process Model that contains six components. After each of the components of the model has been described, four evaluative criteria are defined and their relevance for students, teachers, and administrators explored. It is shown how these criteria, or *curriculum outcomes*, relate to each other as components of a Curriculum Outcomes Model and how the two models are related in a third, Unified Model through the cooperative approach to curriculum development outlined in the body of the paper.

The thesis of this paper is that cooperative relationships are at the heart of a successful curriculum process and are basic to *unity*, conceptualized here as a primary curriculum outcome. It is further maintained that unity is essential for achieving any of the other curriculum outcomes, as it fosters a positive attitude toward improvement and change. Program unity therefore sets up the essential conditions for a continual process of review and evolution, which we term *evaluation*. The ongoing function of evaluation in this sense is to develop and maintain unity within the program and to tie together all aspects of the curriculum process.

This paper breaks new ground in several ways. It is the first published attempt in ESL[1] to define the notion of excellence for language programs in terms of a series of interrelated criteria. It is also the first attempt in the literature to systematically relate curriculum process and curriculum outcomes in the evaluation of a language program. Finally, it is the first published account to systematically develop the thesis that the core of language program success is unification of the interests and efforts of students, faculty members, and administrators through curriculum process.

## The Administrator's Role in Curriculum

The program administrator—whose title may be department chair, director, academic coordinator, or something else—is naturally a central figure in curriculum development. To set the stage for the curriculum process, the administrator needs to establish an atmosphere that allows all interest groups to feel that they are involved in decision making. Such an atmosphere is not always easy to create. It requires a number of qualities on the part of the administrator: an instinct for providing leadership; an ability to foster cooperation; a willingness to relinquish and to assign personal responsibility; the strength to give credit where credit is due; and a capacity to mediate among students, teachers, and outsiders such as parents, sponsors, or other administrators. These qualities all come under the heading of what has been termed *human skill*. Human skill is the administrator's "ability to work effectively as a group member and to build cooperative effort within the team he [or she] leads" (Katz 1974, 92). It is an important element of a successful language curriculum because:

> curriculum development is in large measure a group process. . . .Curriculum development therefore requires a facilitator skilled in conducting meetings and in leading a group to reach consensus or compromise. Human skill comes into play in many aspects of curriculum implementation, which ordinarily involves periodic meetings, as well as presentations, training sessions, observation, and feedback and counseling sessions. (Pennington 1985, 305)

In the curriculum process, the benefits for all members of the program will be directly commensurate with the administrator's abilities in these human skill areas.

While management styles vary widely, an administrator with highly developed human skill can effect change and lead other people to accomplish all that is within their abilities. How the administrator then deals with the multiplicity of variables in language program administration, teaching, and learning will be a unique set of decisions based on the personalities, the institutional priorities, and the constraints associated with a given program. It is possible, nonetheless, to propose a framework within which any program—regardless of the individuals involved—can develop in a coordinated effort beneficial to all participants. Such a framework is described in the next section of the paper.

## Curriculum Process

The approach advocated here applies to either the design of curriculum from scratch or the ongoing maintenance of a program. In either case, it should be viewed as a process within which the students, faculty, and administration can work together successfully. Figure 1 illustrates the curriculum process, which includes six components: *needs analysis, objectives, tests, materials, teaching,* and *evaluation.*

FIGURE 1. CURRICULUM PROCESS MODEL

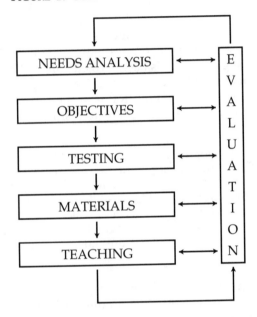

The Curriculum Process Model shown in Figure 1 is adapted from Figure 1 in Brown (1989),[2] which was itself adapted from the systems approach model for designing curriculum of Dick and Carey (1978). It is simplified down to the five basic components (plus *evaluation*) advocated by Mager (1975) in order to facilitate the conceptualization and implementation of language curriculum in specific educational settings.

As shown in the figure, the curriculum process is represented as sequential, beginning with needs analysis, then moving through ordered stages to objectives, testing, materials, teaching, and evaluation. At the same time as it is represented as a step that both feeds into and out of this series of curricular components, evaluation is conceived as a separate dimension that may interact with any of the other components at any point in the curriculum process. This aspect of evaluation is captured by the bidirectional horizontal arrows, which are meant to indicate that evaluation functions as both input and output in the development of each curricular component. Thus, any component may be evaluated and modified at any time in the curriculum process. The *evaluation* component therefore connects the other components of the Curriculum Process Model in a continuous cycle, or process, of revision and potential improvement, while allowing for local changes within components independently of each other as well.

**Needs Analysis.** *Needs analysis* is the gathering and analysis of linguistic and personal information necessary to determine, and ultimately to satisfy, the program-related needs of a group of students, teachers, and administrators within a specific context. In the field of language education, the concept of needs analysis is not new (e.g., Munby 1978; Richterich and Chancerel 1978). In the past, however, such analyses have focused too narrowly on strictly linguistic items and structures. Any needs analysis that does not take into account the characteristics, the goals, and the values of the individuals involved destines the program to failure. Hence, a needs analysis, whether coordinated by outside consultants or the administrators and teachers themselves, must include meetings, interviews, and/or questionnaires aimed at gathering information on the individual and collective needs of administrators, teachers, students, parents, and other relevant parties (see Bernbrock 1979, and Chapter One, this volume, for useful procedures).

Successful curriculum development, then, starts with research into the needs and desires of the student population served by the program, as well as into the interests, abilities, and characteristics of the faculty and other relevant constituencies, such as students' sponsors, parents, future employers, or higher-level administrators and policy makers. Other types of data can be valuable in the beginning stages. Different faculty members might research current literature on curriculum design or study existing course plans from other institutions. Useful input might also be gained by contacting other departments or administrators who might have experience in curriculum planning. For an already established program, curriculum team members can gain insights into program structure by visiting instructors' classes throughout the program. In this way, team members can find out the content and methods being used in the home institution and elsewhere, and so learn what is proving successful in different skill areas and levels at their own and other institutions. Such information can provide useful insights for the ongoing evaluation and curricular revision process.

Continuous data-gathering activities may usefully result in a series of meetings in which participants share the insights that they have accumulated. This first phase of curriculum planning, which is primarily for sharing information, also serves the important function of establishing a group process. A viable group process is essential in all phases of curriculum planning and implementation, so that (1) a wide range of viewpoints will be represented in discussion and (2) consensus or compromise can be reached when necessary.

This is not to say that each person's viewpoint must be attended to at all times. In fact, students may be naive about their own linguistic needs, at least from a language teacher's perspective. At the same time, all available sources of information should be utilized to make the best possible overall decisions. Whatever decisions are ultimately made, the cooperative decision-making process itself yields benefits for all participants. By simply asking for their opinions, the administrator has drawn teachers and students into the process and has created an interest in the language program that reaches beyond their individual classrooms.

**Goals and Objectives.** A logical outcome of needs analyses is the specification of *goals*, that is, general formulations of what must be accomplished in order to satisfy the needs that have been identified. Based on the goals that have been formulated from the needs analysis, *objectives* can be written in the form of precise statements about the content, experiences, or skills that are expected to result in attainment of a given goal. Sets of goals and objectives can help to delineate different course series or proficiency levels and serve as a basis for ongoing examination of the curriculum in terms of the efficacy of goals and instructional sequencing.

A debate that has arisen among education specialists concerns how narrowly specified curricular objectives have to be. Opposite ends of the spectrum might be represented by those who favor experiential objectives, which are stated in broad terms describing general experiences that students should have during the course of instruction, and those favoring behavioral objectives, which are stated in specific terms describing observable behaviors that students should exhibit at a certain stage of or at the end of a course. Within the context of language education, authors have either championed the use of objectives (Steiner 1975; Findley and Nathan 1980) or vehemently argued against their use, at least in the strictly behavioral sense (Tumposky 1984). Steiner (1975), for example, believes that behavioral objectives provide the student with a valuable sense of direction and achievement. Tumposky (1984)—advocating a more individualized approach to instruction—argues that language learning cannot be ordered into a uniform sequence of specific behaviors.

While not wishing to advocate one or the other of these positions, we agree with Jarvis and Adams (1979) that statements of goals and objectives are central to the functioning of a language program:

62

Goals cannot be considered an optional component of a second language program. They are essential..., for education is purposeful...Statements of objectives serve purposes beyond clarifying the intent of their formulator: they function as a communication device among all groups involved in the educational process, including teachers, administrators, parents, and other interested parties. (p. 10)

These "interested parties" include the students, who gain focus and motivation through explicitly stated goals and objectives.

Attention to the form that objectives take is not as important in our view as the benefits accrued from the effort of working together as a program to formulate goals and objectives from the needs analysis. In the same way that a needs analysis should be based on as much information as it is possible and feasible to gather, specification of goals and statements of objectives should take advantage of a variety of types and sources of information. Individual teachers and students should be consulted during the process, whether or not they are enlisted in the actual writing of goals and objectives. Their participation at any stage will have the same beneficial unifying effects already discussed. The process can also end in the creation of a set of objectives that are more suitable and realistic than the administrator alone would be able to create. Moreover, working together at the early stages of program development often helps to avoid problems later on.

The curriculum will gradually begin to emerge, based on the experience and values of the individual members of the group as they evaluate all of the information available on all of the components of the program. As participants seek to define general goals and specific objectives, they will come to many decision points about the form and content of these goals and objectives. At each point, choices will have to be made. These choices will each be significant in defining the ultimate character of the ever-evolving curriculum.

**Testing and Materials.** The issues of testing and materials are dealt with separately in Figure 1, since these are two distinct processes in curriculum development. *Testing* must respond to numerous areas of decision making within a program: placement of students into levels, diagnosis of students' strengths and weaknesses, achievement in courses, and overall language proficiency. *Materials* is another large area for choice, as it must be decided whether to create in-house materials designed specifically to meet the objectives of a particular program or to purchase commercially available texts, cassette programs, and so on. If the first option is chosen, then materials may be developed to match curricular levels or course series. Even commercially available texts can be adapted and coordinated to fit the goals and objectives of a particular program. In either case, the creation, purchase, or adaptation of suitable materials is an important matter worthy of much time and attention by program administrators, teachers, and students.

It is essential for tests and materials to be consistent with course objectives, which in turn reflect the needs of the students, teachers, and administrators, as formulated by the curriculum team. Diverse input can be solicited in the process of selecting or creating materials, as in all stages of the curriculum process, so that participants will feel a sense of investment in the program—an investment in shared needs, goals, and objectives. Administrators can draw on any existing strengths within a program to accomplish the adaptation and/or creation of tests and materials appropriate to their student population. Teachers may be identified who already possess the abilities to create and produce tests or materials. Curriculum development may include provision of special training for some members of the staff in one or the other of these specialized skills. It may be necessary to call in consultants in addition to pooling the talents of the entire teaching staff in order to accomplish these demanding tasks.

**Teaching.** The teacher has traditionally been viewed as a "jack-of-all-trades" who was responsible for everything related to the course of instruction. Thus it was up to the teacher to determine the needs and proficiency levels of the students; the goals and objectives for each course; and the tests that should be used for placement, achievement, and promotion. Moreover, the selection or creation of appropriate materials was a central and often time-consuming part of the teaching job. Under these conditions, it is a wonder that language teachers ever had enough time and energy left over for teaching!

It is for the teacher's sake that the administrator must coordinate the curriculum by either (1) taking responsibility for all of the curricular components based on teacher input, or (2) working out ways for teachers to share the load in curriculum development and maintenance, each supporting all the others. A small amount of each teacher's autonomy may be forfeited by such a strategy of working together. However, much can be gained for the program and for the individuals who are part of it from the satisfaction of teachers at being a part of the curriculum team and from pride in their own professional development. The program also benefits by not having each teacher working in isolation, reinventing each of the components independently with varying degrees of success.

The coordination by the administrator of the nonteaching aspects of the curriculum leaves teachers time to concentrate on their main job: teaching. Given strong program support, the teacher is left to focus on the most effective means for meeting objectives that reflect the perceived needs of the students and for helping them achieve those objectives. This requires professional judgments about how best to convey the curricular objectives to the students. These judgments are important as the teacher deals with the myriad linguistic, cognitive, and affective variables that interact with each other to form the unique charactistics of a given class. Administrators must be supportive of faculty members, at the same time encouraging them to function with a high degree of independence and autonomy in their classrooms, allowing them to perform as skilled professionals able to adapt to the constantly changing conditions of individual teaching situations (Pennington 1989).

**Evaluation.** The last remaining element of the Curriculum Process Model is *evaluation*, defined here as the continuous gathering of linguistic and nonlinguistic information necessary to continue meeting the learning needs of a particular group of students. This definition is very close to that given for "needs analysis" above, and justifiably so. The primary difference is that needs analysis is an initial gathering of information while evaluation is an ongoing process of information collection. Evaluation can make use of all of the insights gained in the needs analysis and also draw on all of the information collected at each stage of curriculum development. In this conceptualization, the distinction between *formative* and *summative* evaluation is not necessary. Evaluation is a process devoted to continually improving each component of a program on the basis of what is known about all other components separately as well as collectively.

**The Evolution of the Curriculum.** The systematic approach to curriculum design and maintenance outlined above is flexible and responsive to change because it is a process, not an end stage, or product. It therefore aids administrators in maintaining a program that can adapt to the changing conditions of the world at large, changes in the student body or staff, or revisions in the theory or practice of language teaching. Looking at curriculum development over the long term, periodic input from a variety of sources, including outside evaluators, will ensure a curriculum that is successful in many different ways. Input from sources both within and outside the program is important, since each constituency is likely to have a different perspective on what constitutes a successful curriculum, as well as on the degree to which the current curriculum is succeeding in meeting its stated goals. Continued review and revision are also necessary to maintain relevance and consistency with the program's overall purpose. A curriculum that is continuously evolving on the basis of large-scale input from many different quarters is less likely,

65

moreover, to meet resistance from any individual or group since participation from all is welcomed, and responsibility for the curriculum is shared.

## Curriculum Outcomes

Curriculum development as outlined above is a cyclical process of interrelated activities. On the basis of a *needs analysis, statements of goals and objectives* are developed, and *testing, materials, and teaching* are all geared to these specifications. *Evaluation* provides for continuous monitoring and mutual revision in each of the other curricular components, tying together all facets of the program. A main function of evaluation, then, is to achieve and maintain unity throughout the curriculum process, coordinating the components and ensuring collective responses to problems. The data-gathering function of evaluation is thus complemented by an equally important coordinative function.

In this cyclical system, improvement and evolution of the program are desired and expected outcomes. A favorable attitude toward change and an orientation to progress are engendered, such that administrators, faculty members, and students are always seeking a better result. Thus, the curriculum process outlined here, which centrally involves cooperative decision making, teamwork, and evaluation, leads directly to the pursuit of goals not yet achieved, that is, to a striving for excellence.

The level of cooperation and morale in a program would therefore seem to be a good indirect indicator, or criterion (in the sense of implying other features related to quality), of its overall success. This indicator, which is here termed *unity,* provides a foundation within a language program for achieving the other desirable outcomes of *consistency, efficiency,* and *effectiveness. These four curriculum outcomes,* when taken together, define an orientation to excellence within a language program. When considered separately, they can be seen as individual *indicators of excellence,* or as criteria for evaluation of the curriculum components outlined above. The relationships among these four curriculum outcomes, or indicators of excellence, are illustrated in the Curriculum Outcomes Model shown in Figure 2.[3]

Like the Curriculum Process Model, all but one of the components in the Curriculum Outcomes Model are ordered in a sequence, with the remaining component tying together the others, as both input and output in their development. In this Curriculum Outcomes Model, it is the component of *unity* that ties together the other three components, both individually and in sequence, in the ordered series of *consistency, efficiency,* and *effectiveness.*

Although programs may vary widely in their specific priorities and circumstances of operation (e.g., in the external or internal constraints

FIGURE 2. CURRICULUM OUTCOME MODEL

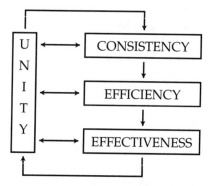

imposed on program structure, budget, and physical resources), it is in the interest of students, faculty members, and administrators alike to work toward achieving unity, consistency, efficiency, and effectiveness throughout the entire curriculum process. In the next four sections, each of the curriculum outcomes will be described in more detail in relation to the interests of students, faculty members, and administrators. This discussion will be followed by an analysis of the relationships among the four components of the Curriculum Outcomes Model in Figure 2, and of the relationship of that model to the Curriculum Process Model developed earlier. It will be argued that the curriculum process leads directly to a striving for excellence, which can be conceptualized in terms of the four curriculum outcomes defined here.

**Unity.** *Unity* in an organization means that people work comfortably together and share common goals and purposes. Unity among participants fosters an atmosphere in which an organization can flourish and so provides a strong foundation for developing a high level of success (Katz 1974). The curriculum model described above promotes a unified vision of the goals and priorities of the language program. Such a vision helps to focus the daily activities of people and to develop in them a sense of loyalty to the group within which they work and of pride in the work that they contribute to help achieve the overall purposes of the organization. Providing a unified vision also helps to develop the qualities of future-orientation and goal-direction that underlie high morale (Roy 1965).

In the process advocated here, unity means that students learn, teachers teach, and administrators manage in a mutually beneficial relationship. The program administrator helps to foster a spirit of partnership by including members of each group in planning and decision making. Through this type of activity, participants learn the skills of negotiation and compromise in reaching mutually acceptable decisions. Along the way, program members start to develop shared goals and a common sense of purpose. They begin to realize that the program advances only when individuals consider their own interests in the context of the interests of the group. A unified curriculum effort avoids the problems that result when the administration and the faculty, or individual teachers, work at cross-purposes. As a joint effort, curriculum becomes a reflection of many individual personalities and a consolidation of a wide range of interests, needs, and points of view.

**Consistency.** *Consistency* relates to the stability of results within a particular context. In the systematic approach to curriculum described here, consistency means having reliable mechanisms for achieving and assessing program goals and objectives. This reliability is a precondition for sound measurement of any kind in language testing and evaluation (see Perkins and Angelis 1985). It is in the interests of all three main constituencies for the program to have consistent procedures and measurable standards against which progress can be judged and instruction planned and evaluated.

A consistent system for testing and placement of students goes a long way toward ensuring high-quality instruction and benefits the students and faculty in a number of ways. For one thing, an explicit presentation of consistent criteria that characterize each level or facet of instruction will help to keep the different aspects of instruction distinct, while providing for continuity from level to level and course to course. Consistent standards therefore help eliminate the problems of grossly misplaced students, mixed-level classes, and substantial overlap in the content of adjacent levels or related courses. It also helps to avoid the situation in which an instructor at one level has to teach what students should already have mastered at another level of instruction or in another part of the program. Moreover, in making course standards explicit, both instructors and students will know what they are aiming for and so may have a greater chance of succeeding. When their efforts are evaluated, they will be fully aware of the basis on which their performance is measured.

A testing system that provides for consistent and explicit standards against which performance can be judged is the fairest system for both students and teachers. Moreover, such a testing system serves the administrator well, as it represents a means of monitoring program quality and provides useful information for the ongoing process of curriculum development. Once the standards of instruction are made explicit, materials and teaching can be geared to explicitly stated goals and objectives in each facet or level of the program. In this way, teaching and learning time can be put to the most efficient use.

**Efficiency.** *Efficiency* in any operation means that resources will be used as productively as possible in pursuit of organizational goals and objectives. This implies that individuals within the organization will not utilize their time or energy working on areas that are not consistent with its purposes and that the organization will not suffer major upsets that threaten stability. An efficient organization achieves a sort of equilibrium that protects it from internal and external disturbances. Such an organization can accommodate unexpected problems without large-scale changes or great infusions of human or financial resources.

A curriculum built around goals and objectives based on needs analysis is designed for maximal efficiency. At the same time, it has built-in flexibility and can tolerate adjustments that might be necessary to respond to future conditions. This helps to prevent major upsets in program operation in the short run, while accommodating to gradual change in the long run. The curriculum model outlined here maintains efficiency by continually gauging the appropriateness of goals, objectives, testing, materials, and teaching in relation to each other, and then adjusting each component as necessary to maintain consistency within the entire system (see Akst and Hecht 1980, 264-265, for a discussion of "appropriateness" and "efficiency" in program evaluation).

It is in the best interests of all parties in a language program to have an efficient operation and to avoid frequent, major changes (Pennington 1983). Efficiency means that classroom instruction and study time result in a high level of language proficiency in a relatively short period of time. It is in the students' best interests, therefore, to have a stable and efficient instructional system, so that they will not have to experience major changes or delays in their course of study.

A flexible structure is to the advantage of the faculty, since it provides guidance for instruction while at the same time allowing for creativity and independence in the specific means that can be chosen to reach the desired ends. If faculty members are to have freedom in deciding what and how to teach, then the administrator must ensure that resources are provided for suitable materials and teacher training. To ensure efficiency and equilibrium throughout the program, the administrator must allocate resources to each component in relation to the other components.

**Effectiveness.** A language program is *effective* to the extent that it does what it is intended to do. Effectiveness may be assessed categorically, as when a certain result is achieved or not. Often, however, effectiveness is measured in relative terms. A certain program is judged more effective than another program, for example, to the extent that it achieves better, faster, or more complete results. A particular course is sometimes judged as more effective than another, based on past experience within the same program or a similar program.

From the student's perspective, an effective curriculum makes it possible to advance through classes and levels of the program in a systematic progression of steps. For the student, therefore, an effective curriculum will be organized in terms of a series of explicit objectives specifying skills or tasks that can be mastered in a logical sequence during the course of study. Similarly, instructors have an interest in working with a curriculum that describes learning in terms of well-defined objectives on the basis of which units of instruction can be designed. Specific objectives are also desirable for the administrator, who has an interest in controlling program quality and in testing the effectiveness of instruction. In sum, a program is effective to the extent that its curricular objectives are explicit, specific, and sequenced so as to be learnable (by the student), teachable (by the instructor), and testable (by the administrator).

## Interrelationships within the Two Models

The curriculum outcomes are interrelated in that *unity* provides the starting point for achieving *consistency, efficiency,* and *effectiveness* in turn. It is through the creation of shared goals and a common sense of purpose *(unity)* that consistent standards and procedures can be developed for measuring program outcomes *(consistency)*. Based on these guidelines, resources can be directed most productively to achieve the desired educational purposes *(efficiency)*. A program that follows this system has the best chance of achieving the results it intends *(effectiveness)*. While unity is a causal factor in the development of consistency, efficiency, and effectiveness in a language program, it is also an effect of these curriculum outcomes, both in series and individually. The vertical arrows and the bidirectional horizontal arrows linking *unity* with the other three components indicate that unity of interests both promotes and is promoted by maintaining consistency, efficiency, and effectiveness within a program

Unity in the sense defined here is also a central outcome of the cooperative approach to curriculum described above. It is therefore possible to combine the models of Figures 1 and 2 into a larger model, as shown in Figure 3, in which the component of *unity* bridges the Curriculum Process Model and the Curriculum Outcomes Model.

FIGURE 3. UNIFIED MODEL OF CURRICULUM PROCESS
AND CURRICULUM OUTCOMES

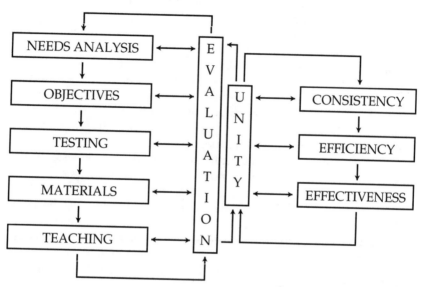

Through the component of unity, the Curriculum Outcomes Model feeds both into and out of the Curriculum Process Model at the *evaluation* component. The arrow going from *unity* to *evaluation* is intended to show that unity and the other curriculum outcomes will inform the evaluation process, as the components of *needs analysis, objectives, testing, materials,* and *teaching* are assessed. The Unified Model also shows a relationship between the two smaller models in the other direction, that is, as an arrow going from evaluation to unity. This aspect of the figure is intended to illustrate the contribution of program evaluation, if conducted in the spirit envisioned here, to developing a more unified vision of the curriculum and greater cooperation among members of a language program.

It is maintained that program unity, in bridging curriculum process and curriculum outcomes as illustrated in the Unified Model, sets up the conditions for achieving excellence in a language program. Specifically, it is claimed that a language program will achieve the outcomes of consistency, efficiency, and effectiveness to the extent that it achieves unity, as its members collaborate to define needs; to delineate goals and objectives; to develop testing, materials, and teaching on the basis of these; and to continually evaluate the goodness of fit of each of these components in relation to the others. In this way, excellence in language education becomes a function of a unifying curriculum process.

## Conclusion

At first glance, the curriculum process and outcomes described above may have seemed abstract and unachievable in the real world of organizing and managing a language program, where differing needs and priorities exist among various individuals and groups. All too often in the field of language education, the interests of teachers and administrators, like those of workers and management, have been thought of as diametrically opposed. At the same time, it is ironic that the concerns of administrators and teachers have often been directly addressed in language programs, while the specific priorities of the students have been ignored or neglected. It has been argued here, however, that this need not be the case and that a spirit of partnership can be established that is in the best interests of administrators and teachers, as well as the students for whose benefit the language program exists.

The mark of an effective administrator is the ability to enlist the active involvement and commitment of faculty members as well as students in all facets of the curriculum process. The key element of this process is evaluation, which connects the components and unifies the curriculum in a continuing process of review and improvement. As Jarvis and Adams (1979, 3) state: "Evaluation activity must be premised on the conviction that conscientious, honest evaluation can lead to better programs and therefore to a more significant role for language educators in the total education process."

It is our contention that an orientation to progress and a unification of interests within a language program grow naturally out of the curriculum process described here. We further contend that the curriculum outcome of program unity furnishes the necessary foundation for developing a variety of other desirable outcomes that may serve as standards or criteria against which language programs can be evaluated. Thus, in curriculum process and curriculum outcomes, it is program unity that is the key to excellence in language education.

## Notes

This article is a substantially revised version of a paper that appeared in 1987 under the title of "Excellence in language education: A function of curriculum process," in *University of Hawaii Working Papers in English as a Second Language*, 6(1), 81–105.

1. Pennington (1987) presented a detailed system for program evaluation in the larger sense that includes administrative aspects outside the realm of curriculum. In that system, the notion of excellence was broken

down into a larger number of criteria that included the four mentioned here. Those criteria are used as the basis for some of the final evaluation questions in Chapter Seven of this volume.

2. The figure that appears in the present article as Figure 1 is a slight adaptation of the Figure 1 that appears in the original version of this article. This figure was developed by Brown as a consolidation of the Dick and Carey (1978) systems model. The box around the *evaluation* component in the present version of Figure 1, which does not appear in either of the other two versions of the figure, was part of the original conception of this figure by Brown.

3. The figures that appear in the present article as Figure 2 and Figure 3 are the original conceptions of Pennington. The Figure 2 that appears in the original (1987) version of this article represents a slight adaptation by Brown of that original figure (which here appears as Figure 3), so that the components of *evaluation* and *unity* are not enclosed in boxes. These differences in the figure represent slightly different conceptions of the status of the elements *evaluation* and *unity* in the model.

# References

Akst, G. and M. Hecht. 1980. Program evaluation. In A. S. Trillin and Associates, *Teaching basic skills in college*, 261–296. San Francisco: Jossey-Bass.

Bernbrock, C. W. 1979. *Determining English-language needs for curriculum planning in a Thai business college.* Unpublished Master's thesis, University of California, Los Angeles.

Brown, J. D. 1989. Language program evaluation: A synthesis of existing possibilities. In Johnson, R. K., ed., *The second language curriculum*, 222–241. Cambridge: Cambridge University Press.

Dick, W. and L. Carey. 1978. *The systematic design of curriculum.* Glenview, IL: Scott, Foresman and Company.

Findley, C. A. and L. A. Nathan. 1980. Functional language objectives in a competency-based ESL curriculum. *TESOL Quarterly* 14(2):221–231.

Jarvis, G. A. and S. J. Adams. 1979. Evaluating a second language program. *Language in Education: Theory and Practice, 19.* Arlington, VA: Center for Applied Linguistics.

Katz, R. L. 1974. Skills of an effective administrator. *Harvard Business Review* 52:90–102.

Mager, R. F. 1975. *Preparing instructional objectives.* 2d ed. Belmont, CA: Fearon-Pitman.

Munby, J. 1978. *Communicative syllabus design*. Cambridge: Cambridge University Press.

Pennington, M. C. 1983. ESL administrators and teachers: Getting together on the curriculum. *TESOL Newsletter* 17:30–31.

_____. 1985. Effective administration of an ESL program. In Larson, P., E. Judd, and D. Messerschmitt, eds., *On TESOL '84*, 301–316. Washington, D.C.: Association of Teachers of English to Speakers of Other Languages.

_____. 1987. Evaluation in ESL programs. Preconference workshop. Annual conference of the National Association for Foreign Student Affairs. Long Beach, CA. May–June.

_____. 1989. Faculty development for language programs. In Johnson, R. K., ed., *The second language curriculum*, 91–110. Cambridge: Cambridge University Press.

Perkins, K. and P. J. Angelis. 1985. Some considerations for ESL program evaluation. *RELC Journal* 16(1):72–92.

Richards, J. C. 1984. Language curriculum development. RELC *Journal* 15(1):1–29.

Richterich, R. and J.-L. Chancerel. 1978. *Identifying the needs of adults learning a foreign language*. Oxford: Pergamon Press.

Roy, R. H. 1965. *The administrative process*. Baltimore, MD: Johns Hopkins University Press.

Steiner, F. 1975. *Performing with objectives*. Rowley, MA: Newbury House.

Stern, H. H. 1983. *Fundamental concepts of language teaching*. Oxford: Oxford University Press.

Tumposky, N. R. 1984. Behavioral objectives, the cult of efficiency, and foreign language learning: Are they compatible? *TESOL Quarterly* 18(2):295–310.

# 5

# Participatory Placement: A Case Study

*Louis J. Spaventa and Janis S. Williamson*

## Introduction

One of the most important aspects of evaluation in language programs is the assessment of the language proficiency of students for placement purposes. It is the thesis of this paper that a placement process in which administrators, students, and teachers participate as subjects of their own learning is better than a placement battery in which they are passive executors and recipients of standardized testing measures. This process-oriented approach is very much in line with the views of Pennington and Brown (see Chapter Four, this volume) on the need for participatory approaches to language program curriculum. Furthermore, we argue that current testing practices, dominated by psychometric rationale, fail to offer solutions to common problems of English language program placement. We offer a three-part placement battery that we believe both achieves fair and consistent placement and involves the participants in ways consonant with humanistic educational goals.

## Theoretical Considerations: Testing Theory

Nearly 30 years ago, Robert Lado (1961, 20) wrote, "What the student has to learn constitutes the corpus of what we have to test. Since the student has to learn language, it is language that we must test." In our opinion, the problem for the administrator/tester in English language programs has been to find a test or to create a test that would gauge language proficiency in such a way as to divide an undifferentiated and largely unknown group of students in a sensible manner, consistent with language learning theory and compatible with a humanistic pedagogy. At the time of Lado's book on language testing, most language teachers who cared to know about theory would likely have accepted Lado's (1961, 22) claim that "language is a system of habits of communication." In the post-Chomskian era, very few would accept this claim. However, the criteria that Lado defined in 1961 have remained central to the literature on testing: validity, reliability, scorability, economy (of time use), and administrability (1961, 31).

Reviewing standard texts on language testing, such as Harris's *Testing English as a Second Language* (1969) and Heaton's *Writing English Language Tests* (1975), one notices the overall similarity to Lado's work—from what is discussed to how that content is presented. *Language skills* (listening, speaking, reading, and writing) are discussed in isolation and in conjunction with what Lado terms *language elements* (phonology, vocabulary, and grammar). Lado saw skills as integrating various language elements. He claimed that it was easier to test an element than a skill (1961, 27). It is not surprising, then, to see the elaboration of step-by-step testing of phonology, for example, and the relative lack of how-to guidance on the testing of skills.

Two English as a Second Language (ESL) tests that have stood repeated use over time, the Michigan Test of English Language Proficiency and the Test of English as a Foreign Language (TOEFL), are discrete-point tests that yield results based on totaling correct answers to largely independent items and that make a psychometric claim of evaluating language proficiency (see Alderson, Krahnke, and Stansfield 1987, for a review of proficiency tests). Even according to Lado's rather strict behaviorist interpretation of language and language learning, the skills one needs to learn are complex, composed of language elements. The problem, particularly for validity claims of discrete-point tests, is that the composition of language skills—their quantitative correlates and their representation in test item choices—have nowhere been specified.

Yet it seems to us that part of the current controversy in language testing revolves around claims regarding what is being tested (see discussion of this point in Chapter Ten, this volume). Moreover, tests such as the cloze test have been rejected on the basis that language competence cannot be captured by one measure, and therefore one ought to revert to a componential (read Lado's *skills*) approach to language testing (see Vollmer 1983 and Bachman and Palmer 1984 for examples of this line of argument). Carroll (1980, 521) outlines four problem areas for testing and declares himself a *conservative* in the matter of test construction, that is, someone in favor of using *traditional* means to assess *language competences* [emphasis provided by authors].

Some researchers seem to view language testing in basically psychometric terms (Vollmer 1983), believing that formulas for reliability and validity justify tests. Such reasoning is often prefaced by observations about the inadequacy of present testing methods as opposed to the continuing refinement of psychometrics. We tend to agree with Ingram (1978), who has criticized standard multiple-choice, discrete-point language testing by noting: "The essential truth about nearly all kinds of tests is that the only theory they are based on is test construction theory, which is a kind of applied statistics" (p. 7).

While the controversy in language testing continues, language programs are faced with the necessity of evaluating their students' skills in order to place them in appropriate levels and dealing with the aftermath, that is, the satisfaction or dissatisfaction that students (and their teachers) feel about their skills vis-à-vis the skills of their classmates. The repeated unsatisfactory experiences of English language programs such as the one described here with placement tests and procedures, and the uncertainty over what is being tested on most tests, have led us to approach the problem of placement afresh, proposing solutions that may or may not turn out to be acceptable from a psychometric point of view. We present our thesis through the study of an actual language program—its placement procedures, its problems, and the changes instituted to improve its placement results.

## Definition to the Problems of Placement

**Description of the Program and Placement.** The program under discussion is a department within the continuing education division of a large public university. It runs several language programs of varying lengths and a TESL Certificate Program. The mainstay of the department is a quarterly 10-week program of English language study that offers students a program of 20 hours per week of classes. The program runs four quarters per year. It is this program on which we will focus.

Students' nationalities vary from quarter to quarter, but most quarters half of the students are Japanese, perhaps a fifth are Swiss, and the rest are from Europe, South America, the Middle East, and Southeast Asia. All have a generally high level of education in their first language. They usually have attended a junior college, a university, or a career training institution beyond the secondary level. Some plan to study at American universities; most learn English to enhance their job opportunities, others for travel or personal enjoyment. The average age of the students is about 23, generally with the youngest at 18 and the oldest at 30.

The program is offered at six levels of proficiency, the lowest level consisting of "false beginners" (see note 2 in Chapter Three, this volume, for a definition), and the highest level enrolling students who score over 540 on the TOEFL. All skill areas are taught in two semi-integrated classes: a grammar/writing class and a reading/vocabulary/listening class. Students also take a special interest class such as Academic Preparation, TOEFL Preparation, American Business Theory and Practice, English Through Plays and Movies, and Conversation Practice. The program emphasizes the development of communicative competence, both orally and in writing. Grammar and vocabulary are developed in context, and a high level of student participation in classes is expected.

On the first day of each quarter, the students are tested, registered, and given a campus tour and a small group orientation to the program, the university, and the community. By the end of the day, the classes have been determined and students begin classes on the second day. In trying to maintain this schedule with a steadily increasing number of students, it was found that the human and technical resources in the administrative area were pushed past their limit, while the teachers were left waiting for the administration to determine classes.

The placement procedure that had been developed consisted of (1) the Michigan English Language Placement Test,[1] which is divided into listening, reading, vocabulary, and grammar subparts; (2) a writing sample in which students wrote for twenty minutes on a predefined topic; and (3) an oral interview of approximately five minutes conducted by a teacher. This interview took place on a one-to-one basis while registration occurred.

There were problems with placement in three different areas. The first was that the placement results were not consonant with classroom performance. This was so endemic as to be viewed as unimportant by some of the teachers. The second problem was that there was a lack of teacher participation in the procedure and in the placement decisions, with a concomitant lack of interest in placement itself and an unwillingness to share responsibility for the composition of any given class. The third problem was that the procedure demanded a high level of involvement from the administrative staff. With an increase in the number of students, the procedure became so time-consuming as to be unworkable.

**Classroom Performance and Testing Measures.** It has been the experience of the faculty that students who come from a Japanese background and students who come from a European background have different abilities in the traditional language skill areas. The Japanese typically score high on standardized tests, particularly tests of discrete grammar points, but are poor in their listening comprehension and speaking ability. On the other hand, the students who speak a European language—whether it be Spanish, French, Italian, Swiss-German, or German—may have high listening comprehension and speaking skills, but a poor knowledge of grammar as evidenced by performance on discrete-point grammar tests of a highly analytical nature.

*The Michigan English Language Placement Test.* The placement test consists of 100 problems: 20 listening, 30 grammar, 30 vocabulary, and 20 reading. In the old testing procedure, a student's level was determined by his or her total score. For example, a range of 35–50 as a total score indicated a low-level student. One result of using the Michigan English Language Placement Test on the student population has been that students in the same class could vary widely in their ability to understand the teacher's oral directions and to participate in the lesson activities. These genuine and deep differences in speaking and listening skills existed to compound the normal and expected cultural differences in classroom behavior of the Japanese as compared with the Europeans.

In an effort by the administration to get a better reading of students' proficiency levels, the Michigan test scores were decomposed into individual subtests. Through this procedure, it was found that the discrepancies among students' skills for a given overall test score was very high. For several quarters, the scores for the listening portion of the test were isolated in an effort to control for listening comprehension. A simple analysis yielded some surprising results. First, there was no relationship between a student's listening score and his or her overall score on the Michigan English Language Placement Test. For example, two students with scores of 74, who were placed in a low-advanced class, had listening scores of 17 out of 20 and 10 out of 20, respectively. Second, nationality was found to have some effect. Swiss students showed a positive relationship between their listening scores and their total scores, while for the majority of students there was no relationship. Furthermore, these listening scores did not match up with teacher assessment of student classroom performance. As a heuristic device, the administration then began to reduce the Michigan scores of the Japanese students by a certain amount to see if this would result in more homogeneous ability groupings. Although this procedure did improve homogeneity, discrepancies still remained. The fundamental problem was that the Michigan test score gave the scorer no concrete understanding of the individual's competence in understanding oral English in the classroom.

*Oral testing.* There were also problems with the oral testing measures. At first, oral assessment was made while the teacher oriented groups of students to the program. Not all students got equal time, and teachers did not always have confidence in their scores using this method. Also, teachers were unconsciously and sometimes consciously applying different standards for the Japanese students and for the non-Japanese students. They might speak, for example, of an intermediate-level Japanese student versus an intermediate-level European student. This lack of standardization of evaluative criteria compounded the difficulties with placement.

At one point in the history of the program, teachers giving individual oral interviews adopted the Foreign Service Institute (FSI) scale. Our interrater reliability using this scale was very poor, and for reasons of time and staffing, it was not possible to allocate more than one interviewer per student. Moreover, some teachers reverted to describing the student's oral ability in terms of our six levels (101–106). Others worked with the FSI evaluation system (0–5), but came away with very little information because they had to score and interview at the same time.

*Writing sample.* The third part of the placement battery was the writing sample. The student writing sample was evaluated holistically by two teachers, and if there was a difference in evaluation by more than one class level, a third teacher read the sample. This part of the procedure seemed the least problematical and the most reliable.

**Teacher Participation.** Teachers were not happy with placement because the procedure was not giving them the sort of results that they needed for homogeneous classrooms according to ability. They were also unhappy with the long periods of time that they and their anxious students were required to wait until test results and class assignments were processed and integrated by the administration. Teachers felt that they were outside of the placement process and consequently took little responsibility for it. Though they were integrally involved in the oral testing and gathering and scoring of the writing sample, they did not feel in control of placement.

**Administrative Problems.** Placement itself required about two quiet, uninterrupted hours if a satisfactory job was to be done; no matter what testing measures are used, the actual placement of students in classes should not be rushed. However, the system became practically unmanageable when the attempt was made to gather together all the information (Michigan English Language Placement Test score, writing sample score, oral test score) about each student so that the actual placement of students into classes could begin. The Michigan English Language Placement Test took approximately 75 minutes to administer. Students recorded their answers on Scantron forms. Scoring those forms took approximately 50 minutes. Michigan scores were then transferred to a master list. It took 45 minutes to evaluate the writing sample. The oral interviews took over two hours to complete. Even with constant minor tinkering to improve procedures, the placement of students did not begin until the end of the first working day of the quarter.

One change that was made was to reduce the time allotted for the writing sample from twenty to ten minutes since it was found that this did not lead to any appreciable loss of reliability in scoring. Another change was that the writing sample was given to the students before rather than after the Michigan English Language Placement Test, so that teachers could start evaluating them right away. At the same time as certain measures were taken to economize on time in the placement process, other measures were taken to improve the reliability of the process. The major improvement of this type was that the program began to use a database that allowed us to rank students based on their scores. Input of all the data required several hours. Oral scores, which came in on lists from several different teachers, took more time to input. In fact, by the time the oral scores were available, some preliminary work on placement had usually begun, and because these scores had been shown earlier not to have a high level of interrater reliability, they did not weigh as heavily in the placement process as they might have otherwise.

All the problems enumerated above, from those of the students to those of the teachers and of the administration, indicated that it was time for a change in our placement process. It was clear that we needed to save time, to increase reliability, and to involve both teachers and students more extensively.

### The Proposed Remedy

**Changes in the Testing Measures.** *The C-Test.* Despite the current unresolved nature of language testing theory and its application, a "new" set of test types has come into use over the last decade. "Old" tests such as dictation, once dismissed by Lado (1961) as being *poorly motivated* and unreflective of ability in a language, have returned to use as "new" tests, championed by testing experts such as Oller (1973, 1975). A second type of test, the cloze test, in its numerous variations from nth-word deletion to selective deletion, and in its alternative scoring methods—exact word and acceptable word—became for a while the leading candidate to replace the syntax-vocabulary-reading comprehension batteries found in most multiple-choice, discrete-point tests, such as the Michigan English Language Placement Test. Oller (1973, 1975) was among the first to point to the usefulness of the cloze. Hinofotis (1987) continues to see it as an important testing tool.

However, while initial enthusiasm for the cloze test was high, it soon became apparent that there were some problems with the claims that all cloze tests were alike (Brown 1984; Klein-Braley 1985), that nth-word deletions produce a random sample of linguistic elements of the text, that actual deletion rate is irrelevant, and that all cloze tests are reliable and valid because they all randomly sample authentic language texts (Klein-Braley 1985). Klein-Braley (1984, 1985) and Raatz (1984) have developed a test similar to the cloze in that the text is damaged and redundancy in discourse is reduced through deletion. Yet it is different in that, with the exception of words in opening and closing sentences that are left intact, every other word is altered by removing one or more letters after the first so as to reduce acceptable responses to only one—or almost only one—correct response. This test is called the *C-Test*.

C-Tests are created from "contemporary, nonliterary, discursive, argumentative, or narrative text with no particular idiosyncrasies or special terminology" (Klein-Braley 1984, 97). According to Klein-Braley, C-Tests are constructed in such a way as to reflect levels of readability. A typical C-Test will start with an easy passage and end with a hard one. Easy and hard are defined by sentence complexity (length) and type-token ratio (number of different words used in the text to the total number of words used in the text). Grotjahn (1987) outlines the procedure for determining the readability order of passages on a C-Test by using statistical evidence from experimental testings. Klein-Braley says that she has shown the C-Test to be "objective, highly reliable, and acceptably valid" (1984, 84) and has worked out justification for its construct validity (1984, 84–89). Raatz (1984, 126) has conducted studies in German secondary schools that indicate to him that the C-Test measures general language proficiency and some other cognitive skills. For Raatz (1984, 126), the C-Test measures the same thing that complex batteries measure, and predicts the same judgments about students as experienced teachers in L1 teaching make (1984, 126). Klein-Braley and Raatz make a convincing case for using the C-Test, providing a tester accepts the underlying assumption that one type of test can accurately reflect a global sort of language proficiency. (See the discussion in Hughes and Porter 1983, on the unitary competence hypothesis, and in Grotjahn 1987, on C-Tests.)

The program chose to replace the Michigan English Language Placement Test by a C-Test of its own devising.[2] Several passages were tested and the final outcome was a four-passage C-Test with passages in ascending order of difficulty based on the above readability formula, as shown in Appendix 1.

*Oral placement.* While we chose the C-Test based on theoretical grounds and on its feasibility, we changed our method of oral placement for more practical reasons. Our program has a strong oral component in nearly all skill areas. Face-to-face communication is stressed daily. We had previously used an approximation of the FSI oral interview test, as discussed above. A more promising tool, we have now found, is a total, synchronous discussion exercise involving most of the teaching staff and all of the entering students. The procedure was first developed by the first author when an English course administrator in Canterbury, England. It will be described briefly below under testing procedure (for a more detailed discussion of the procedure, see Spaventa 1980).

*Writing sample.* The third component of placement is a short writing sample based on several titles offered by the testers, including titles suggesting abstract ideas ("Shapes, Colors, and Sizes"), as shown in Appendix 2. The writing sample is elicited under a time constraint of ten minutes. We feel that the writing sample offers an opportunity to gauge a student's ability to generate language beyond the sentence level within the parameters of specified, yet generalizable contexts. Thus, it completes a placement process that incorporates an oral placement procedure designed to gauge face-to-face communicative skills, a C-Test designed to discern the level of understanding of written discourse, and a writing sample designed to gauge a student's ability to generate language beyond the sentence level.

**Scorability, Economy, Administrability.** Not the least of theoretical considerations in using this three-part procedure for placement has been our concern with scorability, economy, and administrability. We wanted to empower teachers by having them take charge of the scoring process rather than having to wait for the results of a machine-scored test, the precise meaning of which is never clear because item analysis is not carried out for each student. If item analysis were undertaken, it would only add to the loss of time incurred in placement testing using standardized tests such as the Michigan. Throughout the process of revising placement procedures, economy of testing has continued to be a strong consideration. It was felt that a long testing period was counterproductive for student-faculty relations and for the student's first impression of the program. Finally, administrability was framed in terms of control. Who had control over the procedure? Using a standardized test, both testers and students gave up some measure of control. In our three-part system, we gained back some of that control over the terms and the environment of placement testing.

**Participatory Testing.** One new criterion might be added to theoretical considerations of testing. It is the notion of *catalytic validity*. According to Lather's (1986) definition, catalytic validity is "the degree to which the research [testing] process orients, focuses, and energizes participants toward knowing reality in order to transform it" (p. 272). Echoes of such concerns can be found in the writings of Curran (1977) and Gattegno (1978) among language educators; the notion of catalytic validity itself owes much to the work of the Brazilian theoretician and literacy educator, Paulo Freire (1981). In our view, most current testing procedures disempower both teachers and students and leave them none the wiser for having been a part of the testing process, unless a practice effect or "testwiseness" (Henning 1987) is considered to be a positive result. We feel that the gradual drifting of testing over the years to a principally statistical domain has a lot to do with the practicality of standardization and the ease of communication in moving test score information from institution to institution. It has less to do with student progress and test usability as a pedagogical tool by teachers. But once catalytic validity is admitted as a criterion, standardized, discrete-point tests such as the Michigan English Language Placement Test become less attractive and are theoretically of diminished value.

In creating a process model of participatory testing, we have attempted to consider the relationship between testing and teaching, especially in regard to the sociolinguistic implications of a communicatively based view of performance in language (Canale 1984; Wallat 1984). Testing becomes more focused on the concrete circumstances of both teachers (in their role as testers, too) and students when performance in the act of communication is kept in mind. Students logically have the right to question testing procedures. Teachers have an investment in creating, performing, scoring, and evaluating placement results. The circumstances of our placement testing became empowering, in the sense that the opportunity now exists for participants to act on themselves and their environment in order to change it and themselves, thereby gaining knowledge more closely attuned to their reality. It is in this sense that we agree with Ingram (1978) when she says, "Testing is an educational method" (p. 12).

## Implementation

**Creation of an In-House C-Test.** We devised two different C-Tests to administer to our students at the midpoint of the quarter before we decided to replace the Michigan English Language Placement Test with the C-Test. Because of the inherent variability in difficulty of C-Tests due

## TABLE 1
### CLASS LEVEL AND CLASS AVERAGE ON C-TESTS 1 AND 2

| Class | C-Test 1 | C-Test 2 |
|-------|----------|----------|
| 101 classes | 19.7 | 23.3 |
| 102 classes | 25.58 | 30.2 |
| 103 classes | 27.0 | 33.47 |
| 104 classes | 29.0 | 40.47 |
| 105 classes | 35.5 | 52.38 |
| 105+ class | 38.57 | 66.5 |
| 106 classes | 45.32 | 69.0 |

to their context-sensitive nature and thus to varying levels of grammatical and lexical complexity, we expected that determining C-Tests appropriate for placement purposes would require some experimentation. The initial success of the tests as measures of general language proficiency was heartening. The results of the administration of two C-Tests during the winter 1988 quarter are presented in Table 1.

In Table 1, Class 105+ represents a class we regarded as a very "strong" 105 class, that is, one almost high enough to be a 106-level advanced class. The first C-Test was given to 99 students and the second to 105 students. Class size ranged from 9 to 16 students. While the rank-order of scores on both C-Tests corresponded exactly to class levels, the C-Tests themselves proved to be difficult. The raw scores in Table 1 translate to scores ranging from 20 percent to 52 percent out of 100 percent as percentages of correct answers on C-Tests 1 and 2. Because of this low score range, we decided to administer a third test. The students did much better on this test. The average scores for each level of these three tests are summarized in graph form in Figure 1. The close similarity in test results for the three tests indicates that the C-Test is capturing some consistent differences between levels of proficiency, thus supporting the validity of this test type as a measure of English language proficiency.

The results are instructive. First, as the scatterplot in Figure 1 shows, passages do range in difficulty. It was decided that the first two C-Tests were too difficult and could discourage students. On the other hand, the third pass at test construction had given the program a C-Test that was too easy. This third test would also not provide a range of scores suitable for placement purposes. The value of having a series of graded passages was apparent. The program continued to test various passages in individual classrooms. By the end of the quarter, a C-Test had been

FIGURE 1. DATA FROM TRIAL C-TESTS, W88

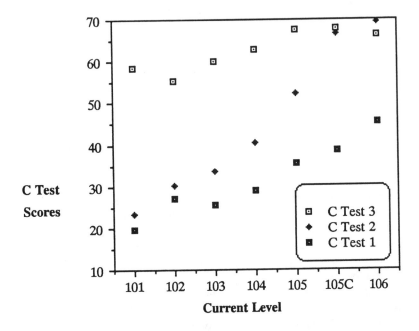

created in which the testers had enough confidence to use as part of the first-day placement process.

**Description of the Placement Procedure.** At present, the testing process begins with the oral component after a brief introduction by the program director. New students are assembled in a large room, and the academic supervisor tells students that they are going to participate in a placement test. The procedure for oral testing requires some advance preparation. Before students arrive, signs are placed on the walls of the room about every 15 to 30 feet. These are usually lettered from "A" to "F" to reflect the six levels of the program. A student who goes to level A would consider himself or herself an elementary-level oral communicator in English, while one who goes to level F would consider himself or herself an advanced one. The signs follow in direct succession. One or two teachers are positioned at each level station. Through experience we have found that the greatest number of teachers are needed at the low to intermediate levels. A few other teachers are assigned the roles of floaters: testers who move around from station to station to help sort students and suggest that they move up or down.

When the oral procedure begins, students are asked to go to the

86

station that they think best approximates their ability to communicate in English. After they have positioned themselves at one of the stations A–F, they begin conversation with the teacher stationed there and, importantly, with other students. No topics are suggested or set out beforehand. Most of the students discuss the sorts of things people talk about when they first meet. After about 20 minutes, groups are formed, and each student is given a letter designation determined by the teacher(s) at his or her station on a sheet that includes some administrative questions, asks for information about the student's native language and nationality, and has the topics for the writing sample on the back. Students then find a seat in the room and take ten minutes to complete the writing sample.

After the ten minutes are up, the writing samples are collected and most teachers begin to evaluate them in a classroom. A few remain to administer the C-Test. The C-Test paper has three damaged texts of ascending difficulty, all created by teachers, and all tested and critiqued in advance for problems such as idiosyncratic or specialized vocabulary and possible ambiguities of interpretation. Students have 15 minutes to complete the C-Test, which typically includes approximately 90 deletions. The whole procedure takes less than an hour to administer—less than the time needed to administer the Michigan English Language Placement Test, which, it should be remembered, was only part of the testing process under the old placement system.

On the first day of the spring 1988 quarter the new testing procedures were introduced. Testing began with the oral communicative exercise described above, followed by the writing sample for 10 minutes, followed by the C-Test for 15 minutes. In 45 minutes, over 100 students had been tested in all oral, writing, and reading skills. The students were then free to register and to complete other first-day activities, as the teachers retired to a classroom to evaluate the two tests. In just under two hours they had evaluated, collated, and ranked the students' tests in a spirit of camaraderie and humor, sharing the responses of students and conferring with each other. The placement process proceeded much more satisfactorily than in the past, even though class level ranges had not been predetermined.

**Michigan English Language Placement Test and C-Test.** In case the new procedure failed to provide a basis for satisfactory placement, the program administered the Michigan English Language Placement Test on the fourth day of the first week in the program's grammar classes. Michigan test results were available for a level-switching meeting, normally held at the end of the first week. Perhaps surprisingly, the C-Test scores correlated with the students' Michigan English Language Place-

FIGURE 2. C-TEST VS. MICHIGAN PLACEMENT SCORES

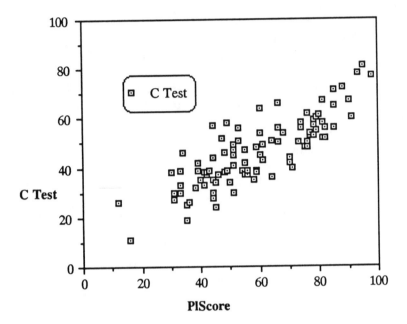

ment Test scores at 0.826 using a Pearson Correlation Matrix. Figure 2 above illustrates the high correlation in a scatter plot graph. Because final class placement involves factors other than C-Test scores—for example, nationality, sex, relative strengths in oral communication and writing, to name the more obvious ones—one cannot expect a strict linear correlation between C-Test score and class level. Figures 3 and 4 below show the average writing sample and C-Test scores for each class, respectively. Note that the class levels 104c, 105a, and 105b had virtually the same C-Test scores. Here the class placements were based on the writing skills of the students.

As a result of instituting the new testing procedure, teachers felt that the wide extremes in communicative skills in the classrooms had lessened. In addition, there were fewer level changes than previously. Interestingly, when individual discrepancies between Michigan scores and initial placement arose, teachers preferred the initial placement. For example, a Japanese student in a high-intermediate class scored as borderline high-advanced (a potential difference of two levels). Both he and the teacher felt he should stay in his initial intermediate class.

FIGURE 3. WRITING SCORE VS. CLASS AND LEVEL

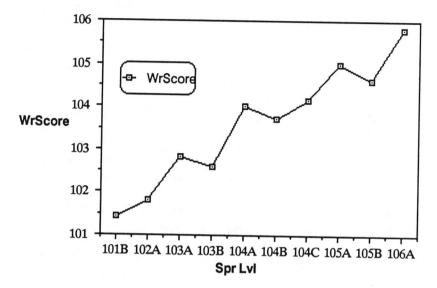

FIGURE 4. C-TEST VS. CLASS AND LEVEL

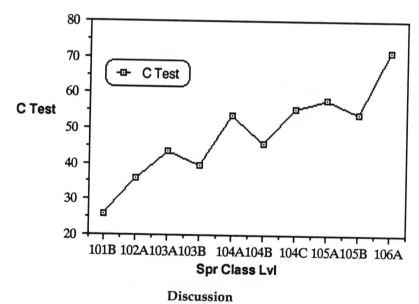

## Discussion

From the first time it was used, this three-part procedure for placement was economical of time, simple to administer, and quick to score. It has

89

now been used for five quarters without any substantial modification. During this period the cutoff points on the C-Test for the class levels were refined, the oral communicative exercise was lengthened to 20 minutes, and calculators were brought in to aid in the scoring of the C-Tests. The C-Test scores have conformed to classroom placement and level evaluation, and they have correlated with external standardized tests. Moreover, the use of the C-Test has reduced the number of level changes made in the program.

Through this three-part procedure for placement, a number of things are accomplished. The foremost among these is that the placement procedure has become a gradual series of exercises in getting acquainted with students, and the initial oral procedure has set the tone for personal communication among program participants: students, teachers, and administrators. Teachers meet students first as walking, talking wholes, not as a series of number two pencil markings on Scantron scoring paper. Secondly, students take some responsibility for assessing their English communicative ability in conjunction with teachers, and they are able to experience the range of ability across the whole program. This establishes the learning process as a mutuality of effort, not as a "banking process" (Freire 1981). Next, teachers are involved in a process that makes use of their skills and expertise. Having been engaged in the construction of the testing process, they are also involved in its administration and its evaluation. They are working cooperatively in a collegial community. They report to each other on writing evaluations, C-Test scores, and impressions from the oral procedure. They make decisions in concert. Finally, the academic administrator is able to save time to fine-tune class makeup and to reevaluate test results, as well as to receive multiple inputs on problem placements from the community of teacher-testers involved.

### Conclusion

The features of our testing mechanisms and procedures, in our view, justify the claim that we have created a process model of participatory testing. However, the most constructive and valuable result of the testing process has been the implementation of a placement procedure that is philosophically consonant with the spirit of the instruction that the language learner receives in the program. In this sense, our testing procedure has gone beyond applied statistics to become a truly valid process for assessing students' abilities and beginning their integration into their English language program.

# Notes

1. This test, which was traditionally used in the English program described in the present article, is an old ("retired") instrument consisting of 100 items developed at the University of Michigan for placement purposes. Test items are discrete-point, multiple-choice items similar to those in the Michigan Test of English Language Proficiency and the Michigan Test of Aural Comprehension reviewed in Alderson, Krahnke, and Stansfield (1987).

2. The C-Test was constructed based on one of Klein-Braley's tests and the authors' understanding of the procedures for test construction as described in Klein-Braley (1985) and as adapted for the purposes of their particular program context.

# References

Alderson, J. C., K. J. Krahnke, and C. W. Stansfield, eds. 1987. *Reviews of English language proficiency tests*. Washington, D.C.: Teachers of English to Speakers of Other Languages.

Bachman, L. F. and A. S. Palmer. 1984. Some comments on the terminology of language testing. In Reveir, C., ed., *Communicative competence approaches to language proficiency assessment: Research and application*, 34–43. London: Multilingual Matters, Ltd.

Brown, J. D. 1984. A cloze is a cloze is a cloze. In Handscombe, J., R. A. Orem, and B. P. Taylor, eds., On TESOL '83: *The question of control*, 109–122. Washington, D.C.: Teachers of English to Speakers of Other Languages.

Canale, M. 1984. A communicative approach to language proficiency assessment in a minority setting. In Reveir, C., ed., *Communicative competence approaches to language proficiency assessment: Research and application*, 100–121. London: Multilingual Matters, Ltd.

Carroll, J. B. 1980. Foreign language testing: Persistent problems. In Croft, K., ed., *Readings in ESL, 2d ed.*, 518–530. Cambridge, MA: Winthrop Publishing Co.

Curran, C. A. 1977. *Counseling-learning: A whole person model for education*. Apple River, IL: Apple River Press.

Freire, P. 1981. *Pedagogy of the oppressed*. New York: The Continuum Publishing Corporation.

Gattegno, C. 1978. *Teaching foreign languages in schools the silent way*. New York: Educational Solutions.

Grotjahn, R. 1987. How to construct and evaluate a C-Test: A discussion of some problems and some statistical analysis. In Grotjahn, R., C. Klein-Braley, and D. K. Stevenson, eds., *Taking their measure: The validity and validation of language tests*, 219–253. Bodrum: Brockmeyer.

Harris, D. P. 1969. *Testing English as a Second Language*. New York: McGraw Hill Publishing Company.

Heaton, J. B. 1975. *Writing English language tests*. Essex: Longman.

Henning, G. 1987. *A guide to language testing*. Cambridge: Newbury House.

Hinofotis, F. B. 1987. Cloze testing: An overview. In Long, M. H. and J. C. Richards, eds., *Methodology in TESOL*, 412–417. New York: Newbury House.

Hughes, A. and D. Porter, eds. 1983. *Current developments in language testing*. New York: The Academic Press.

Ingram, E. 1978. The psycholinguistic basis. In Spolsky, B., ed., *Approaches to language testing*, 1–14. Papers in applied linguistics: Advances in language testing. Series 2. Arlington, VA: Center for Applied Linguistics.

Klein-Braley, C. 1984. Advance prediction of difficulty with C-Tests. In Culhane, T., C. Klein-Braley, and D. K. Stevenson, eds., *Practice and problems in language testing*, 97–112. Occasional Papers 29. University of Essex: Department of Language and Linguistics.

Klein-Braley, C. 1985. A cloze-up on the C-Test: A study in the construct validation of authentic tests. *Language Testing* 2(1):76–104.

Lado, R. 1961. *Language testing*. New York: McGraw-Hill.

Lather, P. 1986. Research as praxis. *Harvard Educational Review* 56(3): 257–277.

Oller, J. W., Jr. 1973. Discrete point tests versus tests of integrative skills. In Oller, J. W., Jr. and J. C. Richards, eds., *Focus on the learner: Pragmatic perspectives for the language teacher*, 184–199. Rowley, MA: Newbury House.

_____. 1975. Cloze, discourse and approximations to English. In Burt, M. K. and H. C. Dulay, eds., *New directions in second language learning, teaching and bilingual education*, 345–355. Washington, D.C.: Teachers of English to Speakers of Other Languages.

Raatz, U. 1984. The factorial validity of C-Tests. In Culhane, T., C. Klein-Braley, and D. K. Stevenson, eds., *Practice and problems in language testing*, 124–139. Occasional Papers 29, University of Essex: Department of Language and Linguistics.

Spaventa, L. 1980. Testing people and placement. *Modern English Teacher* 7(4):28–31.

Vollmer, H. 1983. The structure of foreign language competence. In Hughes, A. and D. Porter, eds., *Current developments in language testing*, 3–29. New York: The Academic Press.

Wallat, C. 1984. An overview of communicative competence. In Reveir, C., ed., *Communicative competence approaches to language proficiency assessment: Research and application*, 2–33. London: Multilingual Matters, Ltd.

# Appendix A

## Sample C-Tests (p. 1)

INTENSIVE ENGLISH PLACEMENT TEST

ORAL_____

WRITING_____

C-TEST_____

Family Name_____

First Name_____

### C-TEST

<u>Directions:</u> In this test, you must complete the missing letters in each word. There are three different paragraphs.

<u>Example:</u>

English is the native or official language on one-fifth of the land area of the world. It i_s_ spoken in N_orth_ Amer_ica_, Great B_ritain_ Australia, a_nd_ New Zealand. In S_outh_ Africa a_nd_ India i_t_ is o_ne_ of t_he_ official la_nguages._

# Sample C-Tests (p. 2)

1. John is a wonderful kid. He al_____ has a sm_____ on h_____ face, a_____ he i_____ always ki_____ to peo_____. He h_____ made a l_____ of fri_____ at sch_____ because h_____ is s_____ easy t_____ get al_____ with. His mo_____ seldom ge_____angry wi_____ him; h_____ father can_____ wait t_____ see h_____ at t_____ end o_____ the d_____ and his li_____sister i_____ happy wh_____ he pla_____ with he_____.

2. Baking bread is not difficult to do. I le_____ to ba_____ bread ma_____ years ag_____. I us____ to ba_____ every we_____. When I h_____ finished ba_____, I wo_____ give so_____ of m_____ bread t_____ my fri_____. Sometimes, I wo_____ trade bre_____ for a fri_____ home-m_____ beer. The_____ days I se_____ bake bread because I am quite busy.

3. I haven't had a vacation in a long time. I cou_____ go anyw_____ last ye_____ and alth_____ I a_____ now re_____ to ta_____ another tr_____, I ju_____ don't ha_____ enough mon_____. My wi_____ doesn't mi_____ staying ho_____ though. L_____ July, h_____ parents c_____ to vi_____ us. W_____ spent so_____ time a_____ the bea_____ and th_____ we we_____ to vi_____ my pa_____.

4. After many years of decline, American cities are beginning to enjoy a revitalization. For ex_____, thousands o_____ people w_____ had le_____ for t_____ suburbs y_____ ago a_____ moving ba_____. They a_____ attracted b_____ the gr_____ quantity o_____ professional oppo_____ in the cities a_____ well a_____ all t_____ different k_____ of enter_____ big c_____ can o_____.

96

# Appendix B

## Sample Writing Test

INTENSIVE ENGLISH PLACEMENT TEST

Name _____ Date _____

Please write as much as you can in 10 minutes on *one* (1) topic. (*Do not* write on all topics.) You may choose one of the following topics, or make up your own.

_____ My favorite year          _____ My favorite dinner

_____ My flight to the U.S.     _____ Colors, shapes, and sizes

_____ My plans after the ELP

# 6

# Evaluation of Culture Components in ESL Programs

*Christine Winskowski-Jackson*

## Introduction

It is a truism that a language cannot be taught independently of its culture. Culture teaching can take many forms: explicit lessons on history, beliefs, and customs, or the underlying presuppositions and implications of language use. Indeed, culture teaching can take the subtlest of forms, as when attitudes and points of view are unconsciously displayed by an instructor. Culture and its manifestations pervade the language learning setting, forming its ecology. The business of culture teaching is thus a unique sort of endeavor.

Culture teaching and culture learning are unlike the teaching and learning of the classic four language skills of reading, writing, listening, and speaking. While some methodology has emerged from the international business and foreign service fields, culture teaching is something of a new field by comparison. Moreover, while culture can be treated as an independent, teachable topic, it also intersects, reinforces, and in some cases may detract from other aspects of classroom and out-of-class learning. International students cannot avoid being aware of manifestations of culture in their environment, explicit and implicit, and can hardly avoid taking in this pervasive information and reacting to it.

For a teacher of culture or a curriculum supervisor in an English as a Second Language (ESL) program, there are a number of important questions, such as what cultural input is needed at various stages of the students' sojourn, what aspects of culture are teachable, what amount of culture orientation is sufficient, what amount of cultural input is optimal, and how cultural information will be integrated with the language learning that is the backbone of the language program. Still other questions arise, such as whether the substance of the culture curriculum is comprehensive, whether all channels of culture learning are being optimally employed, how the culture and language learning experience interrelate in such a way as to enhance and reinforce one another, and where culture should be treated as a topic in its own right, separate from the language curriculum.

The avenues for teaching culture in a university-level intensive English program or in similar ESL programs are many. In most programs it is considered productive to conduct an orientation for newly arrived foreign students, where immediate survival, self-management, and social needs are addressed. Culture courses and seminars have presently come into vogue in ESL programs, as evidenced by the increasing number of culture-centered textbooks available. *Settling In* (Shapiro 1985), for example, is an introduction for immigrants to the practical aspects of living in the United States. *The American Way* (Kearny, Kearny, and Crandall 1984) is an introduction to basic North American values as they are manifested in our institutions and daily lives. The nature of culture itself has generated texts, like *Face to Face* (Zanger 1985), that are unlike traditional ones. This text, with its focus on the shaping of communication and attitude, incorporates case studies, guided interviews with native speakers, ethnographic observations, research projects, field trips, and other activities with a cultural focus.

In traditional language skill courses, cultural explanations have always been needed, though language skills lend themselves differentially to inclusion of cultural content. For example, learning conversational conventions integrates nicely with learning the culture of social exchange; reading involves culture, though to varying degrees, depending on the content of the text. Additionally, international students in a college or university environment naturally undertake all sorts of culture learning that is not part of the curriculum.

The purpose of this article is to guide readers' evaluation of culture teaching in ESL programs. To this end, different aspects of the culture teaching enterprise are described, pertinent issues are raised, and a range of elements are identified that might be productively incorporated into each cultural component. Because formal preparation for teaching culture tends to be minimal for most ESL instructors, the exposition begins with a discussion of professional development in this area. Aspects of program structure are addressed next, including curricular infrastructure, orientation, and culture courses. Culture components in language skills courses are then considered, followed by a discussion of the evaluation of program effectiveness as measured by indicators of students' acculturation. In each of these sections, specific suggestions are offered; these suggestions are further detailed as a series of checklists in the Appendix. The checklists are not intended to be prescriptive; rather, they provide readers with an opportunity to compare the cultural elements of their own program with those identified in the checklists, and thereby to evaluate their own program's goals and effectiveness.

## Evaluating Culture Components in ESL Programs

### PROFESSIONAL DEVELOPMENT

It is taken for granted in the TESL (Teaching of English as a Second Language) and TEFL (Teaching of English as a Foreign Language) fields that speaking a language does not necessarily qualify one to teach it. The cultural corollary of this truism about language would probably be equally accepted, namely, that growing up in a given culture does not necessarily qualify one to teach it. In both cases, it can be argued that teaching requires systematic knowledge and understanding as well as pedagogical training. Indeed, Gregory Trifonovich, in describing his life sojourns across cultures to a student group (1986), offered his realization that culture is a secret—so secret, in fact, that it is hidden from conscious awareness, until people find themselves in a foreign culture.

The need for education in the substance of the target culture and appropriate teaching methods seems self-evident. Yet a look at teacher training programs in the United States shows comparatively scant attention paid to this aspect of teacher preparation. The *Directory of Professional Preparation Programs in TESOL in the United States, 1986–1988* (Frank-McNeill 1986) lists 120 Master's degree programs. The number of course titles in the directory with phrases indicating cultural content are few. These are as follows (the number of required courses is indicated in parentheses): culture and language, 14 (7); culture/miscellaneous (e.g., culture studies, culture of target language), 6 (2); culture teaching, 3 (1); American culture, 3 (1); Hispanic/French culture, 7 (0); intercultural communication, 11 (3); cross-cultural awareness, 2 (2); sociolinguistics, 44 (18); ethnography/ethnolinguistics, 3 (0); multiculturalism, 1 (0); bilingualism, 13 (3); multi/bicultural education, 9 (3); history of English, 29 (7); literature, 14 (2).

While cultural content in teacher training courses may not always be indicated by course title, the number of titles that appear to include such content is remarkably low. Courses actually titled "Culture Teaching" number three in this 1986-88 directory. The number of culture-related courses that are required in various programs unmistakably place this topic out of the mainstream of ESL teacher training. As Dunnett, Dubin, and Lezberg (1986) point out, "TEFL training programs are pro-

100

viding a good preparation in theoretical backgrounds to second language teaching, applied linguistics, and in-class practice teaching, but very little in the way of intercultural training" (p. 158). They recommend that teacher training programs provide opportunities for student teachers to gain culture teaching experience.

So many ESL and EFL teachers have had some cross-cultural contact—from the Peace Corps, from previous teaching experience, from sojourns abroad—that perhaps a cultural element in teacher training is considered unnecessary. However, teachers in the field can benefit from a variety of in-service training opportunities, a number of which are identified by Dunnett, Dubin, and Lezberg (1986, pp. 158-9): among them exposure to workshops, courses, and publications offered by such professional organizations as TESOL (Teachers of English to Speakers of Other Languages), ATESL (Administrators and Teachers in English as a Second Language) in NAFSA (National Association for Foreign Student Affairs), and SIETAR (Society for Intercultural Education, Training, and Research). Specialized gatherings, such as the annual East West Center Summer Workshop for the Development of Intercultural Coursework (University of Hawaii) or the annual Summer Institute for Intercultural Communication (Stanford University and Maryhurst College) are of particular interest.

No one course or workshop, however, can do justice to the wealth of knowledge available about culture. Ultimately, a teacher must self-educate on an ongoing basis (see discussion in Chapter One, this volume). A survey of program staff expertise on areas of the target culture might be helpful for evaluation. These areas can be compared with those described below (and summarized as a checklist in Appendix A) to evaluate the adequacy of coverage. Areas that are weakly represented but deemed useful might be apportioned to interested staff members for study.

**Conversational Conventions.** Conversational conventions are generally considered the domain of sociolinguistics, and include conversational openings and closings, topic changes, politeness rituals, levels of formality, telephone procedures, service encounters, and the most common speech formulae (Richards and Schmidt 1983). Happily, this sort of information is now finding its way into textbooks such as Kasser and Silverman (1981) and Levine and Adelman (1982); additional material from sociolinguistic research, or simply from brainstorming, can serve as reference files. Conventions used in academic settings may be of particular interest for many students.

**History.** A general familiarity with North American history is desirable, although the need for specific events and dates may be fulfilled by most college-level history texts. Of deeper interest are "culturological histories," that is, historical studies that provide insight into the influence of certain events on the American character or on American English. For example, many foreigners find Americans' penchant for probabilistic thinking curious. It is likely that such statistical thinking has roots in the U.S. government's census endeavors, the insurance industry's development of statistical mathematics, and the development of standardized measurement in clothing and other industries, as described by historian Daniel J. Boorstin (1974). Other well-documented American values and characteristics (independence, frontier mentality, etc.) may receive helpful explanations from historical accounts.

**Contemporary Anthropology/Popular Culture.** The myriad of expressions, personas, themes, and topics that have saturated the American consciousness from cinema and television are a revealing part of contemporary anthropology and popular culture. Anthropologists' investigations of contemporary American culture present a wealth of information on advertising, food, dress, work, lifestyle, education, religion, and so on. Some examples are found in chapter titles of a volume edited by Montague and Arens (1981), including "Football Games and Rock Concerts: The Ritual Enactment of American Success Models" and "Homes and Homemakers on American TV."

**Religion/Spirituality.** It is puzzling that many fine books on American culture (e.g., Stewart 1972) provide only the briefest treatment of American religion and spirituality. This may be due to the perceived sensitive nature of the subject, or to the proliferation of religious traditions in this country. However, given the historical role of religion, its pervasive influence on secular values and customs, and the potentially interesting implications of the religiosity of Americans today, the particular forms that American spirituality has taken might well be part of the culture curriculum. Materials giving surveys of American religious beliefs are useful (e.g., Kearny, Kearny, and Crandall 1984), as well as works that are "culturological" in the sense described above. For example, an understanding of the western religious precept of personal responsibility for thoughts as well as deeds helps to explain the current "self-destiny" ethic, that is, the notion of an individual's responsibility for inner states and happiness (a notion evident in the "Self-Help" sections of bookstores). It goes without saying that any discussion of spiritual or religious topics must be conducted by the instructor with objectivity, respect, tact, and discretion.

**Psychology.** Descriptions of the American (U.S.) national personality abound (e.g., Spindler and Spindler 1983), and can provide a rich reference collection for the instructor. ESL textbook writers are becoming increasingly sophisticated in their incorporation of this sort of material. Studies contrasting American culture with other cultures are helpful (see, for example, those in Valdes [1986]). A caution should be raised here against a unitary view of the North American character. While there is a dominant, mainstream set of characteristics, the instructor must retain a realistic perception of regional differences (e.g., the Southwest versus the Northwest, or Hawaii versus Alaska), and demographic changes in the ratio of minority to majority populations, even within one generation. Another focus with which the instructor should be well acquainted is the psychological process of acculturation, including culture shock. A recent, comprehensive treatment of this subject is Furnham and Bochner's *Culture Shock: Psychological Reactions to Unfamiliar Environments* (1986).

**Ethnosemantics and Pragmatics.** This category is meant to describe an ability in identifying the real-time functions and significance of spoken or written text: identifying speech acts, functions, and formulae, presuppositions, implications, and meaning; and identifying the sequential development of argument or reasoning and other functional labeling of language events (see, for example, discussions in Jakobovits 1970; and in Myers, Brown, and McGonigle 1986; Richards and Schmidt 1983). This ability also involves identifying where the larger influences of history, ethnicity, contemporary culture, belief, and personal history intertwine and are manifested in a given moment of language expression. Yet such perceptions are simply the normal (albeit often unconscious) rendering of culture-specific meaning, though perhaps more explicitly and systematically expressed than in ordinary conversation.

Ethnosemantic and pragmatic knowledge are called into play to help interpret the world of English discourse to the international student. This kind of knowledge goes beyond the surface-level coding of discourse events, such as "inquiry," "apology," and "raising of a new topic," and focuses on the significance of discourse events in the context of the speakers' relationships and the events of the moment. The ability to make use of ethnosemantic and pragmatic knowledge in interpreting language allows the language learner to move from a position of merely recognizing the overt "morphology" of cultural manifestations in social events (i.e., how people may be expected to behave with each other in a given setting) to understanding uniquely expressed meaning on particular occasions.

**Curricular Infrastructure: Toward a Taxonomy of Culture and Accultura-
tion Content for Individual Programs.** Culture interweaves language
intimately, and acculturation processes intimately interweave language
acquisition processes. It is important for administrators and instructors
to be clear about whether culture teaching and learning are apportioned
optimally among orientation activities, language classes, culture classes,
social encounters, non-ESL classes, or other experiences. A comprehensive taxonomy of the elements of cultural content in an ESL program
can be most helpful in identifying the location of the cultural elements
in the various program components. This kind of taxonomy facilitates
the evaluation of the distribution and appropriateness of cultural components in the program, and helps to determine whether they are suf-
ficiently spiraled at various levels of the curriculum. Additionally,
identified elements of the taxonomy can be compared to schemes of
cultural content from other sources to determine whether elements need
to be added to the cultural aspects of the ESL program.

There are many useful schemes that may be taken both as starting
points for the identification of a taxonomy of culture elements, as well
as points of comparison for later development. One such scheme is the
*Outline of Culture* (1971) developed by Murdock et al. for the Human Area
Relations File. It is an excellent starting point—basic, objective, and
complete—into which other lists, taxonomies, and compendiums can
be integrated according to the needs and purposes of individual programs. Another list of cultural content comes from the appendix of
Hirsch's *Cultural Literacy: What Every American Needs to Know* (1987). This
is a list of words and phrases identifying events, people, places, concepts, quotations, and so on, "intended to illustrate the character and
range of the knowledge literate Americans tend to share" (Hirsch 1987,
146). While the list is probably too detailed for complete absorption into
a culture curriculum, it is a useful reference for the teacher or
administrator.

Textbooks in recent years have grown increasingly sophisticated in
their presentation of culture components, and these provide a third and
complementary source for the development of a program's cultural infrastructure. One example is Stewart's *American Cultural Patterns: A Cross-
Cultural Perspective* (1972). It focuses primarily on Americans' beliefs and
behaviors (rather than institutions, history, language, etc.) and is a
valuable, in-depth treatment. Another example is Shapiro's *Settling In*
(1985), which offers a detailed and comprehensive cultural orientation
for entrance into daily life activities in the United States. Texts like these

will contribute depth and detail to the cultural taxonomies of individual programs, according to their needs.

Other kinds of texts, often reading or conversation texts, use culture as the content vehicle to teach language skills. Unfortunately, some of these tend to offer superficial treatments of culture topics of the "friends-telephone-shopping" variety. While useful as language texts and for providing elementary information about culture, they are unlikely to contribute substantially to the development of an ESL program's curriculum in culture learning.

The identification and development of a cultural infrastructure in the form of a taxonomy of culture content will, and ought to, take time, in order to be shaped to program needs. The various parts of a program in which sections of the taxonomy may manifest themselves will be addressed now.

**Orientation.** Orientation is likely to be the first form of official welcome and introduction an international student receives from an institution. While the student may be happy to be beginning a new academic career in a foreign country, this is probably also a time of anxiety. Many questions about the student's obligations may be in mind, matters of the daily routine and living may still be unsettled, and of course the pain of separating from family and home may still be fresh. Orientation must begin to address these circumstances and to foster the student's assimilation into the academic community.

Barnes describes the development of a program designed to orient foreign teaching assistants (FTAs) at Drexel University (1986). Originally, the program involved sightseeing and activities orienting the FTAs to aspects of their campus life and to aspects of general daily life (e.g., nutrition). These activities were evaluated by FTAs (both by their physical presence, which was optional, and by survey feedback), and the program revised. The activities retained were those that helped students to "get down to business" (e.g., "learning about the teaching assistant program and getting a feel for the campus," p. 35), and those that helped students "organize the days and weeks to come" (p. 35). This study indicates that information and activities that help people in a foreign environment gain control of and familiarity with their schedule and with the environment are those that help minimize initial culture shock. Below is a description of elements that may be usefully included in an orientation. (These are summarized as a checklist in Appendix B.)

*Tour of environs.* The first step is a tour of all locales on campus where the student may need to conduct business, such as dining areas, campus store, faculty offices, registrar's office. The next step is a tour of corresponding locales off campus, such as post office, drugstores, bus stops, and so on.

*Conventions of routine service encounters.* Here, the patterns for service encounters are addressed, including using public transportation, dining in a restaurant, using the post office, and general inquiry and politeness strategies.

*Academic procedures.* The student will likely need familiarizing with important academic procedures, such as registration, consultation with advisors, financial matters, library cards, campus I.D.'s, health clearances, and campus employment procedures.

*Conventions of academic culture.* The international student may encounter many differences in the American academic system, such as in role expectations, requirements, and obligations for students, professors, teaching assistants, and classmates (e.g., North American professors may appear to be quite friendly and informal, yet expect course requirements to be taken seriously); in routine classroom behavior; in understanding course syllabi, requirements, grading policies, and work standards (plagiarism is an issue here); and in campus policies and rules.

*Socialization.* Though listed last, this may be most important for fostering international student assimilation. Social events should be planned with both nonnative and native students, dorm and student leaders; introductions to key staff must be made (nurses, librarians, freshman professors, counselors); contact with and access to churches, community agencies, and organizations must be provided; and homestay families must be made available.

**Culture Courses and Seminars.** *Content.* After the initial flurry of the semester's activities have passed and students have settled into something of a class routine, semester-long courses or seminars on culture offer deeper, ongoing support and learning for the student (see Brislin and Pedersen 1976). In the first year of an international student's sojourn, the stresses of culture shock emerge, sometimes with dismaying effects. In what is probably the most comprehensive literature review on the subject to date, Furnham and Bochner (1986) describe the prevailing theories on the causes of culture shock. According to these authors, there are extensive literatures attributing culture shock to (1) a sense of grief and bereavement at the separation from family and surrounds; (2) a sense of lack of control over one's environs; (3) the stress of major life change; (4) the absence of one's support from relationships; (5) the mismatch between the sojourner's expectation and the reality confronted; and

(6) differences between the values of the sojourner and the host nationals. Actually, the explanation of culture shock that the authors favor points to a lack of social skills of the sojourner, and recommends training to promote competency in social interaction (Furnham and Bochner 1986, 200ff).

Institutions have developed a variety of solutions for the task of providing extended cross-cultural training for international students and a variety of methods of implementing them. Many such efforts are described in a volume edited by Byrd (1986). Three learning levels described by Jakobovits and Nahl-Jakobovits (1987) characterize important aspects of culture training: affective learning, cognitive learning, and learning of psychomotor skills. These three aspects of learning will be returned to periodically through this paper. Affective learning refers to the understanding and personal skills involved in cross-cultural adjustment. First, it involves understanding the nature of culture, its deep roots in one's psychology, and the psychological disorientation of culture shock. It also involves reinforcing productive attitudes, such as tolerance for difference and ambiguity. Finally, it involves a willingness on the part of the foreign sojourner to use effective coping strategies (see, for example, Archer 1986; Diemar 1986; Furnham and Bochner 1986; Hughes 1986; Seelye 1984).

Cognitive learning involves acquisition of information about the culture, its roots, and its people. It may involve the use of North American informants or counterparts to provide pertinent cultural information (see, for example, Bell et al. 1986; Comer 1986; Davis 1986; Maggio and Gay 1986). Of particular interest are the major contours of North American cultural characteristics, history, customs, daily life and popular culture, religious beliefs, and so on. Also important are communicative strategies for various social settings and discourse events.

Psychomotor skills comprise the ability and awareness to practice socially interactive competence. Training may include roleplaying (Genzel and Cummings 1986), interviews (Zanger 1985), and ethnographies completed by the student in classrooms or other relevant settings (Hickey 1980; Zimmerman 1987).

These elements are briefly detailed in a checklist in Appendix C. Program evaluation of these learning foci may involve considering whether each focus is adequately represented and integrated with the others. For example, the extent to which specific points of affective or cognitive knowledge are applied in the practice of psychomotor skills may be a focus of evaluation.

*Culture materials and resources.* Culture courses have a unique feature, namely, that the environment can serve as a text. Actually, the last decade has seen the emergence of ESL texts in which culture is the content itself rather than a vehicle for language content. Kasser and Silverman's *American Cultural Encounters* (1981), Levine and Adelman's *Beyond Language: Intercultural Communication for English as a Second Language* (1982), and Stewart's *American Cultural Patterns* (1972) are all examples. Dunnett, Dubin, and Lezberg (1986) have argued that materials that present culture learning in a two-dimensional fashion, that is, contrasting the target culture with that of another culture, help to prevent implicit cultural bias (p. 153). They go on to suggest that "one-dimensional" materials (noncontrastive descriptions of the target culture) can be supplemented and that successful teachers can inject an "intercultural ethos" (p. 156) into the class.

Their point is well worth considering, although the exclusion of one-dimensional materials would seem a great loss of cultural realia. There is a tremendous wealth contained in publications of every sort that might be found in an average household, a bookstore, or even a rummage sale. The solution is, as Dunnett, Dubin, and Lezberg (1986) suggest, in the instructor's framing the materials' presentation as an impartial—perhaps comparative—investigation of cultural information and artifacts. Archival materials of every sort might be collected for this endeavor (Winskowski 1985).

One category of materials might be called "informant collections" (Gordon 1977), that is, collections, categorizations, and enumerations of knowledge that a native speaker (or informant) would be aware of. These collections might be in published form, such as almanacs, telephone books (the yellow pages), social registers, lists of various types of information, and educational curricula. Informant collections might be unpublished as well, such as student-generated ethnographies of behavior and language use in local settings, videos of gestures, assessments of North Americans by native speakers and by nonnative speakers. Informant collections are also exemplified by student assignments for an undergraduate social psychology course described in Jakobovits and Gordon, (1978): transcripts of mental conversations with oneself, as well as thoughts during conversation with others; logs of daily activities; inventories of wallets, closets, and drawers; and descriptions of behavior. A related category of materials is reference books such as dictionaries, manuals, cookbooks, books on folklore, idioms, and proverbs. Archival collections can further be expanded with items such as common household "junk" mail, appliance instructions, application forms, magazines, comic books, and documents.

A checklist of sample materials is detailed in Appendix D. Administrators and instructors may use this checklist for a point of comparison to determine the degree to which similar materials are available to students in their programs.

108

*Methods.* With the growth of cross-cultural training for international business and diplomacy, a variety of new methodologies have been joined with traditional ESL teaching methods to address the unique topic of culture learning. Because the learning of culture is so broad a task, it is a good idea to combine teaching approaches to deal with the various aspects of culture learning. The benefits and drawbacks of the various approaches are discussed below.

The traditional lecture is useful for clear and direct dissemination of cognitive knowledge. By itself, however, it can rarely generate a full appreciation and understanding of culture points that contrast greatly with corresponding points of the student's own culture. The lecture method needs to be complemented by in-depth discussion, readings, and various types of exercises.

There are times when no other method can offer the value of informal discussion for flexibility and serendipitous discovery. This mode of learning especially addresses affective and cognitive needs, and it has the merit of spontaneity for both instructor and student. It may provide the occasion for generating understanding, for catharsis, and for resolving confusion that no other format provides.

Reading and interpretive exercises can offer a nonthreatening way to confront cultural differences of all sorts. *Culture capsules* and *culture clusters* are designed to present situations to the student, who is asked to consider the appropriateness of various behaviors; implications and significance of each alternative are then revealed and discussed (see, for example, Kasser and Silverman 1981). Short stories whose characters' motives and behavior can be subject to interpretive analysis can serve the same purpose. These types of exercises foster cognitive and affective understanding. Finally, elements of culture can be directly taught with explanatory readings.

Cultural awareness training can comprise a learning focus in its own right. For example, groups may be primed with hidden agendas, and left to accomplish a task jointly; in a debriefing the hidden agendas are revealed, leading to a discussion on misinterpretation of meanings, motives, values, and the like. These kind of exercises facilitate the development of affective tolerance and coping skills. It is important to note, however, that these may follow a primarily Western psychological tradition and must be examined for the potential of psychological threat to non-Westerners.

Student-conducted ethnographies prompt first-hand student learning (Hickey 1980; Zimmerman 1987) that is at once detailed and holistic. Ethnographies of the classroom, of the dormitory, and so on, allow the student to consciously focus on what is familiar and what is not; follow-up discussion presents an opportunity for deep culture analysis.

Finally, the use of counterpart native speaker students paired with international students provides learning for both. They may be assigned to special tasks, such as an ethnographic investigation (e.g., of music, of college populations, or of life histories as described by Davis 1986); or they may conduct weekly routines together (e.g., studying). At least partial structuring (of the interaction is preferred, rather than simply socializing. Profound affective and cognitive developments are likely with this method, and psychomotor skills get a good workout as well.

Any evaluation of a culture course can benefit from an analysis of methods used, their appropriateness for program goals, and the way in which various methods used complement and reinforce each other.

**Culture Components in Language Skills Courses.** Language courses must, of course, focus primarily on (1) the development of skills in reading, writing, speaking, or listening, or (2) language content: phonology, vocabulary, grammar. Attention to linguistic forms, combined with or applied to meaningful content, provides an optimal context for learning. Where content is a necessary vehicle for language examples, applications, and exercises, it seems a pity to employ only abstract, contextless text. A grammar point can be exemplified with an idiom, a useful conversational formula, or a bit of history as easily as with the conventional textbook type of example. Annotations may need to be added to explain the cultural content; however, these provide supplementary or reinforcing material to the main focus of class.

In some classes the content may be predetermined. For example, a pre-university preparatory writing or reading course may necessarily focus on academic reading or writing. It is easy to overlook the fact that academia (or indeed any social setting where specialized English is used) is a subculture unto itself, and that the impersonal tone of textbook prose and the citation conventions of academic writing are conventions of the scholarly subculture. Indeed, they may be more meaningful if taught as such. Below is a discussion of ways in which cultural content can be incorporated into language skills courses so that everything in the instructional setting counts.

These cultural elements that may be incorporated into language skills classes can be found in a checklist in Appendix E. The reader may note that some of the elements listed echo those listed for culture courses, or in other checklists. This is appropriate, for given the pervasive nature of culture learning, some redundancy is desirable. As suggested above, a program evaluation may take into account the extent to which learning of cultural elements is recycled and reinforced at progressively more sophisticated levels.

110

*Speaking.* Speaking courses probably lend themselves most readily to the incorporation of culture teaching, since so many of our attitudes, values, beliefs, and so on emerge in speech. In addition, what constitutes politeness, patterns of affect, and conventions of reasoning are inherent in spoken discourse. Materials should contain authentic, appropriate, and colloquial language samples, clearly tied to specific social roles and social settings. Tape recordings of spontaneous speech (for intermediate and advanced students) and materials from the radio and television are rich in cultural content. Study, analysis, and imitation of these materials will supplement and help prepare for the primary practice that students will ultimately need: spontaneous conversation with native speakers.

*Listening.* A cultural focus in a listening course might center around recognizing nuances of meaning colloquially expressed (e.g., in idioms and formulae), expression of meaning through intonation and stress, the expression of emotion and affect, and finally, the variations on these in regional accents. Text materials can profitably be supplemented with students' exposure to and analysis of spontaneous conversation and television or film dialog.

*Reading.* In a reading course, a cultural focus might well begin with the traditional forms of rhetoric and the historical roots and valuation of text in the West (see Kaplan 1986). Carefully selected fictional literature is a rich source of cultural information, as Valdes (1986) points out, though students may require help with interpretation. Household reading items, such as those described in Appendix D are also a rich source of cultural information. Finally, of course, readings may be selected to directly instruct the student about some aspect of culture. The instructor of academic reading may wish to focus on academic textbooks and textbook-type discourse conventions. Both slow, intensive reading and rapid, broad, extensive reading may be appropriate.

*Writing.* Cultural content in a writing class might frequently focus on the forms used in the academic subculture, including exposition, rhetorical forms, research conventions, and citation and bibliographical forms. Conventions of letter writing or business communication might also be useful.

*Academic culture and classroom conventions.* Academic culture and classroom conventions may be treated in any of these language classes, though college preparatory programs may devote part of their schedules exclusively to this. It is important to ensure that aspects of academic culture are explicitly dealt with somewhere in the curriculum. These might include principles of independent inquiry ("learning to learn"); conceptual organization and use of library systems (Jakobovits and Nahl-

Jakobovits 1987); conventions of classroom discussion and argumentation; etiquette of visits to a professor's office; understanding of student and instructor roles.

## Evaluating the Effectiveness of the Cultural Program

Just as culture teaching itself is rather complex, assessing a program's effects on students' cognitive knowledge, affective states, and psychomotor skills is not generally a clear-cut or simple matter. Probably the most straightforward aspect of this endeavor is the testing of cognitive knowledge, which to a large extent can be done through traditional, objective testing procedures. Valette (1986) provides a variety of models for test items that respond to these learning goals: knowledge of the target culture, command of the culture's etiquette, understanding differences between the target culture and the student's home culture, and understanding the target culture's values (p. 181). These goals incorporate cognitive knowledge about historical facts, events, people, and customs, as well as cognitive knowledge about values and the manifestation of affective patterns in daily life.

The affective development of the student—successful coping with culture shock, coming to terms with changing perceptions, nonjudgmental understanding of the target culture, tolerance of difference and ambiguity, and other aspects of a developing bicultural identity—is harder to assess. This assessment may depend largely on self-reports of students or on evaluations by others, such as teachers or advisors who are in close contact with students.

Psychomotor abilities—performative abilities—are fairly easy to determine when witnessed. However, logistical problems arise in this area: one cannot necessarily follow the students around on their daily circuits of activity. Psychomotor abilities may therefore also need to be self-reported or evaluated in classes through simulated tasks and situations.

Below is a final discussion suggesting specific foci of culture learning that can be evaluated initially and then at approximate intervals of three months, six months, one year, and two years (see also a description of four levels of cross-cultural awareness in Hanvey 1979). The discussion is necessarily general, and caution is warranted in using the suggestions offered here, for the pace and nature of each sojourner's acculturation will vary. It is assumed here that the student has had basic to intermediate language training prior to enrolling in the language program. A student who has had more extensive preparation than this can achieve linguistic, cognitive, and perhaps other competencies more quickly than is indicated in these descriptions. The reader's own experience, especially in light of specific program goals, will help validate

112

these descriptions of acculturation, or help to adjust them in appropriate ways. These competencies are summarized in a checklist in Appendix 6.

**Initially.** Assessment of a student's acculturation may productively begin soon after the student's arrival. Within a week or two, international students should be able to find their way around and function at the most basic, survival level in the campus and off-campus locales most important to basic daily routines. These include eating, shopping for personal items, participating in class, and knowing who is available when help is needed.

**Three Months.** At three months, a student should be able to carry out routine service encounters with some ease and should feel comfortable with classroom routines. At this time, too, the student should recognize any adverse effects of culture stress or culture shock—such as homesickness or excessive fatigue—and understand that these effects will pass.

**Six Months.** At six months, the student should be able to productively cope with any negative emotional states (though this does not necessarily mean eliminating such states) and should be able to cope effectively with linguistic or cultural misunderstanding. Some general features of the target culture such as national characteristics, major ceremonies, and general history and geography should be recognizable to the student. Daily routines, service encounters, personal business, and simple conversations should all be manageable at this point.

**One Year.** At the end of a year, students should have considerable ease and familiarity in their daily life and relationships with native speakers with whom they have much contact. While the student may not agree with or approve of all the cultural differences encountered, at this stage, the sojourner should usually be able to view them with tolerance and some objectivity. The international student should at this point be substantively familiar with national characteristics of the the target culture, and with politeness patterns, customs, normative behavior in school and public settings, recent history, popular culture, and general philosophical or religious beliefs. Finally, the student should have a general competence in routine social or business interactions and be able to identify and remedy misunderstanding.

**Two Years.** A university-level sojourner who has dwelled in a foreign environment for two years can be expected to be relatively fluent in the target language and competent in social interaction. The student should have come to terms with cultural differences that cause stress, and indeed, be well on the way to the reconsolidation of a social identity, integrating newer elements of the "target culture self" with the "native culture self." At this stage, abiding friendships with members of the target culture will have been formed, and the international student will have some appreciation of and empathy with the deeper elements of the target culture (perceptions, values, beliefs, etc.) that are manifested in native speech and behavior.

### Conclusion

The evaluation of a student's acculturation is a rather uncertain business. It is a simple enough matter to test the details of a person's external acquisition of facts about the target culture, such as major holidays and their historical origins. However, those who have sojourned abroad for any length of time know that the most significant changes resulting from acculturation are internal, and deeply so. They are in the nature of (1) background knowledge so pervasive that actual responses are automatic; (2) a wide knowledge of details of the target culture that are applied easily in particular situations; and (3) a subtle understanding and acceptance of—even empathy with—target culture events. The difficulty of measuring such developments in a person are self-evident. At the same time, an administrator or instructor experienced in dealing with international students can often tell with fair precision, after some period of time in conversation, the degree to which the student has absorbed the perspectives, patterns, attitudes, and so on of North American culture.

The purpose of evaluating the culture components in an ESL program and their influences on international students is to become more effective in our culture teaching. With the increase in cross-cultural contact in the world today, ESL programs have a prime opportunity—and an obligation—to take a leading role in culture teaching, and ultimately to serve as models in facilitating cross-cultural orientation and training for the rest of the academic establishment.

# Note

Thanks are due to Bill Potter and Pamela Zimmerman for helpful suggestions.

# References

Archer, C. 1986. Culture bump and beyond. In Valdes, J. M., ed., *Culture bound: Bridging the cultural gap in language teaching.* Cambridge: Cambridge University Press.

Barnes, G. A. 1986. Toward a model for cross-cultural orientation. In Byrd, P., ed., *Teaching across cultures in the university ESL program.* Washington, D.C.: National Association for Foreign Student Affairs.

Bell, L., P. Lee, D. Nelson, and R. Rutkowski. 1986. University of Wisconsin-Milwaukee: Cross-cultural components in an intensive ESL program. In Byrd, P., ed., *Teaching across cultures in the university ESL program.* Washington, D.C.: National Association for Foreign Student Affairs.

Brislin, R. W. and P. Pedersen. 1976. *Cross-cultural orientation.* New York: Gardner.

Boorstin, D. J. 1974. *The Americans: The democratic experience.* New York: Vintage.

Brown, G. 1977. *Listening to spoken English.* London: Longman.

Byrd, P., ed. 1986. *Teaching across cultures in the university ESL program.* Washington, D.C.: National Association for Foreign Student Affairs.

Comer, E. D. 1986. Macalester College: The American language and culture program. In Byrd, P. ed., *Teaching across cultures in the university ESL program.* Washington, D.C.: National Association for Foreign Student Affairs.

Condon, J. C. 1986. ". . . So near the United States." In Valdes, J. M., ed., *Culture bound: Bridging the cultural gap in language teaching.* Cambridge: Cambridge University Press.

Davis, V. 1986. Culture partners in symbiotic education: U.S. and foreign students learning together. In Byrd, P., ed., *Teaching across cultures in the university ESL program.* Washington, D.C.: National Association for Foreign Student Affairs.

Diemar, T. T. 1986. Ohio State University: The American language program cross-cultural training project. In Byrd, P., ed., *Teaching across cultures in the university ESL program.* Washington, D.C.: National Association for Foreign Student Affairs.

Dunnett, S. C., F. Dubin, and A. Lezberg. 1986. English language teaching from an intercultural perspective. In Valdes, J. M., ed., *Culture bound: Bridging the cultural gap in language teaching.* Cambridge: Cambridge University Press.

Frank-McNeil, J. with C. R. Byrne, ed. 1986. *Directory of professional preparation programs in TESOL in the United States 1986–88.* Washington, D.C.: Teachers of English to Speakers of Other Languages.

Furnham, A. and S. Bochner. 1986. *Culture shock: Psychological reactions to unfamiliar environments.* London: Methuen.

Genzel, R. B. and M. G. Cummings. 1986. *Culturally speaking: A conversation and culture text for learners of English.* New York: Harper and Row.

Gordon, B. Y. 1977. Personal communication.

Hanvey, R. G. 1979. Cross-cultural awareness. In Smith, E. C. and L. F. Luce, eds., *Toward internationalism: Readings in cross-cultural communication.* Rowley, MA: Newbury House.

Hickey, L. 1980. Ethnography for language learners. *Foreign Language Annals* 6:475–481.

Hirsch, E. D., Jr. 1987. *Cultural literacy: What every American needs to know.* Boston: Houghton Mifflin.

Hughes, G. 1986. An argument for cultural analysis in the second language classroom. In Valdes, J. M., ed., *Culture bound: Bridging the cultural gap in language teaching.* Cambridge: Cambridge University Press.

Jakobovits, L. A. 1970. *Foreign language learning: A psycholinguistic analysis of the issues.* Rowley, MA: Newbury House.

Jakobovits, L. A. and B. Y. Gordon. 1978. *Society's witnesses: Experiencing formative issues in social psychology.* Department of Psychology, University of Hawaii at Manoa.

Jakobovits, L. A., and D. Nahl-Jakobovits. 1987. Learning the library: Taxonomy of skills and errors. *College and Research Libraries* (May):203–214.

Kaplan, R. 1986. Culture and the written language. In Valdes, J. M., ed., *Culture bound: Bridging the cultural gap in language teaching.* Cambridge: Cambridge University Press.

Kasser, C. and A. M. Silverman. 1981. *American cultural encounters.* Hayward, CA: Alemany Press.

Kearny, E. N., M. A. Kearny, and J. A. Crandall. 1984. *The American way: An introduction to American culture.* Englewood Cliffs, NJ: Prentice-Hall.

Levine, D. and L. Adelman. 1982. *Beyond language: Intercultural communication for English as a second language.* Englewood Cliffs, NJ: Prentice-Hall.

Maggio, M. and C. W. Gay. 1986. Intercultural communication as an integral part of an ESL program: The University of Southern California experience. In Byrd, P., ed., *Teaching across cultures in the university ESL program.* Washington, D.C.: National Association for Foreign Student Affairs.

Montague, S. P. and W. Arens. 1981. *The American dimension: Cultural myths and social realities.* 2d ed. Sherman Oaks, CA: Alfred Publishing.

Murdock, G. P., C. S. Ford, A. E. Hudson, R. Kennedy, L. W. Simmons, and J. W. M. Whiting. 1971. *Outline of cultural materials.* 4th ed. New Haven, CT: Human Relations Area Files, Inc.

Myers, T., K. Brown, and B. McGonigle. 1976. *Reasoning and discourse processes.* London: Academic.

Richards, J. C. and R. W. Schmidt, eds. 1983. *Language and communication.* London: Longman.

Seelye, H. N. 1984. *Teaching culture: Strategies for intercultural communication.* Lincolnwood, IL: National Textbook Co.

Shapiro, T. 1985. *Settling in: A competency-based curriculum for U.S. cultural orientation,* vols. 1 and 2. Brattleboro, VT: Experiment in International Living and World Education.

Spindler, D. and L. Spindler. 1983. Anthropologists view American culture. *Annual Review of Anthropology* 12:49–78.

Stewart, E. C. 1972. *American cultural patterns: A cross-cultural perspective.* Yarmouth, ME: Intercultural Press.

Trifonovich, G. 1986. Learning culture. Freshman Colloquium lecture at Hawaii Loa College, Kaneohe, HI. March.

Valdes, J. M., ed. 1986. *Culture bound: Bridging the cultural gap in language teaching.* Cambridge: Cambridge University Press.

Valette, R. M. 1986. The culture test. In Valdes, J. M., ed., *Culture bound: Bridging the culture gap in language teaching.* Cambridge: Cambridge University Press.

Winskowski, C. 1985. On the role of teaching culture in ESL: What do we need to be cultural informants? Paper presented at the Annual Hawaii Council of Teachers of English TESOL Roundtable Conference, Honolulu, HI. February.

Zanger, V. V. 1985. *Face to face: The cross-cultural workbook.* Cambridge, MA: Newbury House.

Zimmerman, P. 1987. ESL student as ethnographer. Paper presented at the Hawaii Association of Language Teachers/Hawaii Council of Teachers of English Joint Combined Annual Conference and Roundtable, Honolulu, HI. April.

# Appendix A

Checklist for Instructor's Areas of Cultural Knowledge,
Competencies, and Resources for Culture Teaching

## Conversational Conventions

—— conversational openings
—— conversational closings
—— topic switching mechanisms
—— politeness rituals
—— formal speaking

—— informal speaking
—— telephone conventions
—— service encounters
—— appropriate topics
—— common speech
formulae

## History

—— general North American history
—— commonly known dates and events
—— "culturological" historical accounts
   —— frontier mentality
   —— individualism
   —— personal freedom
   —— achievement orientation
   —— probabilistic thinking
   —— other

## Contemporary Anthropology/Popular Culture

—— family relationships
—— work
—— social roles
—— stereotypes
—— food
—— current events in popular
consciousness

—— religion
—— education
—— lifestyle
—— dress
—— leisure

Religion/Spirituality
- _____ religions
- _____ philosophies/metaphysical beliefs
- _____ sects
- _____ beliefs
- _____ practices
- _____ values

Psychology/National Characteristics (based on Spindler and Spindler 1983)
- _____ individualism, self-reliance
- _____ achievement orientation
- _____ equality before the law, equality of opportunity
- _____ conformity to community norms
- _____ sociability and friendliness
- _____ personal and corporate honesty and integrity
- _____ competence in work and daily life management
- _____ optimism about the future
- _____ usefulness of work, value of hard work
- _____ suspicion of authority

Ethnosemantics and Pragmatics
- _____ implications, presuppositions
- _____ speakers' background knowledge
- _____ speakers' relationship and occasion
- _____ elements of argument structure
- _____ implicit and explicit meaning

# Appendix B

## Checklist of Elements for Cultural Orientation

### Tour of Environs

#### On campus

_____ dormitories
_____ head resident's room/office
_____ dining hall(s)
_____ campus store(s)
_____ mail office
_____ libraries
_____ registrar's office

_____ faculty offices
_____ health clinic
_____ lounges
_____ financial office
_____ classrooms
_____ laboratories
_____ other

#### Off campus

_____ drug stores
_____ grocery stores
_____ post offices
_____ bus stops and main transportation routes
_____ recreation spots
_____ immigration office
_____ medical and dental offices/clinics
_____ other

### Conventions of Routine Service Encounters

_____ bus fares and transfers
_____ mail room services/post office services
_____ cafeteria/restaurant services
_____ shopping routines
_____ general inquiry and politeness strategies
_____ illness or emergency procedures
_____ other

### Academic Procedures

_____ registration
_____ consultation with advisors
_____ financial matters
_____ campus employment procedures

_____ campus ID cards
_____ health clearances
_____ library cards
_____ other

Conventions of Academic Culture

_____ expectations, requirements, and obligations for students, professors, teaching assistants, classmates

_____ routine classroom behavior (lecture, questions, discussion, late class entrance, exams, deadlines, etc.)

_____ cultural contrasts in role performance of students, professors, teaching assistants

_____ interpretation of course syllabi, requirements, grading policies, and work standards (with special attention to plagiarism)

_____ campus policies and rules

_____ other

Socialization

_____ social events with international and native students

_____ dorm and student leaders

_____ introduction to key staff (nurses, librarians, freshman professors, counselors)

_____ contact with and access to churches, community agencies and organizations, and homestay families other

# Appendix C

Checklist of Components for Culture Courses or Seminars

Affective Knowledge and Coping Skills

_____ understanding of the nature of culture and its effects on the individual

_____ culture awareness and cross-cultural coping skills for international students

_____ tolerance for difference and ambiguity

_____ continuing discussions and exercises to identify and resolve misunderstandings, conflicts, and discomforts

_____ recognition of affect in native speakers

_____ other

Cognitive Knowledge

_____ use of North American informants or counterparts

_____ North American cultural characteristics

_____ history: ethnicity of Americans, events which underlie national characteristics (e.g., the "frontier mentality"), connections between events and common language patterns and formulae

_____ daily life and popular culture: food, time and space, work, family relationships, education, clothing, celebrations and festivities, etc.

_____ religious and philosophical beliefs and practices

_____ normative behavior in the daily activities, with special attention to the students' setting

_____ communication strategies for various social settings and discourse events

_____ other

Psychomotor Skills

_____ roleplays and practice conversations

_____ structured interviews

_____ excursions to special events, as well as participation in ordinary events (e.g., studying) with a native speaker counterpart

_____ ethnographic investigations of the classroom or other relevant social settings

_____ interaction assignments, e.g., a bank transaction, a consultation with a professor or staff member

_____ other

# Appendix D

Checklist of Culture Materials and Resources Archive
(based on Winskowski, 1985)

## Informant Collections
### Published Examples
_____ *The ESL Miscellany.* R. C. Clark, P. R. Moran, and A. A.
Borrows (Pro Lingua 1981). A valuable compendium of
lists of linguistic, communicative, and cultural information,
e.g., on eating, human relationships, superstitions, and
sports teams.

_____ *Success with Words.* (Reader's Digest 1983). Style, usage,
dialects, topical vocabulary collections, word lore and
history, etc.

_____ *Native Tongues.* C. Berlitz (Grossett and Dunlap 1982).
Grandson of the founder of the Berlitz method, the author
provides a delightful compendium of nontrivial but little-
known language facts.

_____ *The Bible Book of Lists.* J. MacKenzie and S. Bledsoe
(Zondervan 1984). Decidedly "one-dimensional"; a
valuable source for common Western religious notions,
e.g., angels, religious symbols and celebrations, famous
characters, common expressions, etc.

_____ *The New Reading Teacher's Book of Lists.* E. B. Fry, D. L.
Fountoukidis, and J. K. Polk (Prentice-Hall 1985). A
wonderful collection of anything and everything to do with
reading.

_____ *Why Did They Name It. . .?* H. Campbell (Fleet Press 1964).
An entertaining history of brand names, with reproduc-
tions of old-time advertisements.

### Other Material
_____ school textbook samples for all grade levels
_____ inventory of popular symbols in the media
_____ inventory of common gestures, body language, and facial
expressions on videotape

Other Material cont.

_____ assessments of North Americans by native and nonnative speakers on videotape, developed by the teacher and other program staff members

_____ inventories of household items (wallets, purses, desks, drawers, closets, etc.)

_____ microdescriptions of behavior and thinking diaries of daily activities

_____ indexes of community knowledge (telephone book yellow pages, library classification schemes, educational curricula, etc.)

Reference Collections

_____ dictionaries of all types

_____ phrase books (e.g., of two-word verbs, prepositional phrases, etc.)

_____ how-to manuals (e.g., cookbooks, gardening books, hobby and craft manuals, college catalogues, etc.)

_____ collections of idioms and their meanings

_____ books of names and their meanings

_____ reference collections on North American culture and language (folklore, fairy tales and mythology, proverbs, idioms, customs, humor, holidays, etc.)

_____ other

Other Household and Homemade Collections

_____ junk mail

_____ forms (job applications, merchandise order forms, bank forms, post office forms, tax forms, etc.)

_____ comic books (one sample each of several types)

_____ magazines (one sample each of several types)

_____ community agency publications (leaflets, pamphlets, coupons, brochures, tickets, etc.)

_____ newspaper and magazine human interest articles on North American culture, history, institutions

_____ instructions on merchandise packaging, clothing, in appliance manuals, etc.

_____ commercials and advertising from television, magazines, and newspapers

Other Household and Homemade Collections cont.

_____ videotapes of representative movies and television programs, classic and current (of course, these cannot be kept for more than a short period of time without violating copyright statutes)

_____ legal documents (sales contracts, wills, rental agreements, warrantees and guarantees, etc.)

_____ tape recordings and transcripts of conversations (among friends, family members, coworkers, all combinations of sexes and ages, regional and ethnic backgrounds, etc.)

# Appendix E

## Checklist of Cultural Components in Language Courses

### Speaking

#### Content

_____ conversational formulae (openings, closings, topi shifts)
_____ comprehensive presentation of politeness rituals, with implications and presuppositions
_____ politeness levels according to various status combinations of the participants; appropriateness of topics as a function of participants and occasions
_____ other conversational rituals (reciprocity of information exchange, etc.)
_____ values and beliefs emergent in talk
_____ speech acts, functions, and notions
_____ the structure of argument (rhetoric and pragmatics)
_____ sentence and argument intonation
_____ expression of emotionality
_____ other

#### Materials

_____ textbooks with authentic-sounding dialogue
_____ dialogue appropriate to social roles
_____ colloquial speech
_____ tape recordings of spontaneous conversation (preferably with transcripts, for easy classroom analysis of meaning)
_____ identification of common modes of conversational humor (both professional humor and ordinary, spontaneous humor)
_____ feature films involving conventional scenarios (family, boy-girl, cops and robbers, etc.)

### Listening

#### Content

_____ clause and sentence intonation
_____ stress or rhythm as a function of meaning
_____ distinction between topic of speech and function of speech

_____ redundancy, cohesion, and paraphrasing
_____ expression of emotionality
_____ common conversational formulae
_____ structural indications of argument
_____ compendium of colloquial referents
_____ regional accents
_____ interpretation of meaning
_____ other

## Materials

_____ conventional listening materials for sound recognition, word recognition, and basic sentence intonation (e.g., clause-end intonation versus sentence-end intonation)
_____ audiotapes and videotapes of conversation, lectures, and speeches
_____ tape-recorded readings
_____ audiotapes and videotapes of television and radio dialogue

# Reading

## Content

_____ survey of types of text and rhetorical forms
_____ historical roots of western text and its valuation
_____ context and redundancy
_____ colloquial forms
_____ customs, behaviors, conventions
_____ literary forms, allusion, metaphor, simile, etc.
_____ structure of formal argument (evidence, claims, presuppositions and implications, etc.)
_____ descriptions of culture
_____ other

## Materials

_____ ESL textbooks
_____ academic textbooks
_____ literature
_____ household reading realia

# Writing

## Content

_____ rhetorical forms
_____ nature of evidence, claims, presupposition and implication

Materials
_____ writing texts
_____ professionally-generated and student-generated models

# Academic Culture and Classroom Conventions (for all classes)

_____ value and practice of independent inquiry (learning to learn)

_____ use and organization of information systems (e.g., library classification schemes, periodical index headings and subheadings)

_____ expectations and obligations of student role

_____ expectations and obligations of instructor role

_____ conventions of classroom discussion, questions, and debate

_____ etiquette of visits to a professor's office (appointments, conduct, problem resolution, etc.)

_____ scholarly conventions of citation and avoidance of plagiarism

_____ other

# Appendix F

## Checklist for Evaluating Progress in
## the Student's Acculturation

### Initial Survival Skills

_____ knowledge of important locations on campus and off campus

_____ ability to carry out basic service transactions (e.g., simple shopping, mail service, food service, etc.)

_____ ability to get around by bus, taxi, or other appropriate mode of transportation

_____ knowledge of basic daily round procedures (e.g., dining, dormitory, classroom, etc.)

_____ ability to carry out greeting and leavetaking, express lack of understanding, and ask for help

_____ other

### Three-Month Competencies

_____ competence in class routines

_____ general competence in daily service encounters

_____ general awareness of possible stress effects from culture shock

_____ ability to carry out routine service encounters without assistance

_____ other

### Six-Month Competencies

_____ understanding of culture shock effects; recognition of effects in self

_____ ability to cope productively with negative emotional states and disorientation

_____ ability to cope effectively with misunderstanding

_____ competence in routine conversational interaction of a basic nature (language ability permitting) with native speakers

_____ ability to manage routine personal business (shopping, post office, etc.) with fair facility

_____ knowledge of major national characteristics of members of the target culture, and recognition of their common manifestations (e.g., in routine conversation)

_____ knowledge of major ceremonies, customs, and holidays that have been experienced during the sojourn
_____ knowledge of basic local geography and major features of history of the target culture
_____ other

## One-Year Competencies

_____ substantive familiarity with national characteristics of the target culture and how they manifest themselves in the members' behavior and language
_____ sense of ease in the presence of familiar members of the target culture; development of some sustained friendships with members of the target culture
_____ competence with politeness rituals in formal and informal social interaction
_____ facility with daily conversation in the target language; competence with major conversational conventions
_____ competence with most colloquial language in daily conversation
_____ general knowledge of recent history and popular culture of the mainstream of people in the target culture
_____ competence in active problem solving for misunderstandings, and competence with politeness remedies
_____ awareness of manifestations of philosophical or religious values or beliefs in daily life
_____ other

## Two-Year Competencies

_____ good general language fluency (e.g., academic program entrance level or better)
_____ recognition of and competence with most colloquiality in talk, humor, implications and presuppositions, etc.
_____ facility in exercising customary behavior
_____ competence in academic classroom and coursework performance
_____ ease and competence in most social interaction
_____ development of abiding friendships with target culture members
_____ recognition of deep culture manifestations of perceptions, values
_____ integration of "target culture self" with "native culture self" in personal and social identity
_____ other

# PART THREE
# Assessing Noninstructional Aspects of the Program

EVALUATION OF STUDENT SERVICES IN ESL PROGRAMS
*Geoffrey C. Middlebrook*

CREATING AND OPERATING A STATISTICAL DATABASE FOR EVALUATION IN AN ENGLISH LANGUAGE PROGRAM
*Roger Ponder and Bill Powell*

DESIGNING AND ASSESSING THE EFFICACY OF ESL PROMOTIONAL MATERIALS
*Frederick L. Jenks*

# 7

# Evaluation of Student Services in ESL Programs

*Geoffrey C. Middlebrook*

## Introduction

International educational exchange is not a recent phenomenon. On the contrary, cross-cultural education has a long and well-documented history that can be traced far back into classical antiquity (see Breitenbach 1970; Brickman 1965; Cieslak 1955; Deutsch 1970; DuBois 1956; Fraser 1968). In the United States, the established presence of foreign students goes back several centuries to Francisco Miranda, from Spain, who studied at Yale in 1784 (Jenkins 1983). Much has changed since the days of Miranda, most noticeably, the number of students who now go abroad. The end of the Second World War precipitated an explosive increase in the transnational movement of students (see Institute of International Education 1988). In particular, the United States, due to the fortunate position it occupied in relation to other nations at the close of that conflict, saw tremendous growth in its international student population, and for several decades the United States has been the world's leading host country for international students (Altbach, Kelly, and Lulat 1985).

Research reveals an array of competing factors involved in overseas study (see Altbach, Kelly, and Lulat 1985). In many instances, individuals, governments, and businesses have as a principal motivation for going or sending someone abroad the desire for intensive English language training. For some, this training is an early or initial step in a larger academic, vocational, technical, or professional agenda; for others, the training is an end unto itself (Institute of International Education 1982). Whatever the reason or reasons for coming, international students in English language programs represent a significant and prominent presence on many campuses and in many communities in this country. In response to the strong and growing demand for in-country English language study, existing programs have been modified and expanded, and new programs have been developed. In 1978–79, there were 163 programs nationwide offering students 15 hours per week or more of English language instruction; in 1987–88, that number had risen to 392 (Institute of International Education 1988).

Even a cursory examination of these many English language programs reveals a wide variety of administrative structures and services. I will be concerned in this paper with those English language programs that include within their scope a student services component, recognizing that not all programs will deliver, in-house, the full spectrum of services discussed below. In particular, it is my intention to provide a set of guidelines for the evaluation of student services in ESL (English as a Second Language) programs. There are a variety of reasons why this focus is appropriate. While evaluation has long been a part of good ESL programs, the emphasis has been, perhaps too narrowly, on the language dimension, as noted in Chapter Four of this volume. When programs admit international students, they assume certain responsibilities and obligations beyond language training that it would be improper to ignore (Cieslak 1955; Diener and Kerr 1979; Spaulding 1988; Woolston 1983). Given the importance of these obligations and responsibilities to the well-being of international students and to that of the field of international educational exchange, it is critical for a host institution and its clientele to know the extent to which they are being successfully addressed.

## Evaluation of Student Services in an ESL Context

**Evaluation of Educational Services.** Evaluation has met with a mixed response in the academic community. There are those who question the applicability of what are seen as fundamentally business and government concepts such as management and accountability to the field of education, which has its own set of values and control mechanisms, traditionally quite separate from those of both government and business (Giamatti 1988). The opponents of evaluation contend that education and the cluster of services that attend it are by their very nature outside the purview of objective measurement and assessment. Some (e.g., Martin, Overholt, and Urban 1976) have argued that the evaluation movement is not in fact educational but political, fueled by the economic concerns of budget-minded decision makers. Others (e.g., Elton 1988) point out that even well-meaning evaluation can result in unanticipated and less than beneficial effects: when a primary and desired change is introduced into one part of a system, that change can frequently spill over and spread into other parts of the system, producing unwanted and undesirable secondary results.

By contrast, evaluation in education is seen by others, probably the majority of program administrators in ESL and a large proportion of the wider NAFSA constituency as well, as the sine qua non of effective and ethical professional services. Those who advocate educational program evaluation argue that it provides the means for establishing and maintaining institutional standards and for the proper assignation of responsibility (Reichard 1983). It is further argued by those who favor evaluation (e.g., Brislin and Pedersen 1976; Deegan 1981) that it performs a vital function in educational services, because no system can achieve its potential, assess its performance, or modify its practices in an informed manner in the absence of evaluation (Brown and Pennington, this volume; Stufflebeam and Webster 1988). In view of the recent calls for professionalism in the field of international education (Reid 1988), it is the opinion of this author that the objections to evaluation in education, while not unfounded, are overridden by the need to determine the merit and effectiveness of the services offered.

**The Place of Student Services in an ESL Program.** In the early academic institutions, located primarily in Europe, there were virtually no student services; in fact, there was an almost complete lack of administrative support services (Altbach, Kelly, and Lulat 1985). In stark contrast, very early on in their history, institutions in North America began to assume responsibility, in loco parentis for numerous areas that are to this day not assumed by similar institutions in many other countries, in part out of concern for nonacademic development in an increasingly secularized world, (Deegan 1981; Leonard 1956). While the formal doctrine of in loco parentis is largely a thing of the past, these responsibilities remain and have evolved into the unified infrastructure of student services characteristic of education in the United States. Many of these services have been incorporated in some form and to some degree into English language programs as a way of responding to the extralinguistic needs and interests of ESL students.

A vast array of aggregate figures is available on foreign students; though useful and interesting, Altbach (1988) points out that they tend to obscure the enormous variation in the motivations and experiences of international students. One reason for this variation is the fundamental heterogeneity of the foreign student population in the United States (DuBois 1956; Oyen 1985); another is the complex of factors and determinants that affect the study-abroad sojourn (Deutsch 1970; Halls 1971). While generalizations on international students are elusive, it is nonetheless possible to speak with some confidence of general areas and a relative hierarchy of international student needs and interests (see Lee, Abd-Ella, and Burks 1981; Spaulding and Flack 1976). In an ESL program, the identification of these areas provides the program with guiding principles for the establishment, maintenance, and evaluation of student support services.

It is not surprising that more than one pattern of organization exists in ESL programs, for no single structure is necessarily best in all circumstances (Pennington 1985). The response to the needs and interests of ESL students should differ across programs, because this response will be a function of such factors as program type, size, location, and funding, and must take into account the priorities of students, faculty, and staff (Deutsch 1970; Woolston 1983), as well as those of governments, sponsoring agencies, and relevant and affected communities (Brown and Pennington, this volume; Spaulding 1988). In short, the administrative response to international students must reflect the program's unique culture (Tierney 1988).

**Evaluation of Student Services within ESL Programs.** The field of student services can be analyzed in a number of ways and from a number of perspectives. While student services can be viewed as a coherent whole, it is helpful, if the intention is evaluation, to think of the different services as discrete. With this perspective in mind, the approach taken here will be to develop a model of student services within ESL as a set of conceptually separable services. The presentation of the model begins with the identification of those components of student services that are deemed to be necessary in some form and to some degree in English language programs located outside the student's home country, with the awareness that not all of these components may be present in the program proper. Although some services may not be a direct part of a program, it is essential for administrators to be aware of them and to have an appropriate mechanism in place for providing them through other means. Each of these dimensions is described, and the salient issues associated with it discussed. The student services components to be considered and their order of presentation are as follows:

- recruitment
- admissions
- orientation (academic and cultural)
- employment
- advising (academic, legal, and personal)
- financial aid
- housing

- health services
- campus and community life programs
- alumni relations

For each of these areas, a set of four evaluation questions is derived from an overview of concerns expressed in the published literature. The questions are summarized and extended in the final section, where general and specific guidelines for the evaluation of student services in an ESL program are provided.

## The Components of the Student Services Evaluation Model

**Recruitment.** The central issues arising in ESL student recruitment have to do primarily with ethics and information. In the past decade, a number of ESL programs, faced with both increased competition and the potential for increased revenues, have reacted in what many consider to be an unethical manner by recruiting international students solely on the basis of their ability to pay tuition and fees—in a sense "selling" students access to the United States (Byrd and Constantinides, this volume; Constantine 1986; Jenkins 1983; Silny 1988). Althen (1983), Jenks (this volume), Michie (1967), and Speakman (1966) have pointed out the great need for international students to be accurately informed about the prospective institution—its costs, its curriculum, the duration of its courses—as well as about the nature of the surrounding community, so that students' expectations can be met. Motives and objectives will naturally differ between students and institutions (Deutsch 1979; Dubois 1956), not to mention governments and sponsoring agencies (Spaulding 1988), and so it is crucial that information flowing in all directions be clear and complete, and that decisions be made in an ethical manner during the recruitment process.

In response to the confusion and transgressions arising out of international student recruitment, the National Liaison Committee on Foreign Student Admissions (NLC) held a colloquium on the subject in 1980 to examine current practices and establish future guidelines (Thackaberry and Liston 1986). The NLC located several problem areas of particular relevance to English language programs. These included the use of per capita placement agencies for overseas recruitment and the failure to accurately represent the institution in advertising, informational materials, and interviews. The NLC recommended that institutions avoid contractual arrangements with fee-for-enrollment recruiters and that they provide full and realistic figures and statements to prospective applicants (National Liaison Committee on Foreign Student Admissions 1980).

Based on the foregoing discussion, a number of general questions regarding ESL recruitment processes can be derived:

## Evaluation Questions for Recruitment

1. Are the recruitment practices of the program ethical?
2. If recruitment is performed by a contracted agency, on what basis is that agency remunerated?
3. Are the recruitment practices based on the needs and interests of the program and its clientele?
4. Does the program provide clear and complete information via all mailings and other media to its prospective clientele?

**Admissions.** The most frequently discussed issues in the admission of international students are admissions criteria and the evaluation of overseas credentials. Every program must decide the bases for admission, and these should be the result of a high degree of institutional self-awareness, extending from a stated program philosophy, combined with a sure sense of present and future program goals and objectives and of what is required to realize them. One consideration is purely quantitative: How many students can the program handle and still provide the necessary level of education and services? Related to the question of sheer numbers are demographics: What relative mix of gender, age, ethnicity, nationality, and first language is desired in the ESL student body? Another admissions criterion is the degree of importance to be assigned to such factors as level of proficiency, academic, social, and psychological readiness, and test scores. One way to establish the extent of compatibility between an applicant and the ESL program is to require the completion of a thorough questionnaire as part of the application process.

The problems associated with the evaluation of overseas credentials can be acute; quite simply, it is not always possible, even in the best of circumstances, to ascertain with any degree of certainty whether an international student has adequate preparation for a program. There are many reasons for this, among them being simple translation problems, differences in academic nomenclature and the meaning of credentials, and profound differences in educational systems (Halls 1971; UNESCO 1982). There are several resources available to help alleviate these difficulties. The Institute of International Education (1981) and NAFSA (1979) have both published evaluation manuals. Of course, standardized, norm-referenced English language proficiency tests such as the TOEFL (Test of English as A Foreign Language) are of enormous assistance, but they do not measure all factors, and not all programs are in a position to require or administer these tests. In the final analysis, the most important question to ask when making admissions decisions is, to what degree are the needs and aspirations of the student congruent with the resources

140

and emphases of the ESL program and/or the institution (if any) in which it is situated (Christensen and Thielen 1983)?

Extrapolating from the foregoing discussion, one can identify the following questions as central to the evaluation of ESL program admissions:

## Evaluation Questions for Admissions

1. Are admissions criteria well articulated and consistent?
2. Is the evaluation of students' credentials thorough and accurate, and is admission based on a mutual compatability between the applicant and the program?
3. Do admissions decisions reflect the goals and objectives of the ESL program and, if relevant, the larger institution in which it is housed?
4. Are admissions staff knowledgeable about INS regulations concerning the issuance of I-20 forms (for students on F visas), IAP-66 forms (for students on J visas), and other such documents?

**Orientation.** Academic, social, and psychological adjustment issues are a frequent topic in much of the literature on international students (Altbach 1988). As visitors, international students are expected, if not to assimilate, at least to accept and conform to the dominant dynamics of the program and the surrounding community (Guiton 1977). Research on the effectiveness of orientation programs is, generally speaking, inconclusive (Lee, Abd-Ella, and Burks 1981; Spaulding and Flack 1976); however, it would be difficult to find a professional who did not advocate some form of transitional program for newly arrived international students. Most authors in the field of international educational exchange emphasize that orientation, while not a panacea or a vaccination for international students against problems and confusions, is a way of anticipating and preparing students for multiple adjustment issues. Moreover, there is a widely held belief that students' success in language learning is intimately tied to their success in cultural adjustment (Winskowski-Jackson, this volume).

Orientation of ESL students should not be thought of as a one-time event, but rather as an ongoing series of events—a continuous and integrated process available for the duration of and concurrent with the program of study (Deutsch 1970; Murphy 1956; Spaulding 1988; Winskowski-Jackson, this volume). Nor should orientation be limited to new students; it should be a way to introduce or reintroduce students, new and continuing, to the possibly very different world, academic and cultural, in which they find themselves (Althen 1983; Brislin and Pedersen 1976). In planning and implementing an orientation program,

141

Brislin and Pedersen (1976) remind us that while a good orientation covers the full spectrum of academic, social, and psychological adjustment issues, the best orientation stresses those particular areas that may have special importance due to the unique characteristics of the students, the program, or the community.

These considerations lead to an examination of questions such as the following as a basis for evaluation of the orientation component of an ESL program:

### Evaluation Questions for Orientation

1. Is the orientation comprehensive?
2. Is the orientation well organized and comprehensible to ESL students?
3. Is the orientation focused on areas of special importance related to the characteristics of the cultural and, if applicable, the institutional situation in which the program finds itself?
4. Is orientation an ongoing and flexible process available to new as well as to continuing ESL students?

**Advising.** The phenomenon of culture shock is well accepted in educational exchange. Many professionals (e.g., Brislin and Pedersen 1976; Winskowski-Jackson, this volume; Woolston 1983) make the point that international students must adjust to both the academic and the larger cultural contexts. This adjustment process will be more or less difficult as a function of several interacting variables such as age, gender, marital status, English language proficiency, academic level, sponsorship, length of stay, country of origin, size of program, type of orientation, living arrangements, and previous international experience (Klieneberg and Hull 1979; Lee, Abd-Ella, and Burks 1981; Spaulding and Flack 1976). Deutsch (1970) states that it is unrealistic to strive for a trouble-free environment for foreign students, and so the mechanisms must be in place to effectively address difficulties when they arise. Oyen (1985) argues that an experience free of problems is not only unlikely but also undesirable for foreign students. The nature of overseas education rightly assures that the sojourn will be demanding and quite possibly highly emotional.

As concerns academic advising, for many reasons foreign students may be wholly unfamiliar with the academic milieu of the ESL program in such diverse and important areas as expectations regarding class participation, appropriate and acceptable relations with faculty and staff, and central program requirements. Cadieux and Wehrly (1986) take the position that solid academic advising is the means to ensure program relevance for international students. With respect to legal advising, the status of international students is by definition legally distinct, and is defined and regulated by U.S. immigration law. This law is extremely complicated, frequently ambiguous, and easily confusing, and so it is critical that ESL students and their host institutions be familiar with the law as it relates to them. Further, ESL students should be aware of the more general laws that govern the behavior of the entire community. In terms of personal advising, ESL students present several challenges (Altbach, Kelly, and Lulat 1985). Many international students experience strong reactions to and during the adjustment process (see Klieneberg and Hull 1979). For cultural, linguistic, or other reasons, international students often do not seek out help when they need it (Sue 1978). Moreover, because of cross-cultural dynamics, effective counseling of international students can be a difficult enterprise (Althen 1983).

The following questions are relevant to the assessment of the advising area:

### Evaluation Questions for Advising

1. Is advising designed to prevent as well as resolve ESL student difficulties?
2. Is advising available on an ongoing basis, either within GK the program or in another unit to which the ESL student has access?
3. Does advising incorporate academic, legal, and personal concerns and issues?
4. Is the advising sensitive to the special needs of ESL students?

**Employment.** The employment of international students is subject to immigration regulations and is, with few exceptions, limited to work at the school site, which may not legally exceed 20 hours per week, except during interim breaks and in the summer. Dependents of international students may or may not work, depending on the student's visa type. In intensive English language programs in this country in 1988, 76.2 percent of international students were on the F visa, which prohibits the employment of dependents, while only 5 percent of international students were on the J visa, which allows the employment of dependents (Institute of International Education 1988). Thus, as Joshi (1983) puts it, international students are not really in a position to work their way through school. The purpose of these restrictions is ostensibly to moderate the impact of international students on local economies, for there are those who question the wisdom of employing international students or their dependents if this results in the displacement of local workers (Spaulding 1988).

The financial needs of international students are often underestimated. While figures are not available for students in English language programs, one can look to the situation in higher education in this country for a parallel. A recent study found fully 65 percent of all international students supported by personal or family funds (Institute of International Education 1988)—funds that are subject to the vicissitudes of family, political, or economic events far outside the student's sphere of control. Beyond the fiscal aspect, however, is another dimension to the employment of international students. Many studies (see Altbach, Kelly, and Lulat 1985; Lee, Abd-Ella, and Burks 1981; Spaulding and Flack 1976) have revealed that one of the strongest and yet least frequently satisfied desires of international students is the practical opportunity to use their training through working. A related argument in favor of fewer restrictions on international student employment contends that by working, international students enrich their overseas experience via greater exposure to the host institution and the community, and that in the process the program and the community are in tangible and intangible ways also enriched (Joshi 1983).

In evaluating ESL student employment, questions such as those provided below may prove useful:

## Evaluation Questions for Employment

1. If employment is available to ESL students, are the tasks involved safe and respectful of all constituencies?
2. If employment is available for students in the ESL program, are they fairly compensated for their efforts?
3. If employment is made available, does it provide the ESL students with an opportunity to use the target language?
4. Do the program and the community benefit from the employment of ESL students?

**Financial Aid.** Foreign students are not eligible for much of the financial assistance, in the form of government grants and loans, that is accessible to domestic students. Not surprisingly, many studies (see Lee, Abd-Ella, and Burks 1981) have found that financial problems and concerns are a recurrent issue for international students. Foreign students must plan in all likelihood for most of the following expenses: application fees, standardized test fees, travel to and from the United States, passport and visa costs, tuition and fees, books and supplies, room and board, support of dependents, insurance and medical costs, and incidentals (Joshi 1983).

Since most international students—particularly those undergoing full-time English study—are self-supporting and have limited employment opportunities, it is important for the institution and the student to collaborate on ways to make English study affordable. Some alternatives might be for the program to offer or help locate for ESL students a relatively inexpensive homestay that includes room and board. If a program anticipates a large number of students from a single country or region, it may be possible to arrange a charter or discount rate with an airline. A program may be able to negotiate reduced meal costs for its students at a school cafeteria or a local restaurant. Certain schools may be in a position to offer a work-study option to their international students, thereby allowing them to work on site for pay or for reduced tuition.

In considering the issue of financial aid for ESL students, the administration of an ESL program might wish to address these questions:

## Evaluation Questions for Financial Aid

1. Does the institution or program have available some form of financial assistance for ESL students?
2. Does the institution make an effort to render the program affordable to international students?
3. Are options in place for ESL students who may unexpectedly need financial assistance during the course of the program?
4. Does the program or institution make use of community resources to assist ESL students?

**Housing.** In their review of the literature and in their own findings, Lee, Abd-Ella, and Burks (1981) found that living arrangements during the study-abroad sojourn play a significant role in overall international student satisfaction. In general, students who were in accommodations that provided them with an abundance of contact with domestic students, international students from different countries, or others from the host country tended to view their overseas experiences in a more favorable light. Of course, it is important to remember that for a multitude of personal, social, religious, dietary, or other reasons, some foreign students may have little or no interest in this kind of contact (Woodhall 1988). Some programs may require or make available institutional housing as part of their package; if this is the case, the institution must be fully aware of and make provision for student preferences. If housing is not a part of the program proper, then the program can demonstrate its commitment to student welfare by making available information on housing options, the advantages and disadvantages of these options, and the fine points of leases, contracts, and utilities (Althen 1983).

The following questions can be kept in mind when evaluating the housing component of an ESL program:

## Evaluation Questions for Housing

1. Does the program provide or make available information on housing?
2. Are the needs and interests of international students considered and respected in the area of housing?
3. Do housing options avoid the problem of isolation of ESL students?
4. Do housing options take into account the resources of ESL students in terms of funds and transportation?

**Health Services.** A conspicuous omission in educational exchange research can be found in the area of health. Very little is known about patterns of wellness and disease, physical and mental, among international students (Altbach, Kelly, and Lulat 1985). The majority of studies have dealt with the comparative use of institutional health services by domestic and international students. For example, Ballard (1988) found that whereas international students tend to "underuse" counseling services, they "overuse" health services; the assumption is that the latter is a reflection of the myriad difficulties that often accompany international student adjustment. As with issues that relate to counseling services, international students may have very different perceptions of what should be done and who should do it when they become ill (Althen 1983). It is not to be expected that all or even most programs will provide students with health services, but for those that do, personnel should be trained and sensitive to the quite possibly different health needs of international students. Those ESL programs that do not provide health services must at the very least be able to recommend in a confidential manner the services of appropriate health professionals in the community. In addition, ESL programs or the larger institutions in which they might be housed should make every effort to offer some kind of group health plan to their international students.

The issues surrounding the provision of health services for ESL students can be summarized in the form of the four questions below:

## Evaluation Questions for Health Services

1. Are ESL students known to be healthy before arrival?
2. Are ESL students made aware before arrival of health concerns in the host community?
3. Does the program provide or make available information on health insurance or health services?
4. Are the special needs and interests of international students considered with respect to health services?

**Campus and Community Life Programs.** The goal of international student programming may be educational, cultural, or both (Althen 1983). The notion of reciprocity is often built into international student programming; that is, the student is expected to give as well as take. One of the most frequently cited reasons for the existence and continued support of transnational educational exchanges is the cross-cultural learning and understanding that is believed to follow from contact between people of different countries (Dudden and Dynes 1987). Coelho (1958) said from this perspective that the countries that one hates are the countries that one does not know.

A great deal has been written on the idea of foreign students as resources and informants (e.g., Mestenhauser 1976), and this is reflected in much of the frequent and established programming for international students, such as international fairs, food and film festivals, and visits by international students to local schools (Christensen and Thielen 1983), where the host population also benefits from the events. The other consideration, of course, involves the benefits that the foreign students receive from these endeavors. Through effective and creative programming, students in ESL programs can have the opportunity to see and experience the human and physical host community in a unique way, and in the process share of themselves while employing the target language.

The questions relevant to the area of campus and community life programs for ESL students are as follows:

### Evaluation Questions for Campus and Community Life Programs

1. Does the ESL program or larger institution offer educational and cultural programming for international students?
2. Does programming genuinely engage ESL students?
3. Does programming reflect the needs, interests, and resources of the constituencies involved?
4. Do ESL students, the ESL program, and the community all benefit from programming?

**Alumni Relations.** In higher education in the United States there are over 50,000 new foreign alumni each year, and of these over 35,000 return to their home country (Goetzl and Strutter 1980). Yet, disturbingly, foreign alumni networks are markedly missing from most colleges and universities in this country (Kaplan 1983; Spaulding and Flack 1976). While figures are not available on English language programs, it is probably safe to assume that the situation in those programs is not dissimilar.

If so, this absence is unfortunate for several reasons. From the point of view of the institution, foreign alumni could be valuable in establishing or maintaining a program's presence and profile abroad, and could assist in screening and interviewing prospective applicants to the program.

From the perspective of foreign alumni, contact with the alma mater could help to ease post-return reassimilation issues resulting from changes within the student or within the home country during the student's absence (Hood and Schieffer 1983). Good relations and regular contact between alumni and institution, perhaps via a newsletter, is a healthy and logical extension of the study abroad experience.

With these considerations in mind, the ESL program administrator might assess the effectiveness of alumni relations according to questions such as the following:

### Evaluation Questions for Alumni Relations

1. Does the program have an alumni relations network in place?
2. Is contact between the program and its alumni regular and informative?
3. Is communication between the program and alumni two-way?
4. Do both alumni and the program benefit from alumni relations?

## Guidelines for the Evaluation of Student Services in ESL Programs

The evaluation questions that follow are meant to provide a framework for a thorough and focused institutional self-study of student services. Byrd and Constantinides (this volume), in keeping with the position taken by NAFSA (1983) and TESOL (1983 1985), cite the benefits of self-study: (1) the goals of the program are clarified; (2) problems and strengths in the program are identified; (3) personnel, procedures, and resources are reviewed in a systematic fashion; and (4) needed changes are introduced. A broad spectrum of evaluation systems has been developed (see Stufflebeam and Webster 1988), each with its advantages and limitations. The self-evaluation guidelines offered here are no exception: they are intended not to compete with or replace other models or instruments, but to supplement them.

Several features are stressed in these guidelines. The first is the absolute need for a thoughtful, pragmatic, and well-articulated institutional policy in the student services area (Altbach, Kelly, and Lulat 1985; Goodwin and Nacht 1983; Higbee 1961; Spaulding 1988). A carefully considered and clearly stated policy allows for the informed and rational establishment of program goals and objectives. Second is the critical need for the presence of student services and other administrative personnel in possession of the requisite skills and knowledge (Woolston 1983), either within the ESL program itself or in close contact with the program through the larger institution or community. The existence of trained and experienced personnel in key positions ensures the smooth and professional functioning of a program. Third is the crucial need for adequate funding (Thackaberry and Liston 1986). Sufficient funding enables an institution to initiate and maintain programs and structures commensurate with the level of commitment expressed in the institutional policy.

The questions below are designed to evaluate the planning, organizing, budgeting, staffing, and directing of the people and processes involved with each area of the student services component of an ESL program. The questions are divided into general and specific guidelines that reflect questions raised by Deegan (1981) and DeRoche (1987) and evaluative dimensions (unity, efficiency, consistency, effectiveness, cost-effectiveness, importance, image, and potential) developed by Pennington (1987).

## General Guidelines

1. What are the program's guiding principles, philosophy, goals, and objectives, and what is its stated policy with respect to the area of student services?
2. Are the principles, philosophy, goals and objectives, and policy manifest in the actual decisions and practices in the area of student services? If not, what needs to be changed?
3. Do the principles, philosophy, goals and objectives, policy, decisions, and practices in the area of student services accurately reflect the needs and interests of the program and its clientele? If not, what needs to be changed?
4. What is the balance between academic services and student services in the ESL program? Is the balance appropriate to the needs and interests of the program and its clientele? If not, what needs to be changed?

## Specific Guidelines

1. Is this area of student services *adequately staffed?* Is the staff trained, knowledgeable, and experienced in this area? If not, what needs to be changed?
2. Is this area of student services *adequately funded?* Are the funds sufficient to support the people and processes in this area? If not, what needs to be changed?
3. Is the area of student services *unified?* Are all staff members working towards the same purposes and goals? If not, what needs to be changed?
4. Are the services offered in this area *comprehensive?* Do the services represent a complete response to the issues in this area? If not, what needs to be changed?

5.  Are the services offered in this area *accessible*? Are the services obtainable, and is the clientele aware of the services in this area? If not, what needs to be changed?
6.  Are the services offered in this area *coordinated*? Are the services in this area coherently administered and delivered? If not, what needs to be changed?
7.  Are the services offered in this area *continuous*? Are the services in this area provided throughout the duration of the program? If not, what needs to be changed?
8.  Are the people and processes involved in this area *efficient*? Are both practical and effectual in this area? If not, what needs to be changed?
9.  Are the people and processes involved in this area *consistent*? Are both uniform in relation to time and clientele in this area? If not, what needs to be changed?
10. Are the people and processes involved in this area *effective*? Do both contribute fully to the delivery of services in this area? If not, what needs to be changed?
11. Are the people and processes involved in this area *cost-effective*? Do both reflect funding and budget constraints in this area? If not, what needs to be changed?
12. What is the *image* of the area of student services? Is this the image that the program desires? If not, what needs to be changed?
13. What is the *importance* of the area of student services? Is this in keeping with the program's principles, philosophy, goals and objectives, and policy in this area? If not, what needs to be changed?
14. What is the *potential* of the area of student services? What is being done to help realize the potential of this area? What more needs to be done to help realize the potential of this area?

## Conclusion

Many English language programs in the United States offer a student services component. This is not surprising given the large number of programs currently in place, nor is it surprising in view of the historical relationship between an educational institution and its students in this country. These student services can take many forms, and this is as it should be, for the particular administrative arrangement and scope of services offered to ESL students should be a reflection of that program's unique character. However, regardless of the form and range of the student services component, it is extremely important to know the merit of these services and the extent to which they meet the needs and respond to the interests of all the constituencies involved in the language learning endeavor. With this in mind, the purpose of this paper has been twofold: to discuss the various dimensions of student services within the context of how they relate to international students in English language programs, and to provide guidelines for a program to self-evaluate its efforts in the area of student services.

International educational exchange is not a new phenomenon, but in this increasingly mobile and interdependent world it is a growing and ever more important phenomenon. English language programs play a large and significant role in transnational education, and the size and importance of this role make it imperative that these programs and their missions and services be taken seriously. This requires that the elements of professionalism and accountability, and by extension evaluation, be at the center of every program. Reichard (1983) aptly points out that through the exchange of persons, nations have at their disposal a vehicle by which to address the major issues of our time; unless international educational exchange, in all its forms and services, continues to be carefully examined and purposefully enacted, there is the risk of losing the full potential of this magnificent opportunity.

# References

Altbach, P. G. 1988. Foreign student adjustment: Issues and perspectives. Paper presented at the OECD Seminar on Higher Education and the Flow of Foreign Students, Hiroshima, Japan. November.

Altbach, P. G., D. H. Kelly, and Y. G-M. Lulat, eds. 1985. *Research on international students and international study.* New York: Praeger.

Althen, G. 1983. *The handbook of foreign student advising.* Yarmouth: Intercultural Press, Inc.

Ballard, B. 1988. Social and cultural adjustment by foreign students: The Australian experience. Paper presented at the OECD Seminar on Higher Education and the Flow of Foreign Students, Hiroshima, Japan. November.

Breitenbach, D. 1970. The evaluation of study abroad. In Eide, I., ed., *Students as links between cultures,* 70–98. Oslo: UNESCO.

Brickman, W. W. 1965. Historical development of governmental interest in international higher education. In Fraser, S. E., ed., *Governmental policy and international education,* 17–46. New York: John Wiley and Sons, Inc.

Brislin, R. W. and P. Pedersen. 1976. *Cross-cultural orientation programs.* New York: Gardner Press, Inc.

Cadieux, R. A. J. and B. Wehrly. 1986. Advising and counseling the international student. In Pyle, K. R., ed., *Guiding the development of foreign students,* 51–64. San Francisco: Jossey-Bass.

Christensen, G. C. and T. B. Thielen. 1983. Cross-cultural activities: Maximizing the benefits of educational interchange. In Jenkins, H. M. and Associates, eds., *Educating students from other nations*, 210–236. San Francisco: Jossey-Bass.

Cieslak, E. C. 1955. *The foreign student in American colleges*. Detroit: Wayne University Press.

Coelho, G. V. 1958. *Changing images of America*. Glencoe, IL: The Free Press.

Constantine, K. K. 1986. *Higher education marketing*. Chicago: American Marketing Association.

Deegan, W. L. 1981. *Managing student affairs programs*. Palm Springs, CA: ETC Publications.

DeRoche, E. F. 1987. *An administrator's guide to evaluating programs and personnel*. Boston: Allyn and Bacon, Inc.

Deutsch, S. E. 1979. *International education and exchange*. Cleveland: The Press of Case Western Reserve University.

Diener, T. J. and L. Kerr. 1979. Institutional responsibilities to foreign students. In King, M. C. and R. L. Breuder, eds., *Advancing international education*, 179–198. San Francisco: Jossey-Bass.

DuBois, C. 1956. *Foreign students and higher education in the United States*. Washington, D.C.: American Council on Education.

Dudden, A. P. and R. R. Dynes. 1987. *The Fulbright experience: 1946–1986*. New Brunswick, NJ: Transaction Books.

Elton, L. 1988. Accountability in higher education: The danger of unintended consequences. *Higher Education* 17:377–391.

Fraser, S. E. 1968. *A history of international and comparative education*. Glenview, IL: Scott, Foresman, and Company.

Giamatti, A. B. 1988. *A free and ordered space: The real world of the university*. New York: W. W. Norton and Company.

Goetzl, S. and J. D. Strutter. 1980. *Foreign student alumni: Overseas links for U.S. institutions*. Washington, D.C.: National Association for Foreign Student Affairs.

Goodwin, C. D. and M. Nacht. 1983. *Absence of decision: Foreign students in American colleges and universities*. New York: Institute of International Education.

Guiton, J. 1977. *From equivalence of degrees to evaluation of competence*. Paris: UNESCO.

Halls, W. D. 1971. *International equivalences in access to higher education*. Paris: UNESCO.

Higbee, H. 1961. *The status of foreign student advising in United States universities and colleges*. East Lansing, MI: Michigan State University Press.

152

Hood, M. G. and K. J. Schieffer, eds. 1983. *Professional integration: A guide for students from the developing world.* Washington, D.C.: National Association for Foreign Student Affairs.

Institute of International Education. 1981. *Evaluating foreign student credentials.* New York: IIE.

_____. 1982. *English language and orientation programs in the United States.* New York: IIE.

_____. 1988. *Open doors 1987–1988.* New York: IIE.

Jenkins, H. M. 1983. Growth and impact of educational interchanges. In Jenkins, H. M. and Associates, eds., *Educating students from other nations,* 4–30. San Francisco: Jossey-Bass.

Joshi, J. H. 1983. Finances: Finding the funds for international study. In Jenkins, H. M. and Associates, eds., *Educating students from other nations,* 91–112. San Francisco: Jossey-Bass.

Kaplan, R. B. 1983. Meeting the educational needs of other nations. In Jenkins, H. M. and Associates, eds., *Educating students from other nations,* 253–276. San Francisco: Jossey-Bass.

Klieneberg, O. and W. F. Hull, IV. 1979. *At a foreign university: An international study of adaptation and coping.* New York: Praeger.

Lee, M. Y., M. Abd-Ella, and L. A. Burks. 1981. *Needs of foreign students from developing nations at U.S. colleges and universities.* Washington, D.C.: National Association for Foreign Student Affairs.

Leonard, E. A. 1956. *Origins of personnel services in American higher education.* Minneapolis: University of Minnesota Press.

Martin, D. T., G. E. Overholt, and W. J. Urban. 1976. *Accountability in American education.* Princeton: Princeton Book Company.

Mestenhauser, J. A. 1976. *Learning with foreign students.* Minneapolis: University of Minnesota Press.

Michie, A. A. 1967. *Diversity and interdependence through international education.* New York: Education and World Affairs.

Murphy, F. D. 1956. *Orientation of foreign students.* New York: Committee on Educational Interchange Policy.

National Association for Foreign Student Affairs. 1979. *A guide to the admission of foreign students.* Washington, D.C.: NAFSA.

_____. 1983. *NAFSA self-study guide: A guide for the self-assessment of programs and services with international educational exchange at postsecondary institutions.* Washington, D.C.: NAFSA.

National Liaison Committee on Foreign Student Admissions. 1980. *Foreign student recruitment: Realities and recommendations.* New York: College Board.

Oyen, O. C. 1985. "Marginals" versus "centrals". In Allaway, W. H. and H. C. Shorrock, eds., *Dimensions of international higher education,* 63–74. Boulder, CO: Westview Press.

Pennington, M. C. 1985. Effective administration of an ESL program. In Larson, P., E. L. Judd, and D. S. Messerschmitt, eds., *On TESOL '84*, 301–316. Washington, D.C.: Teachers of English to Speakers of Other Languages.

_____. 1987. Evaluation in ESL programs. Preconference workshop at the annual conference of the National Association for Foreign Student Affairs. Long Beach, CA. May–June.

Reichard, J. F. 1983. Summary and agenda for future interchanges. In Jenkins, H. M. and Associates, eds., *Educating students from other nations*, 295–318. San Francisco: Jossey-Bass.

Reid, J. M., ed. 1988. *Building the professional dimension in educational exchange*. Yarmouth: Intercultural Press, Inc.

Silny, J. 1988. *Handbook on establishing an international recruitment program*. Princeton: Peterson's Guides.

Spaulding, S. 1988. *International students in higher education: Institutional policy issues*. Paper presented at the OECD Seminar on Higher Education and the Flow of International Students, Hiroshima, Japan. November.

Spaulding, S. and M. J. Flack. 1976. *The world's students in the United States*. New York: Praeger.

Speakman, C. E. 1966. *International exchange in education*. New York: CARE, Inc.

Stufflebeam, D. and W. J. Webster. 1988. Evaluation as an administrative function. In Boyan, N. J., ed., *Handbook of research on educational administration*, 569–602. New York: Longman.

Sue, D. W. 1978. Eliminating cultural oppression in counseling: Toward a general theory. *Journal of Counseling Psychology* 25:419–428.

Teachers of English to Speakers of Other Languages. 1983. *Standards and self-study questions for postsecondary programs*. Washington, D.C.: TESOL.

_____. 1985. *Statement of core standards for language and professional preparation programs*. Washington, D.C.: TESOL.

Thackaberry, M. D. and A. Liston. 1986. Recruitment and admissions: Special issues and ethical considerations. In Pyle, K. R., ed., *Guiding the development of foreign students*, 29–38. San Francisco: Jossey-Bass.

Tierney, W. G. 1988. Organizational culture in higher education. *The Journal of Higher Education* 59:2–21.

UNESCO. 1982. World guide to higher education. Essex: UNESCO.

Woodhall, M. 1988. *Specific measures and programs for foreign students*. Paper presented at the OECD Seminar on Higher Education and the Flow of International Students, Hiroshima, Japan. November.

Woolston, V. C. 1983. Administration: Coordinating and integrating programs and services. In Jenkins, H. M. and Associates, eds., *Educating students from other nations*, 184–209. San Francisco: Jossey-Bass.

# 8

# Creating and Operating a Statistical Database for Evaluation in an English Language Progam

*Roger Ponder and Bill Powell*

## Introduction

Recordkeeping is a task that administrators in English language programs assume dutifully, if not always joyfully. No one needs convincing that scores and other statistics are essential factors in evaluating currently enrolled students. Most of the time, however, data linked with individual students become superfluous once the students have left the program. Systematically archiving these numbers in a database can extend their usefulness to the program long after the departure of the students who generated them. This article suggests approaches to utilizing the large amounts of data generated by students passing through English language programs for a variety of evaluative purposes. The ideas presented here are meant to be useful for a wide readership—including both those who have a good background in statistics and those who admit to being near novices. Similarly, some degree of computer literacy is helpful, but not required, since the article seeks to demystify the exploitation of computerized databases for evaluative ends within an English language program.

The paper begins with a description of four typical cases in which a statistical database could be used for evaluative purposes within an English language program. Following the cases, various options are described for setting up computerized records for statistical analysis in a program. In the concluding section, we return to the original cases and consider how a statistical database might be utilized in each of them.

# Old Problems, New Solutions: Cases from the ESL Frontlines

The following cases depict situations that frequently arise in English language programs. Each situation illustrates a particular type of problem in evaluation that could be resolved or alleviated through the use of a statistical database.

## Case 1. Alice: The Heartbreak of Placement

Scene: The office(s) of a large English language program
Time:   Late afternoon of testing day

Alice, the program director, sits at her desk, staring joylessly at the columns of numbers on a sheet of paper given to her by her testing supervisor as he left for the evening. The numbers represent scores on entrance tests. Before tomorrow morning when classes begin, she has to place all of the incoming students into groups appropriate to their level as revealed in these tests. She sighs and takes a bite out of her fast-food sandwich. It is going to be a long evening.

Type of Evaluation: Placement
Database Solution: Statistical forecasts of future performance

With little information other than scores on a few placement tests, Alice must evaluate her new students' proficiency and assign each a place in the curriculum. It would be helpful to know what kinds of results incoming students in her program have typically achieved in the past. What kinds of results have students with a score of 50 on an entrance test shown after one term? After two terms? How about students who do well on one type of entry test, but poorly on another type? If Alice knew the answer to these questions, her placement problems would be easier to solve. Statistical projections generated through analysis of a database could help Alice reach correct decisions.

## Case 2. Eric: Trickle-Down Planning

Scene: The office of the director of an English language program
Time:   Any time

Eric, the curriculum coordinator, sinks despondently into the only "good" chair in the office. He has just finished trying to explain—for the third time this term—why the program should be structured into six instructional levels. Now, his boss, the program director, is patiently explaining once more why the program should stick to its present four-level configuration. Eric frowns and slouches into the worn depths of his chair.

Type of Evaluation: Program design and management; administration
Database Solution: Precise records; long-term trends

Eric needs to show that many students at a given level are "over-achieving"—that is, that they regularly outperform their classmates and thus would benefit from work at a higher level. Conversely, he also needs to demonstrate that other students consistently fail to come up to standard and should be accommodated at a lower level. It would also be useful to show that the numbers of actual and potential students indicate that major changes in the structure of the program are warranted. The information in a database could help Eric to support his case—or to realize that the director is right in hesitating to make this change.

Case 3. Lily: Lost in the Stars

Scene: A classroom in an English language program
Time: The future

Lily, a teacher in the program, is passing out corrections to a composition handed in several days before. Her smile is warm and encouraging. In reality, however, she is very disappointed in her students' performance. As a new teacher who came into the program only a couple of months ago, she is not sure whether she is expecting too much or too little of her students. Ali and Xiao failed to turn in papers: "It doesn't help with the TOEFL [Test of English as a Foreign Language]," they say. She sighs inwardly and begins to write on the blackboard.

Type of Evaluation: Instructional standards
Database Solution: Pedagogical history (program "tradition")

Lily needs access to past class records. She needs to know how her students were performing when they entered the program and how they compare with former students at this level. A database could give her the numbers she needs. Much of the information accumulated in a database represents the experience of past teachers in the program. Even though Lily is a relatively new teacher, she can benefit from the records left by her predecessors.

Case 4. Steve: The Struggle for Fame

Scene: The office of the director of an English language program operating on the campus of a large university.
Time: Afternoon of a typically busy day

Steve, the program director, is on the phone with an official from the university admissions office. He grimaces, obviously unhappy with

157

what he is hearing. He has just been told that a score is a score, and that is all there is to it. No, his recommendation on behalf of Nkouka, a very good student in the program's most advanced level after six months in English classes, will not be considered, thank you. Goodbye. He hangs up the phone, depressed and angry.

Type of Evaluation: External validity
Database Solution: Measures of validity

Steve needs to demonstrate the value of his program to his host university. He would like to demonstrate that students who achieve a certain level of performance in his intensive ESL (English as a second language) program go on to become successful students in the university. He believes that his program's recommendation should carry weight since the time spent in the language program is an opportunity to observe a student's performance over a prolonged period and is a more accurate predictor of future accomplishments than a two-hour standardized test. Information from a database can be of assistance in substantiating his contention (as shown in Chapter Three of this volume).

## Basic Definitions

These cases convey some idea of the advantages a database might bring to evaluation in an English language program. At this point, it will be helpful to clearly define several concepts dealt with in this article, especially as these differ from usage in a wider context.

### DATABASE

**General Definition.** The term *database* as used in this discussion is purposely nontechnical and very broadly defined. In general, a database is a collection of data: an accumulation of facts observed over a period of time. Each datum (or fact) is usually (but not always) expressed as a number and is associated with a variable. The number "580" is an example of a fact associated with the variable "TOEFL score" for a given individual. The phrase "648 East Park Avenue" is the fact associated with the variable "address." With the proper coding, almost any feature of an English language program or characteristic of an individual can be incorporated into a database.

In a larger context, the term *database* often appears in advertising and discussions about computer programs. In general, there are two types of database programs. Relational database software programs have the capability of extracting and recombining separate pieces of information from many different computer files to create new files. This power and flexibility is suited to many applications in business and administration. The instructions for applications are written in the database's own programming language. In general, the more complete the program, the more expensive. Database programs without relational capability often use a "flat file" design, a format not unlike keeping information on separate note cards or columnar paper. More expensive programs of this type have various enhancements. With the most powerful, it is possible to some extent to manipulate data from several sources, but these operations never achieve the complexity and versatility of a relational program.

**Administrative (Short-Term) Database.** Any English language program obviously keeps records, on paper or on computer, for its current term, ranging from the personal data of the students, through tuition payments, to the performance of the students. Some of these data may be incorporated as is, or in a modified form, into the statistical (long-term) database (see below). For example, while a student's telephone number and home country are essential bits of knowledge while that student is enrolled, the former is relatively useless upon his or her departure; but the latter is useful either as a term or as a code for computer analysis.

**Statistical (Long-Term) Database.** In this article, the focus is on collections of variables composed of data selected for the purpose of statistical analysis. A computer program for analyzing data usually requires that information be organized in computer files having specific characteristics; even a paper-based database for the purposes of statistical analysis suggests a strict columnar format. In this article, the term *statistical database* will often be used to denote such computer files, especially if they are maintained as independent structures distinct from other record-keeping documents such as the administrative database that we have described above.

## DATABASE MANAGEMENT

The concept of data management involves all procedures for organizing, arranging, updating, or otherwise manipulating the variables in a data collection. It is an activity that can be independent of the database itself. A collection of data on index cards qualifies as a type of database, but obviously it is managed very differently from a collection of data residing in multiple computer files in a university mainframe. In the case of index cards, data management involves physically handling and writing on the cards; computerization requires more elaborate procedures. Each type of database may have a management system appropriate to its structure and purpose.

Analyzing the information in a database involves procedures undertaken to discover characteristics about the data collection as a whole. Even though it may be possible to recover information about individuals from a statistical database, the purpose of analysis is to gain knowledge about large groups of students. Indeed, this concept is central to the concept of statistical analysis. A count of the number of students who participate in some testing procedure constitutes a simple level of analysis. Statistical sophistication is facilitated (but not necessitated) by computer analysis. It is important to note that computer programs that manage databases may not be suitable for analysis. In order to utilize data in an analysis program, it may be necessary to reorganize or reformulate data into a form compatible with the program.

## Designing, Managing and Analyzing a Statistical Database

The creation of a database begins long before strings of numbers are ready to be plugged into a computer for analysis. The decision determining the basic components of the database will be partly conceptual, partly practical, but it will always reflect conditions and policies of the language program involved. Managing a database, especially a sizable one, can be greatly facilitated by computer programs, and for meaningful statistical analysis, appropriate computer packages are imperative.

### CONCEPTUALIZATION AND PLANNING

Adroit planning is critical to the success of a database. Not only must the present operation of the intensive program be taken into account, but its future course as well. In part, decisions in the planning process depend upon the requirements of the data management and analysis systems that are available (George 1986). Ultimately, however, the foundation of a successful database is in the imagination of its planners.

**Criteria for Selecting Variables.** Planning a database for an English language program essentially involves deciding which variables, from among the mass of data assembled for each individual passing through the program, are to be permanently maintained for use in an analysis program. A good starting point for making decisions about the types of data to collect is provided by NAFSA's *Computer Systems in International Education* (1985). In the particular case of the English language program, Munsell (1982) suggests that two types of information be maintained on each English language program participant: *student data* (age, native language, educational aims, test scores, source of sponsorship, "and as much personal information as possible" [p. 103]), and *program data* (class placement, attendance records, evaluation forms, "and other records of methods, materials, experiments, and so on" [p. 103]). While this distinction is useful on a general level, it does not take into account the characteristics of data specifically generated and collected for statistical analysis. Two practical criteria for including a variable in a statistical database are its utility in future analysis and its availability in practice.

*Utility.* A useful variable is one that yields basic information, either about a distinguishing characteristic of an individual or about an individual's performance. The variables "sex," "nationality," and "native language" are inherently interesting and potentially useful facts about individuals, while scores on major proficiency tests, such as the TOEFL (Test of English as a Foreign Language), the TSE (Test of Spoken English), and the Michigan Test of English Language Proficiency, give benchmark information against which other information is gauged, even far into the future. The variable "telephone number," on the other hand, is not obviously associated with other variables, and, apart from its utility during the time the student is enrolled in the English language program, is probably of limited interest for an ongoing statistical database. A useful variable is also flexible, in that it can be used singly or in combination with other variables for statistical analysis.

*Availability.* The logical starting point for selecting computer variables is the information that is already being gathered in the routine operation of the program, perhaps extending back for a considerable period of time. Even data that are several years old can be incorporated into a database, provided that it is reasonably complete. Such information is available at very little cost of time or effort.

In contrast, some information may simply not be obtainable, given the record-keeping resources available to the English language program. Description and coding may also present difficulties. The variable "prior English study," for example, may be thought to be an important contributor to performance; however, objectively describing and coding this variable may not be possible. The inclusion of other variables might entail extensive administrative changes. For example, variables denoting scores on psychological trait tests (such as introversion/extroversion, field-dependence/field-independence) would require administering appropriate tests on a regular basis. Most English language programs would probably find the benefit of such data outweighed by the cost and complexity of the testing procedures required to generate it.

**Types of Variables.** Several factors may motivate selection of variables. The following section suggests categories into which variables may be grouped according to their purpose and utility in the database.

*Individual Tracking.* The main purpose of a database is to show characteristics and information about a program as a whole, and only incidentally to keep track of individuals. Even so, in a statistical database enough labeling of information is needed to be able to differentiate among individuals. Possible variables are the following:

- Name (truncated, if necessary)
- Identification number (perhaps social security number, if available)
- Sequence number (in terms of program history, as individuals are appended to the database)

*Language Learning Theory.* Many theories and concepts regarding the way individuals learn languages have been proposed. Planners of an English language program statistical database may wish to include variables suggested by the language-learning literature. For example, information about an individual's age can be justified, since it is widely believed that older learners generally do not progress as rapidly as younger ones. Analysis of an English language program database may help support or discount this and other notions about how individuals learn languages. Possible variables are the following:

- Age
- Nationality
- Native language
- Sex
- Year of birth (from which age can be calculated)
- Prior English study
- Educational background/level
- Academic status (i.e., graduate, undergraduate)
- Psychological traits (e.g., field dependence/independence, extroversion/introversion, etc.)
- Socialization (to what extent a student integrates into the surrounding culture)
- Motivation (integrative/instrumental)

*Pedagogy.* Direct measures of student performance relate primarily to curriculum and instruction as the outward record of pedagogical policies and practices. Possible variables are the following:

- Test scores (with related dates)
- Teacher evaluations/grades
- Attendance
- Textbooks used
- Level of instruction

- Names of teachers (perhaps coded)
- Placement information

*Administrative Decisions.* Many facts about students, particularly those that reveal biographical data, are useful not only from a language-learning perspective, but also because they can inform administrative and business decisions. Possible variables are the following:

- Fee payments
- Recruitment information (e.g., reason student came to that particular English language program)
- Destination after leaving the English language program
- Student evaluations of the program
- Visa status and actions
- Enrollment dates and circumstances

## DATABASE MANAGEMENT

The collection of data extends over a varying period of time depending on the purpose of database, which also may vary at different times in the collection process. As an aspect of its administrative functions, an English language program often begins assembling information on students months before they arrive. Completed applications put essential tags—such as name, age, and educational level—on potential students, while registration inspires even more earnest accumulation of biographical data. Placement testing furnishes substantiated information on the language-related characteristics of the individual student. Thereafter, periodic in-house evaluation and standardized testing provide increasingly detailed descriptions of students as language learners. The graduation and departure of the student yield further biographical data related to immigration status, final address, destination, and so on, along with summative evaluations of language abilities.

File drawers divided into sections representing past, present, and future students are obviously a basic means of data management. The utility of such a system in the search for specific information on individuals does not apply to large-scale program evaluation and forecasting, except as the source of information for databases.

Columnar ledger sheets including variables outlined above and a hand-held calculator could be a low-technology solution in a small, young English language program. Many calculators, even inexpensive ones, can produce statistical correlations, and models that include procedures for simple linear regression are not uncommon. However, the possibility of error in keying in the data and the difficulty of correcting or confirming calculations (except by repeating each job) severely limit the size and scope of a calculator database.

**Computerization.** Successful programs (in terms of enrollment and longevity) would benefit from the computerization of their data. Outlined below are a number of options, reviewing both access to hardware and software possibilities.

Computerized database management need not entail the purchase of a microcomputer for the office, but rather could draw on the computer resources (human and electronic) of the host institution. Universities and colleges provide access to sophisticated statistical programs through campus terminals connected to mainframe computers. Though complicated, programs such as SPSS (Statistical Package for the Social Sciences) offer powerful analyses of numerical data for the cost of computer time. One drawback of using such programs is the generally rigid format that they demand for data files. In many instances, university computing services provide inexpensive (or free) training in running such programs and may even input raw data and design and run analyses for reasonable fees. Such services are attractive alternatives for those without the money to purchase a microcomputer or without the expertise to run these powerful programs themselves.

Terminals can generally be rented from the institution or a private company, although that option might actually increase costs by necessitating the purchase of a modem and dedicated telephone line. If the English language program can make extensive use of the terminal by drawing on other programs in the institution's mainframe or minicomputer—for example, to keep track of registration and student performance data—the expenses associated with renting a terminal and paying for computer time can be justified.

Micro- or personal computers offer a number of possibilities not only for data access but also for data management because of the flexibility they offer in terms of software use. Indeed, an economical option for using a microcomputer in the creation of a database is to take advantage of the increasing number of computer labs on campuses, where a battery of micros, sometimes with a selection of brands, is available for general use. On many campuses, a variation on the computer lab theme is a "dedicated" computer whose use, memory, and output are reserved for a single application such as the PC version of SPSS. Inconvenience is a general disadvantage of the use of a mainframe terminal, a computer lab, or a dedicated machine, since all usually imply leaving the office to input data or run analyses. However, it should be kept in mind that, if the goal is to retain data on program and student performance over the long run, one would only need to be seated periodically in front of a computer monitor.

As microcomputers become more common in English language program administration offices, their availability lends itself to longitudinal recordkeeping and analysis in addition to use for maintaining records on a term-by-term basis and as word processors. With telecommunications software (needed for linkage by telephone), microcomputers can be used to communicate with a mainframe installation in a "terminal mode" option; moreover, the software worlds of both IBM and Apple products contain numerous programs both for administrative functions and, more importantly here, for statistical analysis. The software capabilities range up to the power of versions of SPSS and MINITAB in the PC world and Statview and Systat on the Macintosh, although such programs can necessitate special hardware additions such as high-volume disks, math coprocessor chips, and so forth, especially if they are sharing the environment with other programs. Microcomputer programs of this nature are almost universally formatted in spreadsheet style, in that a column is assigned to each variable and data can be easily typed directly into the program.

Since information can be transferred between microcomputer programs (though not necessarily easily or cleanly) as well as between micros and mainframes, different software programs may be applied to data files at different stages of the data's existence in order to best utilize, evaluate, and present the information at hand. Depending on the formatting required for use of a particular software program, data files can sometimes be imported directly from another program. For example, SPSS/PC+ can translate files from Lotus 1-2-3 and dBase III, while on the Macintosh, Cricket Graph files can be read directly by Statview+. Many programs can read ASCII or text files generated by other programs. At times a data file may have to be "cleaned up"—reformatted or slightly reworked, sometimes simply in a word processing program or in the text editor of the mainframe—before it can be analyzed within a new program. In any instance, there is an efficient, multifaceted beauty in inputting data once for potential use in a variety of software applications to best meet the daily and long-term needs of an English language program.

The ontogeny of the data influences their management. One path is for data to have a single incarnation. That is, information is stored according to the variables chosen, subject to the requirements of the software program to be applied. If the plan is to use only SPSS on the mainframe or in its PC version, for example, then a data file suitable to the data definition commands of SPSS will suffice. However, if, prior to statistical analysis, information on individual students is to be accessed by other administrative programs (e.g., to keep track of enrollment on a term-by-term basis using information, such as current telephone number, that is not particularly useful for historical analysis), then a strategy of compatibility of data files should be devised so that a single data file may serve more than one software master or so that pertinent data can be effectively extracted from one data file for use in another. Relatively simple database management programs on microcomputers generally allow for the easy deletion of a variable (also termed a *field*), permitting the removal of what might have been important information for the term-based administrative file before data are added to the on-going statistical database. Similarly, essential information for eventual analysis, such as coded data for native language or sex, can be added into either the original file or a file representing the next stage of the data's metamorphosis.

Even though some programs have limits in the number of variables/fields/columns that they can accept, additional variables can be added into larger capacity files in several ways. When both the original and subsequent data files are in a tab-delimited, columnar format, it is relatively easy to add more data for each subject after the data have been transferred to the next generation. If the information is going from a micro- to a mini- or mainframe computer, the original file can be converted to a text file and then reopened in a word processing program. At this point, further data can be entered and the file cleaned up (e.g., the tabs separating variables in the original file, that might not translate distinctly, can be changed into spaces) before uploading to the main-frame via telecommunication. The mainframe's text editor can also be utilized for the addition and shaping of data, albeit somewhat more laboriously.

An illustration of such possibilities may be helpful, though it must always be understood that there are many combinations of possibilities, depending on presently available hardware and software and the fact that tomorrow's developments in computing will certainly offer new permutations. Consider, for example, Microsoft Works, a widely used integrated software program available for both IBM PC-compatible and Apple Macintosh computers. *Integrated* here means that the program includes several applications, specifically, a word processor, a database manager, a spreadsheet, and telecommunications, thus making the program useful for office and record management needed in an intensive English program. The database manager can be utilized to keep track of pertinent information on students during each term. However, the first Macintosh version of Works would accept a maximum of only 60 variables for each student. (The latest version, released while this article was being written, greatly expands size limitations and succinctly depicts the rapidly changing world of computers and their software.) While 60 pieces of information may be adequate for data generated over a single term, students enrolled for more than one session would lead to the accumulation of data beyond the capacity of a single Works file. Since separate files on each term could not be combined for the same reason, no historical overview could take place, and Works does not offer the potential for statistical analysis anyway. Two tacks might be envisaged, each of which is described below.

*Plan A.* A Works database file is kept for each term. At the end of the term, a copy of the file (the original is archived) is made with certain fields deleted (e.g., phone number), other fields transformed (e.g., native language changed from the word for the language to a code), and still other fields and their data added up to the limit. The file is saved as an *export*, or text file, and opened up in the word processor, where more data can be inputted and the file configured according to the specifications of the ongoing file. This latest file, saved in text mode, can then be uploaded to a mainframe, where it is attached to the ongoing file and any "tidying" of the newly appended data is accomplished through the text editor. Statistical analyses are then performed with SPSS, MINITAB, etc.

*Plan B.* After the export/text file is made as in Plan A, it can then be opened directly by Statview+ through its import function. Statview+ accommodates hundreds of variables, which can easily be added in the program's columnar, tab-delimited format. Though not nearly as versatile as SPSS on a mainframe, Statview+ is capable of sophisticated analyses (t-tests, ANOVA, multiple regression, chi square, etc.) useful in the many facets of evaluation in an intensive English program. Saved as a text file or copied to the clipboard on the Macintosh, the Statview data file can be opened or pasted into a Cricket Graph data file, from which impressive graphs and charts of student or program performance can be generated.

## UTILIZING THE DATABASE

Once the data are properly set up in a form analyzable by a statistical analysis program in whatever computing environment, the database should provide the capability to evaluate diverse aspects of the English language program's operations. The case studies in the opening section depicted ESL teachers and administrators in situations familiar to everyone who has participated in an English language program. The predicaments faced by Alice, Eric, Lily, and Steve are each problems of evaluation. As in real life, these four ESL professionals first need access to complete, up-to-date information about their programs, and then the means and knowledge to process and to interpret this body of information.

In search of solutions to their dilemmas, this section makes some suggestions for areas of data analysis. However, it should be recognized that the possibilities are limited only by the data available (and even that can easily be updated in some formats), the analyses included in the statistical software, and the statistical expertise of the users.

**Placement.** Alice, the program director in the case in the first section of this article, could approach placement more confidently if she had some idea of how individuals were likely to perform in the weeks and months after taking the English language program's entry examinations. Had Alice kept long-term records of both entry and exit test scores, she could apply a regression analysis. A regression analysis, which is based on a correlation between the two sets of scores, yields a regression equation, a formula using scores from a test administered in the present to predict performance on a proficiency measure to be administered in the future. Thus, with the assumption that an adequate level of correlation existed, Alice could use her placement scores to forecast future performance (using TOEFL, perhaps). If the correlation between present and future scores was relatively weak, Alice might consider a change in tests. As the database grew, Alice could calculate formulas for different types of students, based on language or educational level, in addition to the general program formula. Although there is a margin of error involved in any application of inferential statistics, statistically predicted performance can contribute greatly to an informed placement process.

**Administration.** In the other cases, Eric (the cheerless curriculum planner pondering the level structure of the English language program), Lily (the new instructor who is unfamiliar with her students), and Steve (the director of an English language program "unrecognized" within its university) are hampered without comprehensive, accurate, and up-to-date information about their programs. Yet, some of their dilemmas could be handled with straightforward descriptive statistics that are relatively easy to calculate (a hand-held calculator would be sufficient computing power in many cases) if they had access to an adequate database. Totals, percentages, means, and standard deviations are sufficient statistics to answer many interesting questions about an English language program, for example, enrollment figures for given periods of time (by country, by language, by sex, etc.), the male-female or graduate-undergraduate proportions, duration of enrollment, group performance on tests, teacher evaluations, and group or class size.

Curricular decisions can be enhanced by observing student performance trends by level or over time. The ongoing adequacy of program structure can be appraised in this manner, as can the vigor of the curriculum in achieving program goals. Should there be evidence, for example, that levels have in some sense collapsed into each other over time, a reorganization of the curriculum may be in order. The program's administrators may then wish to choose among options such as reducing the number of instructional levels (and, consequently, operating expenses), adopting new placement tests that would distinguish more sharply among students, developing more appropriate coursework at each level, reorienting the instructional emphases of the program, or retooling the evaluation of students.

The effectiveness of a program's evaluation system can be further evaluated through correlation with external measures of validity such as the TOEFL or the TWE (Test of Written English). If correlational strength is sufficient, an English language program could better argue for the substitution or addition of its evaluations to the results of standardized testing for admission decisions. (Steve would thereby gain the respect he yearns for.) When an English language program earns (and sustains) a role in the admissions process based on meaningful correlations between the program's evaluations and standardized tests important to the students (e.g., the TOEFL), then both the program's "report card" and, more importantly, its curriculum can attain a substantial practical significance in the eyes of the students, further enhancing the effectiveness of the curriculum.

A database can also serve to bolster internal face validity by providing students with a record of past achievements. The previous accomplishments of students in Level X can be shown to current Level X students either to demonstrate the "successes" emanating from the curriculum (message: "You can do it too") or to foster realistic expectations among those students believing in the impossible, given their current proficiency. For example, an "ideal student" profile can be developed, depicting the characteristics of the "successful" student at a given level in terms of academic performance, skills, attendance, test scores, and so on. Such a profile, used in conjunction with effective and substantiated placement, can educate students in the reality of language learning by confirming perceptions of progress, encouraging greater effort, or avoiding unnecessary heartbreak over not "passing" the TOEFL, especially after that first elementary level.

On the business side of an English language program (although the above discussions also certainly concern "good business"), enrollment trends can be plotted to forecast future program size, either by semester or by year, or to explain historical tendencies. The effect of policy changes both within and outside the program, currency fluctuations, lengths of enrollment, advertising, recruitment, and so on, are all possible candidates for analysis, as they are in the nonacademic business world.

**Research.** The maintenance of a long-term statistical database provides opportunities for the evaluation of current and future language learning and teaching principles. With a database structured along the lines outlined above, for example, research could easily be directed at the performance of different age groups, of students at different educational levels, or of individuals from different cultural or language backgrounds. Information from the database could also be utilized in peripheral studies with students as subjects or in follow-up studies of students' performance once they gain admission to university-level studies. Being able to tap existing data can readily facilitate research, in that much of the information-gathering labor is already accomplished.

SOME COMPLICATIONS

The establishment of a database is not without its pitfalls. A database can encourage curricular stasis, since any changes in program organization or curriculum would suggest recreating the database anew; old information might not address a new situation. In a large English language program the rebuilding of the database might only take a term or two, but small programs might have to function "without" for quite a while in order to build up adequate numbers for meaningful statistical analysis.

A changing student population may no longer fit the picture painted by a historical database. On this point, one has only to compare the home countries of students a few years ago with those of today: in 1979–80, there were over 50,000 Iranian students in U.S. institutions; by 1987–88, that number was down to 10,420, while the Chinese (Peoples' Republic of China) had risen from unranked to second, with over 25,000 students (Zikopoulos 1988, 20). English language program demographics have undergone similar transformations. Using yesterday's data may not best serve today's students.

It is important to keep in mind that people are not numbers, that language is a difficult thing to quantify, and that statistics can only assist in decisions. While quantitative results are suggestive, an English language program needs to take into account the qualitative contribution of the "human factor" in student performance and behavior.

And then, there are always hardware failures, human error, and electrical storms.

## Conclusion

Evaluation within an English language program requires information, that is, a database—whether on sheets of paper in manila folders or in computerized form. One purpose of this article has been to make the

170

term *database* less threatening. Though many readers might find this high-tech word a little daunting, the discussion has attempted to show that the essential concept involves nothing more than the thoughtful and orderly collection of information over an extended period of time, an activity that occurs routinely in English language programs. Another goal of this article has been to convince readers that taking steps to manage data collection by computer requires no more than a minimal level of computer literacy but offers the potential for numerous applications to evaluation of the broad scope of English language program operations.

The article was less than specific for several reasons. First of all, the structure of a database varies according to the evaluative needs of the program and the vision of its creators. Even in a minimal form, a database can enhance the decision-making processes, planning, and general understanding of dynamics within an English language program. Complexity may lead to greater utility, but perhaps at the expense of greater time and effort.

Second, with the great variety in currently available software, databases can be constructed in a number of formats. Similarly, a range of analytical options exists within the domain of statistics. Any attempt to dictate a blueprint for a database or its analysis, beyond some general principles, would ignore the many different options available and limit choices. Moreover, in the rapidly changing world of computers, something new is always in the pipeline, and the next paradigm shift in language learning theory (or English language program evaluation) may open new perspectives on database content.

Finally, if the database world seems confusing, expertise is nearby: in a university computing center, microcomputer support group, user group, computing magazines, and statistical help center—or from a colleague down the hall.

# References

George, Jane. 1986. Designing a student record-keeping system: Some preliminary considerations. Unpublished ms. Department of English as a Second Language, University of Hawaii.

Interassociational Committee on Data Collection. 1985. *Computer systems in international education.* Washington, D.C.: National Association for Foreign Student Affairs.

Munsell, P. E. 1982. An ESL administrator looks at research. In Barrett, R. P., ed., *The administration of intensive English programs,* 99–105. Washington, D.C.: National Association for Foreign Student Affairs.

Zikopoulos, M. 1988. *Open doors: 1987–88.* New York: Institute for International Education.

# 9

# Designing and Assessing the Efficacy of ESL Promotional Materials

*Frederick L. Jenks*

### Introduction

The entire arena of formal education would be radically different if every school and each of its instructors were required to provide instruction on a "free enterprise/free selection" basis. For example, what if students were free, as educational consumers, to enroll in courses according to their own interests, at times convenient to them, taught by teachers that they wanted to have, and offered in locations that were easily accessible and well maintained? To many educational administrators, particularly those who manage public institutions, the very suggestion of this portends revolution. Indeed, the entire bureaucracy of public education is based on a management system in which students are not seen as clients; rather, they are "wards" of the educational system—entities to be grouped, organized, coordinated, counted, and overseen as they are processed through the schools.

Private institutions, on the other hand, strive to address the needs and desires of students on a more individualized basis. In higher education, it is the private sector that has pioneered the "cooperative work-study program," the "inter-semester," flexible scheduling of academic terms, core or thematic curricula, and individualized programs of study. The reason for this responsiveness is that private institutions must attract future students' attention and compete for subsequent matriculation. They are not subjected to legislative control of curricula, funding, and enrollment levels. In short, they are more responsive to their clients' interests.

Generally speaking, intensive English programs, whether or not affiliated with universities—private or public—tend to be client-oriented. The clients, international students, are free to select from many such programs in the United States. However, in order to select, the clients must first be informed.

To inform and to attract potential students, a self-supported school must undertake numerous public relations and promotional activities. Large universities, for example, plan on allocating funds for fundraising (i.e., development), promotional publications, recruitment-cum-travel (e.g., college nights at high schools), and alumni networking. All institutions of higher education—large or small, public or private—engage in activities designed to promote and highlight those features that will attract new students and/or funding.

English language programs may engage in promotional activities similar to those of degree-granting educational institutions. Programs affiliated with degree-granting institutions as language training units for international students follow similar patterns for promoting their programs, dovetailing many of their efforts with those of the parent institution. To attract new students, the small private English program is totally dependent, both directly and indirectly, on promotional activities that emphasize its own characteristics.

Therefore, English language programs—particularly those offering intensive or specialized curricula—are one of the most active types of educational enterprises in the area of recruitment. Given their noncredit status, their short-term preparatory function, and their lack of an easily accessed body of residential students, these programs depend on good public relations and advertising to survive, since few such programs are totally supported by endowments, gifts, or the tax base.

Both proprietary and institutionally affiliated English language programs are, in some ways, unusual entities: they serve international scholars, businesspeople, or other foreign clients only; they award no degrees and often no academic credits; they rarely possess the security inherent in the departmental or unit structures of other educational institutions; they frequently receive little or no fiscal support from institutional coffers; and they battle to maintain their faculty's status equal to that of others in the same institution. In short, English programs are generally very much on their own. Their survival—and, indeed, their development—depends on their ability to recruit international students and to provide them with satisfactory language instruction. To do so, they must market their services internationally and frequently.

This article treats the issue of promotional and recruitment activities within English language programs. The paper includes sections that focus on the processes required to perform pilot and formative assessments of materials, to develop and produce effective publications, and to enhance the quality of a program's print and nonprint products. Throughout the article are recommendations for undertaking self-assessments. These suggestions, it is hoped, will permit program administrators to focus on key aspects of their overall promotional strategies.

## Print Materials

A wide range of printed materials is produced by English language programs. In order to access international markets at a reasonable cost, printed materials serve well. Setting aside those many products that are purely marketing "gimmicks" (e.g., notepads with a particular logo), I will focus on information-based publications. Brochures, advertisements, and posters are primary print vehicles used by English programs, and each genre deserves individual discussion.

**Brochures.** Virtually all active intensive or special-purpose English language programs produce a program brochure that typically contains (1) overview information about the school; (2) basic information about the curriculum; (3) schedule, cost profile, and community information; and (4) an application form and/or application procedures. Embellishments may include photographs of the school/campus, portraits of students engaged in studies, small maps, brief commentary regarding area schools of higher education, and so on. The commonalities found in English language program brochures, however, extend beyond the organization of content. One notes striking similarities in style and design, the majority of brochures having some or all of the following properties:

- Size: able to fit into a standard airmail envelope
- Weight: able to be mailed at ½-ounce rate
- Folded format: several folded segments of one sheet of paper
- Application form: an affixed or inserted copy of an application with instructions

Given that so many English programs produce so many thousands of brochures, it appears that the standard product is the combined result of much swapping and ample borrowing from what we might refer to as the "Eve" brochure—the mother of all English language program brochures. I can only assume that Eve was born at one of the first-generation English programs during the 1950s and then was replicated by younger programs. In addition, the constraints of shipping, handling, and production expense are major factors in the development of the standard pamphlet.

Perhaps the most important questions in determining the efficacy of ESL (English as a Second Language) promotional materials are these: How important is the brochure? Is its primary objective to inform or to solicit applications? Can one small publication serve multiple purposes? Indeed, how effective is a program's brochure in fulfilling any or all of its designated purposes? To whom is the brochure sent or by whom is it used? Let us examine each question separately.

For many programs, a brochure is the primary—and perhaps the *only*— form of publicity. Thousands are distributed annually by individual and bulk mailings, by direct distribution, and by inclusion with other materials sent to students or potential clients. As an example, at Florida State University, the Center for Intensive English Studies (CIES) prints and distributes 4,000–5,000 brochures annually. This is not a large distribution; major proprietary programs produce in excess of 200,000 pieces annually. Through the commercial acquisition of specific international mailing lists, address labels can be obtained for overseas schools, educational counseling centers, governmental agencies, and so on. A small school like CIES responds to daily letters of inquiry from international agencies overseas; these addresses become part of the program's own mailing list thereafter. Also, approximately 25 percent of the program's brochures are inserted into other university mailings to international students. These simple operations are sufficient for small programs; more complex strategies are obviously required for larger multisite organizations.

A program brochure should give some basic information in simple English regarding the curriculum, instructional levels, duration of studies, facilities, staff, and resources. Throughout the copy, the recipient-as-potential-student must be considered first. With this audience in mind, the brochure developer will want to supplement the basic information on the program with information concerning housing, food, clothing, climate, community/school population, and cocurricular activities. All of this material must, of necessity, be comprehensible to the limited-English reader while simultaneously striving to be interesting and to influence the reader to consider applying.

*Assessment of brochures.* Printz (1988) suggested lists of "dos and don'ts" for English language program promotional materials. The suggestions below incorporate these points and some additional items:

1. Find and stress your program's "differential advantage"—what makes your program special.
2. Use uncluttered layout with ample white space to enhance visual appeal and ease of reading.
3. Use easy-to-read type fonts.
4. Keep copy brief: use short phrases and simple vocabulary in order to promote readability.

5. Avoid using words that may have different meanings in British and American English (e.g., tuitions).
6. School seals are a must, particularly for mailings to Japan and the Far East, since official emblems are considered to be signs of stability and prestige.
7. List special features of the program and attractive majors/degrees of the affiliated university or other nearby schools.
8. Spell out state names throughout.
9. Include "U.S.A." in the address.
10. Stress safety and secure environment without making misleading claims.
11. Mention proximity to large cities.
12. Refer to a college as a "university" wherever possible.
13. If you include copy in a language other than English, *triple-check* all translations.
14. Indicate clearly whether admissions to the English program has any relationship to admission to an affiliated university or other institution.
15. Be sure that you have not included idiomatic expressions in your copy.
16. Mention major connecting airlines and/or typical travel routes to your program site or sites.
17. Give examples of typical social and recreational opportunities in the environs of the program.

Some additional suggestions concerning nonprint content are the following:

1. Do not pose students for photos. Use natural classroom, recreational, or leisure shots of students at the program site or nearby scenic locations.
2. Do not use maps of a single state in isolation from the continental United States. Geographical contours of individual states are of minor interest to international readers.
3. Do not use line drawings since they are not as easily interpreted visually as photos.
4. Do not show students of one ethnic group only.
5. Do not show classes seated on the grass; do not include photos of people eating, bare arms and feet, people wearing fraternity/ sorority shirts with Greek letters.
6. Do include photos showing students involved in academic activity, participating in social events, or using high-tech equipment.
7. If possible, use photos of modern facilities rather than of traditional "ivy-covered" buildings.

Even the issue of color selection must be resolved prior to printing materials, since some colors are perceived negatively by specific cultures. Black as a primary brochure color is discouraged; gray and yellow are perceived less positively than most other colors (Osgood, May, and Miron 1975). Blue is acceptable broadly, as is white. Green? It depends on the nationality of recipients.

Having taken into account the suggestions of other programs, the findings of numerous studies in international advertising, and the caveats of Printz and others, our intensive English program produced a brochure using a metallic primary color (i.e., bronze or gold), four-color photographs, and black copy. It has received little negative response and much positive comment; the copy is updated annually, but the format endures.

*Distribution of Brochures.* Distribution of brochures is, perhaps, the most important factor in deciding the degree of success of this medium as a promotional device. Keeping in mind that the goal is to reach overseas students who are seeking a place to study English, the administration of an English language program must make constant efforts to contact these individuals. The more direct (and personal) the contact, the more effective the message; therefore, the following guidelines are suggested to ensure effective distribution of brochures:

1. Every letter requesting information should be answered with a personalized letter and brochure immediately (within 48 hours is suggested).
2. Any requests from advising agencies for program information should be answered with a personal letter and bundle of brochures.
3. For programs housed within larger institutions, every department can be sent a letter and a supply of brochures two to three times per year to be used for direct departmental mailings to international applicants.
4. If a home institution hosts internationally oriented conferences and seminars, the program brochure can be included in all participants' packets of materials.
5. On a yearly basis, packets of materials can be mailed to binational centers, U.S. embassies overseas, and international educational centers (e.g., the Institute for International Education in the United States).

More indirect distributions are discouraged. For example, mass distributions at professional conferences, such as those sponsored by NAFSA (National Association for Foreign Student Affairs) or TESOL

(Teachers of English to Speakers of Other Languages), do not appear to bring the desired results. Also, mailing brochures to other English language programs is of questionable value except to announce the establishment of a program, since the client pool is not being directly informed. Very few English language programs seek ways to transfer their international enrollees to other programs.

*The Process of Developing a Brochure.* The cost of preparing a brochure is considerable. Copy preparation, photography, layout, paper/ink selections, printing, enveloping, addressing, and handling can add up rapidly. Careful writing is required to ensure that the content is comprehensible to potential students; this is a task that cannot be left to those unfamiliar with international learners of English. Prudent photo selection takes a culturally sensitized pair of eyes, not merely the visual opinion of a photographer or layout specialist. In short, cost and skills are combined factors to be considered.

Brochure preparation entails the following steps and approximate costs:

1. Determination of content: What information is of major import (school profile, services rendered, curricular levels, admissions procedures, etc.)?

2. Inclusion of future schedule: For many programs, the EX program schedule must coincide generally with that of an affiliated institution; thus, articulation between both schedules is required. Also, printed schedules must provide the program's dates for applying, arriving, and enrolling at least one year in advance. Otherwise, the brochure will be quickly outdated.

3. Layout: The services of an in-house design office may be available. For a fee, private graphics companies are always eager to assist programs in preparing materials.

4. Printing: At current rates, the printing of 4,000 brochures of the four-fold, four-color photo variety will cost in excess of $1,500. The larger the number ordered, the lower per-unit cost, and vice versa. A prudent administrator will request that several printers submit bids on the project.

5. Mailing considerations: The cost of maintaining a database of international addresses; purchasing airmail envelopes with the program's return address printed on them; preparing mailing labels using a computer; stuffing, sealing, sorting, and postage are all quite significant. For example, the airmail postage rate to send three four-page brochures in one envelope is approximately $1.25. The other costs mentioned above can easily amount to $.40 per letter.

Therefore, 1,500 brochures (printed at an approximate cost of $.35 to .40 each) to be mailed to 500 overseas addresses would cost no less than $2.50 per envelope. A total bill for this small mailing may be $1,500. In short, the estimated cost for mailing one brochure is $1.00, a guideline that other programs may find to be appropriate for their production-mailing cycle.

*Judging effectiveness of promotion by brochure.* How effective is a mailed brochure in eliciting a positive response from a potential student? In order to gain some preliminary information, a simple coding procedure to track the distribution and return of brochures can be instituted. By placing a small colored dot in a lower corner of the application page, the administrator is able to determine how the brochure was originally received by the applicant. The dots can be color-coded in categories such as organizational requests, departmental requests, mailing list (international), front desk request (i.e., a person who walks into the program office and asks for an application brochure), international admissions office requests, and direct requests (responses to letters from interested parties). By keeping track of the number of brochures initially assigned to each category, by distributing them only from the correct category, and by tallying the number/color code for applications received, the administrator is able to broadly determine the "return rate" of mailings.

**Program Advertisements.** A wide range of publications for overseas sale/distribution to potential students may be found in the field of international ESL. Any English program director can expect to receive one letter of solicitation per month from a publisher, many of whom produce guides that focus on one region of the world. In addition to magazine-style publications aimed at students, there are professional directories that are sold or distributed to active members of professional organizations. TESOL, for example, publishes a biennial guide to preparatory programs in TESL/TEFL (Teaching English as a Second/Foreign Language) and intensive English instruction (TESOL 1988).

While the professional directories routinely list most intensive English programs and provide general information about each program at little or no cost to member institutions, privately produced guides sell advertising space. The inclusion of a promotional announcement may cost the program several thousand dollars per entry. Rates vary according to publisher, number of issues printed, quantity of guides printed and distributed, region of the world to which guides are distributed, timeliness, quality of the directory (i.e., photography, color, paper), and reputation of the guide.

These educational guides may range from the frequent program-information surveys by Japanese educational advising agencies, each of which seems to publish its own guide for clients, to international and/or regional guides such as *International Where and How, ECES Directory,* and *Study in the U.S.A.* These and other guides of similar scope may target international markets in predetermined sections of the globe (the Middle East, for example), while others are distributed free or sold worldwide. There appear to be very few—if any—guides that publish different editions for different parts of the world, other than *Study in the U.S.A.*

*Development and assessment of program advertisements.* Suggestions provided earlier regarding the preparation of print materials apply here as well. Advertisements in guides to ESL programs should reflect the most contemporary aspects of the ESL program and the larger institution, if any, in which it is housed; include the institution's seal; provide only the most basic information in an uncluttered manner; and contain portions in the native language of the potential clients (if the destination of the guide is well established by the publisher).

Since most guides contain preprinted forms that interested parties may use to write to the advertising ESL program, it is easy to assess the direct effectiveness of the advertisement: simply count the number of the guide's forms that are received in the mail. By noting the names and point of origin of each form, one can follow that person's correspondence from this initial inquiry through, perhaps, submitting an application and ultimately registering in classes. The cost per enrollee of the advertisement can then be calculated on an annual basis in order to assist administrators in determining whether to rerun their advertisement for another year.

**Posters.** In addition to brochures and advertisements, some programs develop a poster for international mailing to advising agencies, foundations overseas, and embassies. A poster might be expected to meet the following criteria:

1. It must fit into a large manila envelope for mailing.
2. It must portray the mission, the basic program information, the location(s), and any special features of the program.
3. It must be able to yield direct inquiries from potential students.
4. It must be visually attractive.

A 14″ x 20″ poster would seem to be the maximum size for easy mailing; when folded once, the poster fits into a 10″ wide envelope. For sturdiness and for unwrinkled placement on walls, the poster can be printed on heavy glossed paper. Minimal yet important information needs to be included, and photos must be of sufficient size and simplicity to be visually informative from a distance.

In order to make it easy for interested parties to respond, a tear-off pad of postal cards can be attached to the poster. By taking a postal card, filling in one's address, placing a stamp on it, and mailing the self-addressed card back, the sender can receive program information swiftly. One poster can usually support the weight of a pad of 15 postal cards.

*Judging the effectiveness of posters.* The response to the poster can be tallied easily. Upon receiving each postal card, a staff member enters on a chart its point of origin by country. Periodically, the total number of cards received is calculated and the return rate derived. In a mailing consisting of 300 posters with 4,500 postal cards, a return rate of approximately five percent would be considered very good for an unsolicited, indirect request.

The cost associated with taking a poster from its inception through mailing will be approximately $3.50 each or more, depending on the cost of materials, postal rates, etc. At $3.50 each, the cost per response would be about $5.00, a very low capital outlay for an original advertisement. A poster that is well designed can thus be an important part of a program's overall marketing strategy.

**Newspapers and Newsletters.** Many English language programs, particularly those in metropolitan areas, find that advertisements or announcements in local newspapers and organizational newsletters are helpful in displaying their services. Large newspapers, for example, run weekly sections pertaining to education, community learning programs, and so on. Non-English advertisements in internationally oriented newsletters, local ethnic newspapers, and locally based international organizational mailings help to inform area residents of an English language program's offerings. Furthermore, some major U.S. newspapers have both English and Spanish versions. What vehicle could be more desirable for announcing a locally based language program?

A visit to a university library's reading/reference room permits one to look over newspapers from most major international cities. Assuming the reader is fluent in other languages, it requires only a simple search to find the basic editorial office's address on the first page. Given that, a letter to the newspaper requesting information on advertising costs should yield a swift response. Once the rates and requirements for inclusion are known, a second reading of the newspaper is required in order to develop a general notion of the layout. Also, the actual positioning within the newspaper of an advertisement is of major importance; outer corners and the center of a page are prime positions.

It is strongly suggested that one request information from the newspaper regarding its production of special "school" supplements or pages. The dates of inclusion of these sections and the details for submission of advertising copy may be different from the requirements pertaining to general advertisements. Evaluating the success of advertisements is based upon the number of inquiries and preregistrations, as measured against the program's goal for these.

**Assessing the Value of Print Materials for Promotion.** The major outlet for virtually all English language program announcements is one or more forms of printed material. As mailing and handling costs continue to increase, the efficacy of these materials must be considered in order to determine whether expenditures for certain forms of promotion are supported by the response from potential or actual clients. In most instances, very simple procedures permit administrators and staff to tally responses from various kinds of print materials. By color-dotting corners of application brochures, one can determine the original source of the brochure (i.e., mailed on request or taken from the program's front desk) when it is filled in and returned. By charting the number and country-source of preprinted forms found in study guides and by noting the address of senders of the self-addressed postal cards, one can roughly determine the response ratio or the cost-per-response ratio.

All print materials should have as a primary purpose the educating of prospective students regarding the program, its features, and ways to receive further information about it. A rich selection of information should be available to send to potential students, all of which emphasizes the value of the inquiring party and presents its message in a personalized manner, thanks to wordprocessing features that allow the swift customization of form letters.

### Nonprint Materials

**Video.** The design and production of nonprint promotional materials may be beneficial to some programs. In particular, a videotape featuring the program, the community, student housing options, an affiliated institution, and typical school activities (in-class and after school) may become a solid publicity tool. Occasional requests come to English program administrators for such videotaped overviews. The question becomes, then, how does one respond to these requests positively?

Making a videotape is easy; making a good videotape is difficult. Much time is spent outlining the proposed content, preparing a storyboard, writing a script for voice-over narration, arranging and directing the scenes, and doing the actual taping. Estimates of time expended on videotape productions vary, but a standard guideline is five hours of preparation for each minute of final videotape. Thus, a 15-minute tape will probably require nearly two full weeks of staff time to produce.

182

Before considering some caveats regarding videotape production, the reader is advised to carefully consider the purpose of the product and the intended audiences. For example, decisions must be made as to what languages other than English might be used in the narration. If English is not used, additional time must be spent translating the narration accurately and coaching a native speaker of that language to prepare the sound track. Unless tapes with sound tracks in the target languages of the receiving countries are made, their overall usefulness could be diminished greatly. If the video's sound track is in English, it should be carefully scripted so as to take into consideration such factors as speed of speech and clarity of voice, as well as the more obvious factors of complexity of syntax and frequency of vocabulary. Subtitles may indeed be of significant benefit, particularly to introduce new scenes. Sophisticated videotape recorders/players are equipped with a subtitling feature that can be of great value in producing an in-house videotape.

If the tape is to be sent overseas on loan, appropriate mailing cartons complete with instructions for returning it must be obtained. Among the issues that arise in this connection are (1) how much money the program is prepared to expend in order to have videotapes available for loan distribution and (2) to whom they will be mailed, individuals or organizations only.

The desirability of videotaped promotional materials cannot be denied. Their use at international language fairs such as Asia's "Study in the U.S. Fair" or "Mondolingua" in Switzerland is particularly beneficial at exhibit booths sponsored by the English language program. In fact, nothing is better for accurately showing one's school than a video presented to an interested audience. However, several problems exist:

1. In order to do an excellent production job, one needs excellent equipment: a good portable video camera, a playback/recording deck with high-quality audio recording features, a supply of blank tapes on which to record individual scenes, and a videotape editing machine on which to splice scenes into a final master tape.

2. In order to produce numerous copies, a high-speed copier is required.

3. Videotape formats are not standardized internationally. Thus, a videotape produced on the most widely available American equipment (i.e., VHS or Beta) does not play on European or Middle Eastern equipment. It may be necessary—and expensive—to have a videotape rerecorded in a different format, such as PAL or SECAM.

4. Videotapes are inspected carefully by customs agents in many countries, causing delays in final delivery and, in some cases, resulting in the loss or destruction of the videotape. Saudi Arabia, for example, has

stringent regulations regarding the content of videotapes as well as of printed materials.

5. At international language fairs in some countries (e.g., Brazil), renting playback equipment may be virtually impossible. On the other hand, taking one's portable playback deck through international customs may be difficult, and carrying a video monitor is cumbersome, if not physically impossible, under most circumstances.

There are other options for videotape preparation if the program is willing to sacrifice some level of production quality for a more "homespun" style of video. An advanced-level ESL class might undertake the production as a relevant and integrative course assignment that combines many desirable language and planning activities. Under the guidance of an enthusiastic instructor, students can write, design, and produce a tape whose charm emanates from its amateur quality. Indeed, potential students viewing this film overseas may be inspired by the fact that they are viewing an interesting "product" of an ESL class!

Also, if the program is part of a postsecondary educational institution, the affiliated university or college probably has produced its own school videotape for use at college nights and other admissions office events. Starting with this video as a basic source of footage, splicing in portions focusing on the English program and international students can result in a blended tape of reasonably high quality. In this way, the program's overall costs for production should be significantly reduced.

*Assessing video promotion.* It is my opinion that a promotional videotape is an excellent component in an overall marketing system. However, one cannot assume that a few copies will suffice; every copy sent overseas is a copy that will probably never be returned. If played regularly at an advising agency or consular library, the investment is then probably a worthwhile one.

Strategies for evaluating videotapes are not readily found in the professional literature. However, it does not seem inappropriate to revisit the earlier suggestions regarding the evaluation of print and nonprint media, particularly as they relate to illustrations and photographs. As more English programs begin to use videotaped promotional materials, one should expect that materials developers will derive evaluative criteria that take into consideration the aspects mentioned here as well as many others.

## A Promotional Failure

An analysis of the cost of a promotion effort versus its potential benefits in terms of actually enrolled students can help to avoid ineffectual attempts at recruiting students. A general rule is to go directly to the potential student or source of students, avoiding indirect approaches to potential clients. As an example of a failed promotional effort, the administrators of the intensive English program at Florida State University thought it seemed logical for a university-affiliated English language program to contact the university's international alumni by mail, informing them of the program's existence, goals, and interest in their assistance in attracting students. In 1982, having secured the parent university's international alumni mailing list, a special letter accompanied by the brochures of the English language program was sent to all of them. One thousand letters were prepared and mailed to all alumni residing in non-English-speaking countries. The results? No responses whatsoever from potential students were received. However, more than 30 alumni wrote to the program seeking teaching positions and a permanent return to the United States.

## A Promotional Success

A recently completed study (Williams and Scherzer 1988) sought to determine how current and former students of our program first learned about the program. Using a survey instrument, it was found that our promotional materials influenced fewer students in choosing our program than was previously assumed. What was revealed, however, was that the vast majority of enrollees learned of the program by word-of-mouth from former English program students. Again, the existence of a powerful communications network among international students was substantiated, a network that extends from the United States to all parts of the globe and vice versa.

In order to take advantage of this fact, a program can easily undertake specific efforts to provide current and former students with up-to-date information about their English language program *alma mater*. Program events, such as international dinners, may be publicized and all former students invited to participate. As students return to their home countries for vacations, they can be provided with brochures and information that they may disseminate. In the case of the Florida State University program, the realization that our promotional materials were less influential than previously assumed was converted to a more positive strategy for distributing information via one of the best possible vehicles—successful, motivated students.

## Additional Promotional Suggestions

As so often proves to be the case, enhancements of existing promotional materials need not be costly to prove effective. In a recent NAFSA conference presentation, an English language program administrator illustrated how all correspondence with potential students was not only written simply but was written to emphasize the second person singular ("You wrote to us for information about our English program. I am sending this information to you") (Honda 1988). The strategy serves to immediately personalize form letters while presenting its message in simple, declarative sentences.

Small inserts placed within the brochure can provide information of specific interest to students from individual countries. Sometimes written in the language of the country to which the brochure is being sent, a topical insert containing information about local festivals or other events taking place during the coming year may instill interest and confidence in the recipient by reducing the fear of the unknown, the pervasive sense of anomie, and a false notion that the United States lacks a sense of community.

As Bergman-Lanier (1988) stated in a NAFSA conference presentation, a program should make efforts to emphasize its unique or highly positive characteristics in its materials. Furthermore, in so doing, program directors must be responsible for maintaining a high level of honesty and truth in the content of promotional materials. Statements regarding curriculum, facilities, prior students' successes in language study, costs, and procedures must be documentable and supportable if the program is to be protected against the possibility of legal action by students or their sponsors. In fact, several nations, among them West Germany and Switzerland, have stringent laws punishing organizations that falsely represent themselves and their services in advertisements.

The veracity of statements found in promotional materials should be determined by having all of the draft copy of an item carefully and critically read by one or more reviewers and, if possible, by the institution's legal staff. Their concerns should be presented to the program director, who must determine whether documentable evidence exists to support statements deemed questionable by the reviewers.

## Conclusion

Every intensive English program, in addition to all of the other English language programs actively teaching international students, must make its presence known if it is to continue attracting students (Zikopoulos 1988). Proprietary programs expend large percentages of their budgets to produce and place high-quality promotional materials in the hands of potential clients. Individual English language programs must find some funds to produce effective informational materials within their smaller budgets. All English language programs need to seek ways to improve their promotional materials by regularly assessing their costs and effectiveness in attracting students.

Printed material, whether in the form of brochures, advertisements in commercial or organizational guides, or correspondence, will continue to account for the bulk of promotional/informational products. Frequent updating of materials, accompanied by critical analysis of content and format, is necessary; every need to reprint should be preceded by a revising stage. Every revision should be preceded by a reexamination of the product's initial purpose. Does this product contain the information that is most essential to the recipient? Can the recipient understand the language? Are there any portions of the content that may be offensive to receiving parties? Have all the relevant "dos and don'ts" been consulted? Can the program afford to produce better materials?

Can any program afford *not* to produce better materials? This closing question cannot be answered without considering several more subliminal features of promotional materials. For example, truth-in-advertising, honest representation of one's program, ethical procedures for recruiting and educating international students, and accurate depictions of the affiliated campus, city, and nation are absolutely essential. NAFSA's Administrators and Teachers of English as a Second Language (ATESL) section, TESOL, UCIEP (University Consortium of Intensive English Programs), and other associations of language educators continue to seek ways to establish and monitor standards for English language program curricula, services, faculty, administration, and promotion. Their individual or collective ability to establish codes of standards or ethics in these areas may serve as an indicator of their status as professional organizations.

The professional image of every ESL educator is ultimately reflected not only in the classroom, the office, and the community, but also in the publicly displayed representations of the institutions and organizations that he or she serves. Promotional materials are, then, announcements of much more than a place or a program. As such, they deserve to be carefully scrutinized and evaluated according to standards that reflect professionally the substance and image not only of individual programs, but also of the ESL field at large.

# References

Bergman-Lanier, V. 1988. Individual presentation. In Bergman- Lanier, V., G. Honda, and A. Shahbaz. Administration: Prospering by aiming to please. Paper presented at the Fortieth Annual Conference of the National Association for Foreign Student Affairs, Washington, D.C. May-June.

Honda, G. 1988. Individual presentation. In Bergman-Lanier, V., G. Honda, and A. Shahbaz. Administration: Prospering by aiming to please. Paper presented at the Fortieth Annual Conference of the National Association for Foreign Student Affairs, Washington, D.C. May-June.

O'Driscoll, J. E., ed. 1984. *English language and orientation programs in the United States.* New York: Institute for International Education.

Osgood, C., W. May, and M. Miron. 1975. *Cross-cultural universals of affective meaning.* Urbana, IL: University of Illinois Press.

Printz, P. 1988. Program recruitment publications. Paper presented at the Fortieth Annual Conference of the National Association for Foreign Student Affairs, Washington, D.C. May-June.

Teachers of English to Speakers of Other Languages. 1988. *Directory of professional preparation programs in TESOL in the United States.* Washington, D.C: TESOL.

Williams, T. and L. Scherzer. 1988. *A survey of IEP students: How they learn about IEP programs.* Unpublished research report. Tallahassee, FL: Florida State University.

Zikopoulos, M., ed. 1988. *Open doors: 1987/88,* 76–80. New York: Institute for International Education.

PART FOUR

# Reviewing the Performance of Teachers and Administrators

PROCEDURES AND INSTRUMENTS FOR FACULTY EVALUATION IN ESL
*Martha C. Pennington and Aileen L. Young*

EVALUATING THE ESL PROGRAM DIRECTOR
*Robert P. Fox*

ADMINISTRATIVE EVALUATION IN ESL PROGRAMS: HOW'M I DOIN'?
*Barbara F. Matthies*

# 10

# Procedures and Instruments for Faculty Evaluation in ESL

*Martha C. Pennington and Aileen L. Young*

## Introduction

As a central component of an educational system, faculty evaluation has an impact at the level of the program, the profession, and the individual teacher. At the program level, faculty evaluation, conducted regularly and fairly, ensures a sort of communication among administrators, teachers, and students that helps to maintain a good match between student needs and the program's educational goals and instructional approaches. Faculty evaluation supports an educational profession by providing a basis for promoting and upholding its standards. At the level of the individual teacher, evaluation provides a way to reflect on performance, to expand competencies, and to sustain the positive momentum that comes with continued learning.

The faculty of an ESL (English as a Second Language) program is its most valuable asset, as good teachers are the best guarantee of continued success in attracting the two quantities in terms of which educational institutions normally operate: income and academic prestige. A sound ESL faculty evaluation process reinforces these two institutional goals by increasing faculty standards and level of performance, thus enhancing the program's ability to attract income-generating enrollments, a national or international reputation, and other indicators of excellence (e.g., as discussed in Chapter Four, this volume). Looking at ESL teaching as an evolutionary process in which competence and effectiveness increase over time, we can expect the initial investment made in hiring a teacher to increase in value over the years, becoming an "educational annuity" that yields tangible benefits for the students and ensures the long-range security of the program as well.

Faculty evaluation can likewise be viewed as an evolutionary process. Evaluation is first applied when a new teacher is hired into a program and in most cases continues to be applied periodically thereafter throughout the career-life of that teacher. There are many different methods currently in use for faculty evaluation (see Pennington and Young 1989 for detailed discussion). These methods include:

- Teacher interviews
- Competency tests
- Student achievement
- Student evaluations
- Classroom observation
- Peer review
- Self-evaluation

Each of these methods of faculty evaluation can be—and has been adapted to the assessment of teachers of ESL. Individual methods of evaluation, or combinations of these, may be appropriate at different times and under differing circumstances.

*Teacher interviews* are conducted to screen applicants for jobs and as part of the performance appraisal process (Haefele 1981). *Competency tests* such as the National Teacher's Examination (NTE), Pre-Professional Skills Test (PPST), or California Basic Education Skills Test (CBEST) are administered for certification of teachers after completion of training (Eisenberg and Rudner 1988). *Student achievement*, as measured by tests or other less formal means, is one of the most discussed but at the same time one of the most problematical methods of faculty evaluation (Medley, Coker, and Soar 1984). *Student evaluations*, using a set of rating scales or an open-ended questionnaire format, are commonly employed for faculty evaluation at secondary and postsecondary levels and are regarded by many experts as a reliable and valid means of evaluating classroom performance (Aleamoni 1987).

*Classroom observation* by administrators or peers is another commonly accepted method of faculty evaluation at all levels of the educational curriculum (McGreal 1983). *Peer review* of credentials and teaching performance (Nunan 1988) is a central method of faculty evaluation at U.S. colleges and universities that is being increasingly applied in other contexts as well—for example, in public school districts in this country and in English programs overseas. *Self-evaluation* via self-ratings, self-reports, self-study, comparison with the teaching of peers, or videotape/audiotape feedback (Carroll 1981) is considered in some programs to be an important part of the assessment of teaching performance, competencies, and professional development.

The purposes and methods of faculty evaluation in ESL will differ

192

FIGURE 1. STAGES IN FACULTY DEVELOPMENT: THE TEACHING CYCLE

| Curricular assignment | | Professional orientation | Supervisory approach | Sources of input |
|---|---|---|---|---|
| Advanced stages | Initial stages | | | |
| (5) supervising teaching | (1) supervised teaching | training | directive (providing direction) | Su, St Fa |
| (6) developing curriculum | (2) teaching across the curriculum | exploring the curriculum | supervisory (suggesting alternatives) | Su, St Fa, Se |
| (7) developing materials | (3) teaching in favorite areas | specializing | facilitative (providing resources) | Su Fa, Se |
| (8) developing new areas | (4) teaching in new areas | expanding competencies | collegial (sharing resources) | Fa, Se |

*(Su=supervisor, St=students, Fa=faculty members, Se=self)*

(Pennington 1989, 107)

from program to program. They may also differ depending on the stage that the faculty member's career has reached. Pennington (1989) has described a faculty career-cycle divided into initial stages and advanced stages, each consisting of a series of four phases, as shown in Figure 1. As Figure 1 indicates, different kinds of input can be seen as most valuable and appropriate for faculty evaluation at different phases of a teacher's career.

Porter (1988) offers a systematic model of stages in a teacher's career, and states that different kinds of assessments should be made at each stage. The areas that might logically be assessed are ordered as follows (see Porter 1988, 5):

- Prior experience: Does the person have the right training?
- Knowledge and beliefs: Does the person know what he or she needs to know, and does the person have the requisite beliefs and convictions?
- Teacher actions: Does the person carry through on his or her potential by actually doing what is needed?
- Short-term outcomes: How do the students and the teacher react in response to the instruction provided?
- Long-term outcomes: What do the students end up knowing, thinking, and doing as a result of instruction?

In the present article, we explore appropriate instrumentation and procedures for ESL faculty evaluation, offering descriptions and sample forms that can be adapted for use under the differing circumstances in English language programs of various kinds. We begin by describing and assessing several types of instruments available for faculty evaluation. Following this discussion, we outline procedures and provide examples of instruments that may be used to implement different methods of faculty evaluation. Throughout the discussion, we stress the need in the ESL faculty evaluation process for a *professional orientation*, that is, an orientation that (1) is geared toward long-term career development; (2) assesses both teaching and nonteaching aspects of the faculty member's job; and (3) includes input from supervisors, students, peers, and the individual faculty members themselves.

## Instrumentation for Faculty Evaluation

The instruments for faculty evaluation can be described in two broad categories: (1) fluid instruments and (2) fixed instruments. The types of instruments in each of these categories are somewhat different from the classification system of Brown and Pennington (see Chapter One, this volume). The fluid instruments to be discussed are conversations, letters, and essay (i.e., open-ended) questionnnaires. With these instruments, respondents use their own words to communicate their observations and assessments. The fixed instruments include fixed-response questionnaires, rating scales, tests, and various sorts of descriptive data. With these instruments, someone else's words or categories of analysis or description are used, and the respondent communicates by checking boxes, circling numbers, or tallying information. Each of these instruments will be discussed with regard to its advantages and disadvantages.

**Conversations.** Doyle (1983, 107) notes that the conversation is one of the least used instruments for teacher evaluation:

> Yet it is one of the most potent, because it is only through conversations, dialogue, and discussion that issues can be formulated in a common language; that an unlimited survey of the strengths and weakness of a course can be made; that diverse points of view can be clarified, challenged, and revised; and that promising steps toward improvement can be formulated, agreed on, and initiated by all parties simultaneously.

Conversations—which may take place as part of prearranged meetings or interviews with students, peers, or supervisor—have the advantage of being impermanent and relatively unstructured, thus allowing for spontaneous and open exchange of information and ideas. Through conversation, new insights may be gained that would be difficult to uncover using more structured instruments. Their fluid nature makes the conversation an instrument well-suited to formative purposes in evaluation, that is, for purposes of improving performance. At the same time, their impermanence and unstructured nature make them an unreliable source of data for summative evaluation, such as for comprehensive performance review, since the conversations cannot be readily tabulated, normed, or recorded for later use.

194

**Letters.** Letters of compliment or complaint are important to administrators as a source of outside data for evaluating an instructor's reputation. Thoughtful letters can provide useful information on how others perceive the performance and qualifications of an instructor. However, unless letters are solicited from a range of people qualified to judge a faculty member's effectiveness, data from letters should be considered supplementary to more systematically collected data because letters easily give undue weight to "outliers," that is, to isolated, extreme, and unrepresentative views.

**Questionnaires.** Questionnaires consist of questions asked of respondents concerning the course, the instructor, or both. Questionnaires fall midway between open-ended conversations and letters, on the one hand, and fixed-response rating scales and tests on the other. In essay-type questionnaires, respondents are directed to answer a set of questions in their own words.

The advantage of the essay questionnaire is that it is open ended, permitting the respondent to address issues that may not be possible with closed-response instruments. Also, responses may be shown to other people and filed for later use. The disadvantages of this instrument are that open-ended questionnaire responses are "difficult to tabulate, are vulnerable to irrelevancy and ambiguity of response, and cannot be normed. Penmanship can also be a problem along with the elicitation of detailed responses" (Doyle 1983, 109). These take a great deal of time to read and are difficult to summarize.

Questionnaires that allow a limited number of responses—for example, a choice of "yes" or "no," or a predetermined selection of potential responses—are fixed instruments akin to rating scales. They therefore share many of the same advantages and disadvantages as rating scales (other than those associated with using a scale of points such as central tendency error) cited from Doyle (1983, 110–111) in the next section.

A sample of the essay-type of questionnaire as used for evaluation of courses and faculty members in the Department of English as a Second Language at the University of Hawaii at Manoa is shown in Appendix A. The form is divided into two parts, one of which asks for the student's assessment of the course, while the other asks for the student's assessment of the teacher's performance in the course. The form is designed for the purpose of summative evaluation, that is, it serves as input to a periodic departmental performance review and becomes part of the faculty member's permanent record. The form is administered at the end of the semester in every undergraduate and graduate teacher preparation course. It is not administered in courses aimed at ESL students that are part of the English Language Institute (ELI). Different sorts of questions and a different type of format—one in which the responses are more structured—are generally advisable in evaluating English language program courses for reasons such as the following:

1. The goals of those courses are quite different from those oriented to native speakers.
2. Students from other cultures may not be familiar with this type of evaluation mechanism.
3. Students whose first language is not English may have difficulty responding to open-ended questions because of their limited knowledge of the language.

**Rating Scales.** Rating scales that include two endpoints and generally at least one other marked point in between are widely used for collecting observations and opinions. The most frequently encountered scales are graphic scales, adjectival scales (or variants of these), and numerical scales.

A graphic scale consists of a labeled line on which the respondent places a mark at any point to communicate a rating. The line may be labeled with a sequence of adjectives, adverbs, verbs, or phrases, as in the examples below:

| Poor | Fair | Good | Very Good | X Excellent |
|------|------|------|-----------|-------------|

| Always | Often | Sometimes | Rarely X | Never |
|--------|-------|-----------|----------|-------|

| Agree Strongly | X Agree Somewhat | No Opinion | Disagree Somewhat | Disagree Strongly |
|----------------|------------------|------------|-------------------|-------------------|

These types of scales permit fine gradations of opinions but are rarely used in large-scale or routine evaluations because they are difficult to tabulate, as respondents can mark a response anywhere on the scale.

Adjectival scales consist of an unequivocal ordering of adjectives or adjectival phrases from "good" to "poor"—or the reverse—one of which the respondent circles, as in the example below:

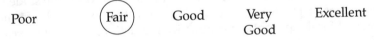

| Poor | (Fair) | Good | Very Good | Excellent |
|------|--------|------|-----------|-----------|

A variation on this type of scale uses adverbs, verbs, or phrases such as those in the graphic scale examples above. These scales may permit fine distinctions—such as good versus fairly good—or gross distinctions—such as, good versus poor. Whatever the distinction, it is important that the semantic differences between pairs of adjacent words or phrases be approximately equal, though it is difficult to ensure such equality (Bailey 1982, 135–136). When the respondents are ESL students, it is also important to ensure that students understand the terms used and how they differ in meaning along a positive-to-negative continuum. Thus, if rating scales are used with nonnative speakers, some preparation and orientation to the evaluation process will be essential.

Numerical scales add numbers to adjectival or other types of scales, as in the following example:

| 1 | 2 | 3 | 4 | 5 |
|---|---|---|---|---|
| Poor | Fair | Good | Very Good | Excellent |

Sometimes the numerical scales are presented alone for each response item on one sheet of paper, along with a separate written key for definition of each numbered point. Having a separate answer sheet tends to increase the reliability of the responses and of the tabulation process. It also facilitates keyboard-based tabulation and machine-aided analysis of responses, such as using a Scantron machine or a computer. This type of scale is attractive because of its simplicity, but it is susceptible to statistical errors, notably that of central tendency—the tendency of respondents to avoid the extremes of rating scales—especially when many scales are laid out in a grid.

A sample faculty evaluation form based on numerical scales is given in Appendix B. This is the faculty evaluation form used in the Department of English as a Second Language at the University of Hawaii at Manoa for formative purposes at midterm in non-ELI courses—that is, in courses for teachers of ESL. The intention of the form is to provide detailed feedback to the teacher on student perceptions of how the class is going so that any necessary adjustments can be made. It is a good example of the categories and types of data that might be collected on a regular academic class from students. However, the form is clearly too complex in language—and perhaps also in format—to be used with nonnative speakers in most ESL courses.

Though there are many rating scales that use a neutral midpoint such as "not applicable" or "no opinion," Doyle (1983) discourages this practice for the following reasons:

1. Rating scales are already prone to central-tendency error.
2. Midpoints tend to draw ratings toward the middle of the scale, exacerbating the error.
3. It is doubtful that raters are truly neutral.

4. Midpoints may encourage superficial evaluation.
5. Using "does not apply" breaks the continuity of the scale.

As an alternative, Doyle suggests that a "not applicable" box be provided to the respondent, but that it be placed physically away from the evaluation scale.

Rating scales, if carefully constructed, can provide a source of useful information in the faculty evaluation process. According to Bailey (1982, 136), "The main thing to remember is that the response categories should be easy for the respondent to answer and should provide just enough detail but not too much." Bailey's practical advice is particularly important to follow when constructing rating scales for use with ESL students.

In using ratings of teaching, program administrators and teachers should be aware of the strengths as well as the limitations of this type of instrument, and this awareness should guide the interpretation of results. The advantages and disadvantages of rating scales in the evaluation of teaching are, according to Doyle (1983, 110–111):

Advantages

1. They can be easily tabulated, statistically analyzed, normed, and stored.
2. They are efficient and inexpensive.
3. They are highly structured.
4. There is a large body of technical literature to guide their construction and use.

Disadvantages

1. Respondents are not able to convey the subtlety or entirety of their thoughts.
2. They are easy to answer, thereby discouraging reflection and thoughtful responding.
3. Because they are so widespread, they may be seen as tedious, repetitive, and marginally relevant to the course at hand.
4. They do not facilitate dialogue.

Ratings of classes and teachers provide a valuable source of data reflecting the point of view of students or other evaluators and identifying gross tendencies or trends in the performance of individual teachers as well as the faculty as a whole. Such ratings can therefore assist the administrator in developing profiles of (individual and group) faculty performance, when used in conjunction with other less prestructured forms of evaluation. Certain types of rating scales are also available for use by teachers to evaluate their own performance and to identify areas in which growth or improvement is desired.

**Tests.** Tests can provide a relatively straightforward way of measuring some aspects of the competence or the performance of students or teachers. Tests may be of the discrete-point, closed-response type, or they may allow for open-ended responses. In either case, when designing or selecting any type of test, questions of reliability, validity, and practicality arise. (For reviews of a wide variety of English language tests according to these criteria and others, see Alderson, Krahnke, and Stansfield 1987.) While standardized tests are practical to use and must receive high ratings for reliability in order to gain widespread acceptance, the question of validity is a perennial one.

The question of whether a certain test is valid can never be definitively answered. There is in fact a sort of unavoidable vicious cycle involving the question of validity. This vicious-cycle problem arises as a result of the procedures used to validate tests. The validity of a test is normally established on the basis of a statistical comparison of the results of one test to those of some other historically accepted measure. Alternatively, tests are validated on the basis of conservative views—that is, the views of established authorities—of what has traditionally counted as an indicator of the knowledge or attribute being tested. Hence, the validity of every new test is open to question whenever (1) the validity of any traditionally validated test or other type of measure in the same domain is called into question, or (2) there is a change in the accepted views of what counts as an indicator of the knowledge or attribute being tested.

As the requirements for knowledge of a second language have been altered over the last two decades to reflect communicative goals for the language learner, some long-accepted tests of English language proficiency have been questioned as measures of communicative competence (see Bachman 1989 for discussion of the issues). Similarly, tests of teacher competency for ESL can be called into question if the test items do not measure the knowledge and skills that are recognized as defining a communicative approach to language teaching. The validity of tests of teachers' professional competency or of students' language proficiency may also be challenged directly, using accepted psychometric procedures. For example, the validity of the old Common Examinations of the National Teacher Examinations (NTE) was called into question by research conducted in the early 1970s showing that scores on these tests did not necessarily predict to other measures of teaching success such as teacher rating scores or student test scores (Quirk, Witten, and Weinberg 1973). Similarly, the validity of a range of new tests of communicative language proficiency will ultimately be challenged if test scores do not predict to ratings of communicative performance in classes, job situations, or other real-life contexts.

Some time ago, Thorndike (1971) argued that tests can be highly reliable and valid if testing procedures are matched to the kinds of learning that are to be measured. For the assessment of both teachers and students in language programs, criterion-referenced, rather than norm-referenced, tests are receiving considerable attention (Bachman 1989; Hudson and Lynch 1984). While norm-referenced tests measure the performance of an individual against a comparison group, criterion-referenced tests measure the performance of an individual "with reference to a specific context domain or criterion of performance. They thus provide information about an individual's mastery of a given content domain, or level of performance" (Bachman 1989, 248).

While criterion-referenced tests may be better suited for the measurement of skills involved in language learning and teaching, they tend to be more difficult to administer than norm-referenced tests. However, this disadvantage is perhaps outweighed by their advantage in terms of validity for both formative and summative purposes (Bachman 1989). Widely accepted criterion-referenced tests for language teachers or students do not exist. However, there is interest in this type of testing within the language teaching profession (Britten 1985), and some individual ESL programs are developing their own in-house criterion-referenced tests of student performance (Brown 1989).

Using student achievement/mastery tests for faculty evaluation is not as a general rule advisable unless all of the following guidelines are met:

1. The tests are developed internally, with teacher input.
2. Separate tests are developed for measuring achievement at each level and for each separate class or skill area of the curriculum.
3. The tests directly measure the degree to which students achieve the objectives at each level and for each separate class or skill area of the curriculum.
4. The tests achieve high reliability through statistical D F means.
5. Teachers agree that the tests measure what they are supposed to measure and have confidence in their validity.
6. The evaluation of teaching effectiveness based on student scores on these tests is in terms of long-term trends, rather than in terms of individual students, classes, or subject areas.
7. Assessment of teaching effectiveness based on student scores on these tests is not the only type of input into the performance review process.

**Descriptive Data.** Descriptive data of various sorts may be compiled as input to a faculty evaluation process. These data may include information on classes taught and number of students attending each; number and type of publications; conferences, workshops, and courses attended; service on committees and boards; and number of citations, grants, awards, and other types of recognition. These types of descriptive data provide proof during evaluation of fulfillment of professional commitments and of continuing career development. The data may be summarized as part of a faculty member's performance review and may become part of a permanent record. An analysis of the data can be conducted for comparative purposes, or to determine if the faculty member meets certain minimum criteria for activity within the program or field.

## Procedures for Faculty Evaluation

A wide variety of methods and instruments of teacher evaluation are in current use within the ESL field. Since every method and instrument has advantages as well as disadvantages (Pennington and Young 1989), a good evaluation system must utilize several methods and instruments in order to realize the purpose of the evaluation. Each institution and program is unique, and each should therefore adopt an evaluation system compatible with its philosophy and the needs of its constituents: the teachers, students, and administrator(s). Cooperative involvement in the design of the evaluation forms and procedures and in the conduct of the evaluation process will help to ensure full relevance and effectiveness of faculty evaluation (see Chapter One, this volume).

Ideally, the methods and instruments adopted would not assess the competence of teachers by means of tests, as that function should already have been fulfilled by teacher training institutions. Once a competent teacher has been hired by means of a careful interview procedure, a developmental approach to faculty evaluation is suggested as the most effective. An approach geared to faculty development allows the most flexibility for the program and ensures individualized assessments of each faculty member's characteristics, teaching performance, and other contributions to the program. Such a developmental approach would utilize the observation method at least twice yearly for neophyte teachers, and once yearly for veteran teachers.

The observation method for ESL faculty evaluation should involve trained peers and administrators, as well as self-evaluation of lessons as a basis for discussion of performance. It is suggested that peers and administrators alternate observations, peers observing for purposes of formative evaluation (i.e., to provide feedback for change) and administrators observing for both formative and summative purposes (i.e., for purposes of employment action). A teacher observation form recommended for use in peer or administrative observation is shown in Appendix C. A self-evaluation form for assessing performance in a class is shown in Appendix D.

In addition, all teachers (above elementary level) can be evaluated by their students with questions appropriate to the purposes and objectives of the program and including a section for open-ended responses. A suggested form that is simple enough for most ESL students above the beginning level and beyond grade 6 and that is general enough to apply to any type of ESL class is illustrated in Appendix E. The *yes/no* answer choice avoids any potential problems associated with use of rating scales by ESL students who have limited exposure to English language and cultural practices. Moreover, the dichotomous *yes/no* choice forces students to decide whether or not the teacher has met their internal criterion for performance on the specified trait. Notice also that the form provides for open-ended comments on each of the ten points that is assessed.

We recommend a periodic performance review in the form of a lengthy interview in which the program administrator or teacher supervisor discusses teaching effectiveness as well as other aspects of the faculty member's job performance. Goldhammer, Anderson, and Krajewski (1980, 210) summarize the purposes of the supervisory conference as follows: (1) to provide adult rewards and satisfactions; (2) to define and authenticate issues in teaching; (3) to offer didactic help (if appropriate); (4) to train the teacher in techniques for self-supervision; and (5) to develop incentives for professional self-analysis.

Adapting from recommendations in the management literature (Moravec 1981), we suggest the following steps for a smooth and comprehensive performance appraisal interview:

1. *Substantiate performance* through such means as observation reports, student ratings, letters, course outlines, and lesson plans.

2. *Reach an understanding* of what it is that the teaching job requires and what other responsibilities the teacher has to the program. This understanding can be established according to a written job description and standards of performance document given to all teachers when they are hired and reviewed as part of the performance appraisal process.

3. *Gain acknowledgement* by the instructor of the issues discussed in the evaluation interview and the need for action or change. This commits the teacher to action and puts an emphasis on future growth, rather than dwelling on problem areas or on any difficulties that the teacher might be experiencing in the present job situation.

4. *Set goals, action steps, and a timetable* for continuing professional growth and for measuring progress toward those goals.

A sample document of "Standards of Performance for Teachers" is provided in Appendix F. That document was developed by the first author in 1981 at the University of California Extension at Santa Barbara English Language Program and approved by the personnel director at that university before its distribution to teachers.

In a professional development approach that emphasizes ongoing training and long-term career goals (Pennington 1989; forthcoming), there should be more to faculty evaluation than assessment of teaching. If teaching is rightly seen as a lifelong career, then it involves much more than teaching individual classes on a daily basis. In addition to the requirements of teaching per se, ESL professionals have a number of other responsibilities that should be considered in faculty evaluation. To assess those aspects of the faculty member's job, a program might adapt forms used for faculty review in academic departments to the situation in that particular ESL program. The faculty review categories of research, teaching, and service shown in Appendix G might be modified for use in an ESL faculty context.

A format developed by the first author in 1983 for evaluation of the yearly performance and professional development of veteran teachers in the English Language Program at the University of California Extension, Santa Barbara, is offered in Appendix H for potential adoption by other programs. As is illustrated in the appendix, programs might explicitly require teachers to uphold standards not only in their classroom performance, but also in their performance of administrative duties and in their relations with other members of the faculty, administrative staff, and students within the program. In addition, career teachers can be expected to take advantage of some type of professional growth opportunity in their field.

## Conclusion

Faculty evaluation is an essential aspect of the management of an educational program and the implementation of its curriculum. Without a fairly and regularly administered faculty review process, an English language program will suffer disorganization and loss of focus that can ultimately lead to disruptive employment actions or to a reduction in enrollments. Thus, faculty evaluation is crucial to the long-range health of an English language program. Faculty evaluation is also an important element in the health of the profession of English language teaching, since it is through evaluation that the field provides for consistent standards and monitoring of those standards. From the perspective of the health of the ESL teacher, too, faculty evaluation is a central concern, since it is the basis for growth and development of individual faculty members throughout their careers. We hope that the overview of instruments and procedures for faculty evaluation provided here will be of value in maintaining the continuing health of English language programs, the profession at large, and the careers of individual faculty members both in the United States and abroad.

# References

Alderson, J. C., K. J. Krahnke, and C. W. Stansfield, eds. 1987. *Reviews of English language proficiency tests.* Washington, D.C.: Teachers of English to Speakers of Other Languages.

Aleamoni, L. M. 1987. Typical faculty concerns about student evaluation of teaching. In Aleamoni, L. M., ed., *Techniques for evaluating and improving instruction,* 25-31. San Francisco: Jossey Bass, Inc.

Bachman, L. F. 1989. The development and use of criterion reference tests of language ability in language program evaluation. In Johnson, R. K., ed. *The second language curriculum,* 242-258. Cambridge: Cambridge University Press.

Bailey, K. D. 1982. *Methods of social research.* 2d ed. New York: The Free Press.

Britten, D. 1985. Teacher training in ELT. Part I. *Language Teaching* 18(2): 112-128.

Brown, J. D. 1989. Improving ESL placement tests using two perspectives. *TESOL Quarterly* 23(1):65-83.

Carroll, J. G. 1981. Faculty self-evaluation. In Millman, J., ed, *Handbook of teacher evaluation,* 180-200. Beverly Hills, CA: Sage.

Doyle, K. O., Jr. 1983. *Evaluating teaching.* Lexington, MA: D. C. Heath.

Eisenberg, T. E. and L. M. Rudner. 1988. State testing of teachers: A summary. *Journal of Teacher Education* 29(4):21-22.

Goldhammer, R., R. H. Anderson, and R. J. Krajewski. 1980. *Clinical supervision.* 2d ed. New York: Holt, Rinehart, and Winston.

Haefele, D. 1981. Teacher interviews. In Millman, J., ed. *Handbook of teacher evaluation,* 41-57. Beverly Hills, CA: Sage.

Hudson, T. and B. Lynch. 1984. A criterion-referenced measurement approach to ESL achievement testing. *Language Testing* 1(2):171-201.

McGreal, T. 1983. *Successful teacher evaluation.* Alexandria, VA: Association for Supervision and Curriculum Development.

Medley, D. M., H. Coker, and R. Soar. 1984. *Measurement-based evaluation of teacher performance.* New York: Longman.

Moravec, M. 1981. Performance appraisal. *Management Review* 70(6):51-54.

Nunan, D. 1988. *The learner-centred curriculum.* Cambridge: Cambridge University Press.

Pennington, M. C. 1989. Faculty development for language programs. In Johnson, R. K., ed. *The second language curriculum,* 91-110. Cambridge: Cambridge University Press.

———. 1990. A professional development focus for the language teaching practicum. In Nunan, D. and J. C. Richards, eds., *Second language teacher education*, 132–151. Cambridge: Cambridge University Press.

Pennington, M. C. and A. L. Young. 1989. Approaches to faculty evaluation for ESL. *TESOL Quarterly,* 23(4):619–646.

Porter, A. C. 1988. Understanding teaching: A model for assessment. *Journal of Teacher Education* 29(4):2–7.

Quirk, T. J., B. J. Witten, and S. F. Weinberg. 1973. Review of studies of the concurrent and predictive validity of the National Teacher Examinations. *Review of Educational Research* 43(1):89-113.

Thorndike, R. L., ed. 1971. *Educational measurement.* 2d ed. Washington, D.C.: American Council on Education.

# Appendix A

Sample Essay Questionnaire for Faculty Evaluation

E-4
(rev. 11/87)

INSTRUCTIONS TO THE <u>STUDENT</u>

## WRITTEN EVALUATION QUESTIONNAIRE FOR ESL COURSES

The written evaluation questionnaire consists of two parts. Please note that the first part focuses on the course and the second part focuses on the instructor.

You will receive two sets of carbonized paper containing two pages each. What you write on the white sheet will automatically appear also on the yellow sheet. The white sheet will be placed in the faculty member's file and made available to the department chair and relevant departmental committees. The yellow sheet will not be give to the instructor until all grades have been recorded for the course.

## Part I. THE COURSE

1. To what degree did this course meet the objective stated in the course syllabus?
2. What is your overall evaluation of the strengths and weaknesses of the course? Consider such factors as the quality and quantity of reading assignments, papers, and tests.
3. What changes, if any, would you recommend be made in this course?

## Part II. THE INSTRUCTOR

1. How able was the instructor in raising challenging questions, promoting independent thought, and encouraging student participation?
2. How able was the instructor in presenting relevant subject matter and clarifying readings?
3. What is your overall evaluation of the strengths and weaknesses of the instructor?

University of Hawaii, Manoa, Hon., HI

# Appendix B

## Sample Rating Scale for Faculty Evaluation

Department of English as a Second Language

IN-PROGRESS EVALUATION
OF
COURSE, MATERIALS, ASSIGNMENTS, AND INSTRUCTION

This four-part questionnaire is meant to provide feedback to the instructor on aspects of the course and instruction while the course is in progress, preferably at about mid-term.

### PART I. CLASSES AND LECTURES
(Do not use this part if you are in a seminar)

Rate the general quality of the classes/lectures on each of the following by circling the corresponding numbers:

| | Excellent | Good | Satisfactory | Fair | Poor | Inadequate | Can't Answer |
|---|---|---|---|---|---|---|---|
| | 6 | 5 | 4 | 3 | 2 | 1 | 0 |
| 1. Held your interest and attention | 6 | 5 | 4 | 3 | 2 | 1 | 0 |
| 2. Covered material at an appropriate intellectual level—neither too complicated nor too simple | 6 | 5 | 4 | 3 | 2 | 1 | 0 |
| 3. Emphasized principles and generalizations | 6 | 5 | 4 | 3 | 2 | 1 | 0 |
| 4. Covered diverse points of view and helped to expand your awareness of alternatives | 6 | 5 | 4 | 3 | 2 | 1 | 0 |
| 5. Instructor's ability to clarify readings and present relevant subject matter | 6 | 5 | 4 | 3 | 2 | 1 | 0 |
| 6. Instructor's ability to raise challenging questions and promote independent thinking | 6 | 5 | 4 | 3 | 2 | 1 | 0 |
| 7. Instructor's ability to encourage broad student participation in discussions | 6 | 5 | 4 | 3 | 2 | 1 | 0 |
| 8. Your own interest, preparation, and participation | 6 | 5 | 4 | 3 | 2 | 1 | 0 |
| 9. Value of classes and lectures to the whole course | 6 | 5 | 4 | 3 | 2 | 1 | 0 |

How many classes did you miss? (1) 1 or none (3) 4–5
 (2) 2–3 (4) 6 +

Were there characteristics of the classes which you found particularly valuable or not very useful? Please explain and, if possible, suggest modifications.
University of Hawaii, Manoa, Hon., HI

# Sample Rating Scale for Faculty Evaluation

## PART II. SEMINARS

Applicable _____ Inapplicable _____

Please rate the general quality of the seminars on each of the following by circling the corresponding numbers:

|   | Excellent | Good | Satisfactory | Fair | Poor | Inadequate | Can't Answer |
|---|---|---|---|---|---|---|---|
|   | 6 | 5 | 4 | 3 | 2 | 1 | 0 |
| 1. Interest to you of the topics covered | 6 | 5 | 4 | 3 | 2 | 1 | 0 |
| 2. Professor's ability to raise stimulating, provocative questions | 6 | 5 | 4 | 3 | 2 | 1 | 0 |
| 3. Professor's ability to encourage broad student participation | 6 | 5 | 4 | 3 | 2 | 1 | 0 |
| 4. Professor's ability to conduct discussions | 6 | 5 | 4 | 3 | 2 | 1 | 0 |
| 5. Degree to which the topics covered were related to one another | 6 | 5 | 4 | 3 | 2 | 1 | 0 |
| 6. Degree to which the topics emphasized the fundamentals of the course | 6 | 5 | 4 | 3 | 2 | 1 | 0 |
| 7. Degree to which you felt a sense of challenge, insight, and discovery | 6 | 5 | 4 | 3 | 2 | 1 | 0 |
| 8. Degree to which you felt a part of a continuing scholarly discussion | 6 | 5 | 4 | 3 | 2 | 1 | 0 |
| 9. General attitude and preparedness of fellow class members | 6 | 5 | 4 | 3 | 2 | 1 | 0 |
| 10. Your own interest, preparation, and participation | 6 | 5 | 4 | 3 | 2 | 1 | 0 |
| 11. Quality of the seminars as a whole | 6 | 5 | 4 | 3 | 2 | 1 | 0 |

How many seminars did you miss?

(1) 1 or none      (3) 3–4
(2) 1–2      (4) 5 +

Were there characteristics of the seminars which you found particularly valuable or not very useful? Please explain and, if possible, suggest modifications.

# Sample Rating Scale for Faculty Evaluation

## PART III. READINGS

Speaking generally, rate the quality of the readings in terms of the degree to which they:

| | Excellent | Good | Satisfactory | Fair | Poor | Inadequate | Can't Answer |
|---|---|---|---|---|---|---|---|
| | 6 | 5 | 4 | 3 | 2 | 1 | 0 |
| 1. Were interesting to read | 6 | 5 | 4 | 3 | 2 | 1 | 0 |
| 2. Were of the right level of difficulty—neither too complicated nor too simple | 6 | 5 | 4 | 3 | 2 | 1 | 0 |
| 3. Clearly presented the relevant subject matter | 6 | 5 | 4 | 3 | 2 | 1 | 0 |
| 4. Covered diverse points of view and helped to expand your awareness of alternatives | 6 | 5 | 4 | 3 | 2 | 1 | 0 |
| 5. Helped you to integrate facts and develop generalizations | 6 | 5 | 4 | 3 | 2 | 1 | 0 |
| 6. Stimulated your intellectual curiosity and provoked independent thinking | 6 | 5 | 4 | 3 | 2 | 1 | 0 |
| 7. Balanced one another and formed a coherent whole | 6 | 5 | 4 | 3 | 2 | 1 | 0 |
| 8. Were relevant and supplementary to the lectures | 6 | 5 | 4 | 3 | 2 | 1 | 0 |

About what proportion of the readings did you do according to schedule?

    (1) All    (3) 1/2
    (2) 3/4    (4) 1/4

About what proportion of the readings did you end up doing?

    (1) All    (3) 1/2
    (2) 3/4    (4) 1/4

Comments:

# Sample Rating Scale for Faculty Evaluation

## PART IV. PAPERS, REPORTS, OBSERVATIONS, LABORATORIES

How would you rate each of the following aspects of the papers, reports, or other requirements?

| | Excellent | Good | Satisfactory | Fair | Poor | Inadequate | Can't Answer |
|---|---|---|---|---|---|---|---|
| | 6 | 5 | 4 | 3 | 2 | 1 | 0 |
| 1. Appropriateness of level of demand in terms of: | | | | | | | |
| a. Number of papers, reports, or other assignments | 6 | 5 | 4 | 3 | 2 | 1 | 0 |
| b. Size or length of paper(s), reports, or problem sets | 6 | 5 | 4 | 3 | 2 | 1 | 0 |
| c. Difficulty of subject(s) | 6 | 5 | 4 | 3 | 2 | 1 | 0 |
| 2. Degree of guidance given by the instructor to choice of topics and suggestions for relevant research | 6 | 5 | 4 | 3 | 2 | 1 | 0 |
| 3. Freedom given to develop topics in a creative, imaginative way | 6 | 5 | 4 | 3 | 2 | 1 | 0 |
| 4 Relevance to the rest of the course | 6 | 5 | 4 | 3 | 2 | 1 | 0 |
| 5. Timing of papers, reports, or other assignments to occur at the most benefiticial time in the course | 6 | 5 | 4 | 3 | 2 | 1 | 0 |
| 6. Overall value of the papers, reports, or other assignments to this course | 6 | 5 | 4 | 3 | 2 | 1 | 0 |

Please explain ratings of *Poor* or *Inadequate* given above and add any further relevant comments you might wish to make.

# Appendix C

Teacher Observation Form (p. 1)

Observer:

Teacher:                          Date:

Type of Class:                    Class Level:

Class Composition:                Number Enrolled/Present:

PREPARATION                                    COMMENTS

  organization

  sequencing

  knowledge of subject matter

EXECUTION

  (use of materials and aids)

  classroom arrangement

  pacing

  instructions, explanations

  answers to questions

  use of examples

ACTIVITIES

  degree of difficulty

  number

  variety

  reality

  cultural focus

# Teacher Observation Form (p. 2)

INTERACTION AND SOCIAL CLIMATE                    COMMENTS

   teacher participation

     amount

     type

   student participation

     amount

     type

   feedback

     amount

     type

   class atmosphere

   degree of stimulation and challenge

TEACHER'S CHARACTERISTICS

   patience and self-control

   confidence

   adaptability

   voice

   use of language

   movement

OVERALL ASSESSMENT OF LESSON

   outstanding aspects

   areas for change or growth

# Appendix D

## Self-Evaluation of Lesson (p. 1)

Teacher:                          Date:

Type of Class:                    Class Level:

Class Composition:                Number Enrolled/Present:

1. Was I well enough prepared?

2. Did I do what I set out to do?

3. Did I adapt as needed to the conditions of the group?

4. Were the activities of the lesson appropriate and well-executed?

5. Was the lesson productive and stimulating for the students?

6. How was the level and type of participation

   —by students?

   —by myself?

7. Did I give appropriate feedback?

8. How did I come across to the students in appearance and actions?

214

# Self-Evaluation of Lesson (p. 2)

Lesson Objectives                    Met/Not Met   Reasons

Strong Points of Class                             Reasons

Weak Points of Class                               Reasons

Comments and Overall Evaluation

# Appendix E

## Student Evaluation Form

Do not write your name on this page!

Teacher _____ Date _____

Subject _____ Level _____

In general, the teacher of this class... <u>Circle One</u>  <u>Comments</u>

1)...came to class on time.  Yes    No

2)...presented well-organized
    lessons.  Yes    No

3)...made good use of class time.  Yes    No

4)...explained the lessons clearly.  Yes    No

5)...answered my questions well.  Yes    No

6)...helped me understand my
    mistakes.  Yes    No

7)...gave me personal help when I
    asked for it.  Yes    No

8)...treated all students the same.  Yes    No

9)...encouraged me to do my best.  Yes    No

10)...helped me to improve my
    English.  Yes    No

# Appendix F

## Sample Faculty Standards of Performance

English Language Program, University of California Extension, Santa Barbara

### STANDARDS OF PERFORMANCE FOR TEACHERS

The University Extension English Language Program Standards of Performance for Teachers has been designed to reflect standards appropriate to English as a Second Language teaching in general, to clarify teacher responsibilities and to make explicit the goals of the program.

These Standards of Performance relate directly to English as a Second Language teaching success and to the maintenance of the quality of the program, according to the administration's perception of teaching and program quality. These are standards against which all teachers will be evaluated. All teachers should read them carefully at the beginning of each quarter and review them as necessary.

### 1. GENERAL CLASS STANDARD
Every class should be one in which the teacher and students are well-prepared and alert; student participation is high; and the lesson is varied, appropriate to the needs and interests of the students, and directed towards a level and goal appropriate for that class. Teachers are expected to perform consistently at this level of excellence and to maintain high standards of student progress and performance.

### 2. THE TEACHER-STUDENT RELATIONSHIP
Students' success in cultural adjustment and language learning is significantly influenced by the atmosphere of their English classes. A good rapport can be established by being friendly and helpful and never "talking down" to students. For teachers to maintain a good working relationship with every individual in their classes, it is necessary to treat all students respectfully and fairly, without bias or favoritism, while requiring respect from every student of the teacher's position and professional qualifications. Since teachers are the representatives of the English

Language Program, they must deal with students in a professional manner at all times, inside and outside of classes.

Teachers can help students adapt to their new environment by encouraging them to develop independence and self-reliance. Teachers should not feel that it is their role or responsibility to provide solutions to students' non-academic problems and should instead refer these to the Student Services Coordinator.

## 3. CLASS PARTICIPATION

In order to succeed at the task of learning English in the program, it is essential that a student participate fully in class. Therefore, it is an important part of the English as a Second Language teaching job to ensure that all students are active participants in every class, that no student dominates or is uninvolved. In order to accomplish this goal, the teacher must act as a facilitator and guide inclass activities, so that the majority of class time is spent in appropriate production of the language involving all students.

## 4. LEVEL OF DIFFICULTY

Students are placed in classes and advanced through levels according to their measured English language proficiency. In order for students to be able to progress and improve in their proficiency, the level of difficulty of class activities must be appropriate to the proficiency level of the majority of the students in the class. If the level of the class is aimed toward the one or two lowest students in that class, the rest of the class will tend to come down to that level. If the lessons are geared to the one or two highest students, the other students will become discouraged and not be able to improve significantly.

Nevertheless, it is better to aim lessons somewhat high rather than somewhat low, as long as all students can keep up and participate in class. In that case, students are being challenged and will show more rapid progress.

To gauge whether the level of difficulty of class activities is appropriate, the teacher should pay attention to signals such as the level of absenteeism, participation in class and completion of homework assignments. In addition, students ought to be asked from time to time whether the level of difficulty of the class is appropriate. If more than a few students think that the level of difficulty is too high or too low, the situation can usually be corrected by speeding up or slowing down the pace of the class. In extreme cases, different materials may seem called for. In such cases, the Academic Coordinator should be consulted.

## 5. MATERIALS

The core materials for a given class are those required texts and other materials stated in the curriculum. The curriculum materials for a given class level have been carefully selected to reflect the goals of that level and to form a sequence with previous and subsequent levels. Therefore, teachers are expected to use any required texts or other materials allocated by the program to that class, unless otherwise stated in the curriculum or agreed upon by the Academic Coordinator. The teacher may not fail to use or at any time in the Quarter stop making regular use of the materials allotted for the given class without permission of the Academic Coordinator. That permission will be given if the Academic Coordinator is convinced that the designated materials are not useable in the particular class and that more suitable materials are readily available.

Teachers are encouraged to communicate with other teachers about their classes and to share activities and resources, as long as this does not result in significant repetition or interfere with the goals of another class. Specifically, teachers should not use materials designated for a different language skill area at the same class level, unless such use is carefully coordinated with the other teacher who is using those materials. To avoid overlap from level to level, teachers are not to use materials in their classes which are required in the curriculum at a different class level.

## 6. COURSE OUTLINE

Teachers are free to develop their own class designs, following the curriculum guidelines. Carefully designing a class in the early stages is important for the smooth functioning of that class and will also be helpful in the coordination of different skills and levels. The goals or plan of a course can then be communicated to the students in the class and shared with other teachers at the same or differen. levels.

In the first or second week of the Quarter, after the teacher has had a chance to gauge the level and needs of the students, an outline of each course being taught must be submitted for approval to the Academic Coordinator. The outline should indicate the planned use and coverage of materials, the goals of the course and how these goals are to be accomplished. A day-to-day lesson plan or detailed outline is not necessary and would in fact in most cases be unrealistic, overly confining, since a teacher must have the flexibility to adapt to changing situations or needs of a class. The outline can be viewed as a flexible frame giving the overall structure and direction of the course.

The Academic Coordinator will review the course outlines in terms of whether the materials, goals and methods are appropriate and realistic for the particular class. If substantial changes are recommended, the outline may need to be revised or amended. When the course outline has been approved, it should be followed unless problems arise. In that case, the teacher should work with the Academic Coordinator to design a revised plan for the course.

## 7. CLASS ACTIVITIES

Class activities should be varied and purposeful, and they should stimulate students into production of the language. Appropriate activities are those which facilitate communication and are geared to a university-level or professional audience. Innovation in techniques of presentation is encouraged, and feedback on the results will be welcomed. To ensure adequate coverage of every language skill area at every level, the majority of class time should be devoted to activities involving the skill area designated for that class period, following the course outline. As a general rule, not more than one quarter of any class period should be spent in "free" discussion or unplanned activities unless these are specifically related to the materials and goals of that class. A few minutes spent in simply talking to students and exchanging ideas is useful for class rapport and morale, but too much of this will be perceived by students as wasting time.

Except in unusual circumstances, all class activities are to take place in the designated English Language Program classrooms. Any plans for class activities which are to take place outside the classroom must be submitted in writing to the English Language Program Director and written approval received before the activity is announced to the class.

## 8. HOMEWORK

The length and difficulty of homework assignments should be appropriate to the level of the majority of students in a given class. The emphasis of the program is on learning in class, and required homework for the combined classes at a given level should be kept at or below an average of 10 hours per week. Even the lowest students in a class should not find it necessary to spend much more than this average amount of time on assigned out-of-class activities. Teachers at a given level will have to coordinate their efforts to ensure that the limits on homework are not exceeded.

Homework need not be assigned every night, and there should be no assignments which are merely "busywork." Homework assignments should be interesting, useful and relevant both to class materials and to the student's life outside of English classes. Students will see the purpose of homework assignments which relate directly to the lesson for a subsequent class or to the overall plan of the course. It should be possible to justify to the students the reason for any homework assignment. Occasionally, teachers should solicit feedback from students to ensure that the assignments are interesting useful, and appropriate to the level and needs of the particular students.

## 9. COMMUNICATION BETWEEN TEACHERS AND ACADEMIC COORDINATOR

The Academic Coordinator is interested in all aspects of the program curriculum and classes and is the teachers' resource for solutions to problems with the curriculum, materials, classes or individual students. The Coordinator welcomes any communication regarding these matters and encourages teachers to discuss any new ideas or suggestions for improvement or changes. If any problems arise in a class, the Academic Coordinator should be consulted to help in correcting or improving the situation. The Academic Coordinator will also periodically make recommendations to teachers based on class observation and feedback from students.

## 10. CLASS PERIODS AND TEACHING OBLIGATIONS

Each teacher is assigned to teach a specified number of classes at certain levels throughout the Quarter. Teachers are responsible for teaching every hour which has been assigned to them unless arrangements have been made with the Academic Coordinator in advance for the substitute from the teaching staff or substitute list. The class periods are 50 minutes. Class will begin on the hour and end 10 minutes before the next hour to allow teachers and students a break between classes. If a class runs overtime, both teachers and students are inconvenienced. Thus, all teachers need to cooperate in beginning and ending classes on time.

## 11. RECORDS OF STUDENT ATTENDANCE AND PERFORMANCE

All students in the English Language Program have made a commitment to full-time study and must adhere to this committment in order to complete their course of study successfully. Although limited amounts of absenteeism, lateness or missed assignments are allowed, excessive delinquency can jeopardize students' visa status and cause problems in their classes. To avoid such problems and to maintain the standards of the program, teachers are required to keep accurate records of student attendance, punctuality, diligence and progress, and to communicate these to the administration as required for attendance records and progress reports.

## 12. SUPPORT OF ENGLISH LANGUAGE PROGRAM POLICIES, PROCEDURES & STAFF

To keep the program operating smoothly, it is necessary for teachers to adhere to stated English Language Program policies and procedures. In addition, teachers are expected to cooperate with and support all English Language Program staff members and other teachers, both within and outside of the classroom, in all matters relating to the operation of the program.

## 13. AFTER-CLASS ACTIVITIES

Each teacher must be present at all meetings and functions described in the Letter of Agreement to teach since those meetings and functions are considered to be an integral part of the program. Other scheduled extracurricular, non-teaching activities such as program parties are optional and do not relate to standards of performance for teachers. Social activities initiated by teachers or students are to be planned outside class time. The English Language Program cannot be responsible for students outside of classes except in scheduled program activities.

## 14. PROFESSIONAL IMAGE

Since teachers significantly influence the public image of the program, they are expected to dress appropriately in class and to maintain a neat, clean, and professional appearance.

Developed by Martha Pennington, Academic Coordinator, January 1981, and approved by UCSB Personnel Office

# Appendix G

## Categories for Evaluation of Research, Teaching, and Service

I. <u>Research Evaluation</u>

A. Evaluation of Publications
[NOTE: Singly authored and refereed publications have greater weight than multiply authored or nonrefereed publications]
1. Major Books
   a. Major original contribution to research or theory
   b. Original graduate textbook (or equivalent software or video)
   c. Original undergraduate textbook (or equivalent software or video)
   d. Overview of previously published research or theory
   e. Edited collection of original articles
2. Minor Books
   a. Edited collection of previously published articles
   b. Original student textbook, test, software, video program
3. Major Articles
   a. Data-based
      i) Report of major original study
      ii) Major synthesis of research with important original insights
      iii) Research review with implications for the field
      iv) Report of minor original study
   b. Non data-based
      i) Theoretical article not explicitly related to research
      ii) Practical article not explicitly related to research
      iii) Full-length book review
4. Minor Articles
   a. Brief research notices
   b. Shorter book reviews
   c. Forum articles
   d. Professional newsletter/magazine articles
5. Research in Progress (unpublished)

B. Evaluation of Overall Research Record
  1. Peer Evaluation of Originality and Importance to Field
  2. Number of Publications in Each Category
  3. Work with Students
     a. Ability to assist students in generating and implementing important and original research
     b. Number of thesis committees chaired
     c. Number of thesis committees served on
  4. Ability to Bring in Grants, Conferences, or Other Forms of Outside Support or Acclaim to the Department

II. Teaching Evaluation

  A. Evaluation Categories
    1. Overall Teaching Effectiveness
    2. Breakdown of Teaching Skill
       a. Relationships with students (supportive, fair, available)
       b. Range of teaching capabilities
       c. Appropriateness of course objectives
       d. Originality and innovation
       e. Scholarly maturity of presentation
       f. Depth and breadth of coverage of material
       g. Appropriateness of level and content in courses
       h. Appropriateness of assignments and grading procedures

  B. Types of Input
    1. Peer Evaluation of Course Outlines, Original Materials and Videotaped Records of Classroom Teaching (if available)
       [NOTE: Peer evaluators may include outside evaluators as well as members of the same department.
    2. Student Evaluations
       [NOTE: Only official student evaluations are to be used as input.]
    3. Teaching Award or Citation
    4. Self-Evaluations of Teaching

III. Service Evaluation

  A. External Service
    1. Editorial
       a. Journal or series editor
       b. Board member of journal
       c. Journal or series reviewer

2. National/International Organizations
   a. President
   b. Board member
   c. Committee/interest section chair
   d. Conference chair
   e. Conference committee member
3. Invited Presentations
   a. National/international conference, colloquium, workshop, etc.
      i) Keynote
      ii) Presenter
   b. Regional/local conference, colloquium, workshop, etc.
      i) Keynote
      ii) Presenter
4. Refereed Presentations
   a. National/international conference, colloqium, workshop, etc.
   b. Regional/local conference, colloquium, workshop, etc.
5. Newsletter Editor

B. Internal Service
   1. University-Wide
      a. Committee chair
      b. Committee member
      c. Participant in fora, lectures, consultancies, etc.
      d. Community liaison
   2. Departmental
      a. Director of institute
      b. Department chair
      c. Conference organizer
      d. Departmental committees and other departmental duties

# Appendix H

Format for Annual Teacher Performance Review

A. Input to Review

    1. List of Subjects and Levels Taught
    2. Annual Self-Review of Activities and Accomplishments
    3. Biannual Course Plans
    4. Observation Reports
    5. Student Evaluation Summaries

B. Areas of Evaluation

    1. Classes
       a. Following the curriculum for the subject and level
       b. Using materials and equipment
       c. Classroom dynamics and atmosphere
       d. Adaptability
    2. Administrative Duties
       a. Testing
       b. Student orientation
       c. Keeping attendance records
       d. Circulating announcements to students
       e. Other
    3. Relationships within Program
       a. Students
       b. Faculty
       c. Administration
    4. Professional Growth
       a. Attendance at workshops, courses, conferences
       b. Presentation or publication of papers
       c. Research activities
       d. Materials development
       e. Keeping up-to-date in the field
       f. Developing new areas of expertise
       g. Contributions to program growth or improvement

C. <u>Summary of Performance Review</u>
  1. Strengths/Outstanding Areas
  2. Weaknesses/Problem Areas/Areas for Growth or
     Improvement

D. <u>Action Steps</u>

Developed by Martha Pennington, Academic Coordinator, June 1983, University of California Extension at Santa Barbara, English Language Program.

# 11
# Evaluating the ESL Program Director

*Robert P. Fox*

## Introduction

> The formal evaluation of academic administrators is quite recent and just now becoming widespread. (Baum 1983, 182)

When Baum wrote this, he was lamenting the fact that the academic community was just beginning to adopt performance evaluations that had been widely used in the business world since the 1950s. Today most academic institutions regularly evaluate administrators at the level of department chair and above, but the evaluation of the college or university ESL (English as a Second Language) program director seems to have lagged to the extent that Baum's 1983 comment is still valid. Since ESL programs have been around for some 40 years, we must ask ourselves what the reason for this is. One simple answer may be that the ESL program is often considered a profit-making unit and not really an academic unit, and therefore it is evaluated in terms of whether it shows a profit or not. The location of a program within the university structure does not seem to influence the attitude one way or the other that it is a for-profit unit.

The director of an ESL program is the chief administrative officer of the unit, regardless of where the program is located—within a department, within a college, or as an independent unit. It is time for the faculty and staff of ESL programs to demand that their administrators be treated as the equals of other administrators and be evaluated on a regular basis. This is not a punitive demand aimed at the director, but a demand that the ESL program be recognized as an academic unit and treated as such.

# The "Well" ESL Director

In 1987, Neugebauer wrote an article entitled "The Well Director" which, although written to help a director perform a self-evaluation, might also serve as a useful basis for examining how one might go about evaluating an ESL program director. Neugebauer cautions directors not to be too hard on themselves, since it is unlikely that anyone would excel in all aspects of administration. An important point to remember in any evaluation is that its primary purpose is to show the director's strengths and weaknesses and to develop a plan to help remedy the weaknesses, not punish the director because of them.

It might be useful to consider Neugebauer's ten points, analyzing each in turn to see how it might apply to the ESL program director.

1. "The well director has a vision for her organization."[1] The ESL program director must be more than an enforcer of rules and regulations and a maintainer of the status quo. The director must have a sense of vision and be creative in developing new ways for the ESL program to interface with the university as a whole. If the ESL program is not already the testing center for all new international students, then steps should be taken to ensure that it will be. This may well involve cooperation with other academic units to establish standards that will be meaningful to them. It may also lead to closer cooperation in developing new programs to meet the needs of students destined for specific programs, and possibly to jointly taught courses. The director "fronts" for the ESL program and must present a vision that inspires not only the ESL program staff but also the staff of other units. The director's belief that the ESL program is an academic unit equivalent to others is not sufficient; it must be promoted on campus so that other key academic administrators will come to hold the same belief. The director must be visible and take an active part in the life of the university by enthusiastically serving on committees and sharing expertise.

2. "The well director achieves results through directing people to accomplish the goals of the organization." The ESL program director works to make a vision into reality. The director works with other members of the organization to establish realistic goals and to communicate those goals to the staff. The director inspires the staff to work to attain the established goals and develop a sense of continuity and enthusiasm. Communication is essential throughout this process (see Chapter Four, this volume). The director communicates with both the staff and the organization and inspires the feeling that the goals can be accomplished through cooperative effort. There are any number of

ways that the director can communicate with the staff, from weekly or monthly meetings and timely memos or office "bulletins" to communiques via electronic mail or brown bag lunches.

3. "The well director is continually assessing the performance of the organization." The ESL program director is constantly assessing the progress of the program toward meeting and maintaining its goals (see Chapter Four, this volume). Again, communication is the key. The "well" ESL program director makes it a point to visit each work area to interact with the staff and students on an informal and regular basis. The director also schedules open office hours to be available to the staff and students on an informal basis. The director does not sit in an office all day, but rather spends a great deal of time out of the office and is available to both the staff and the university at large.

4. "The well director keeps in touch with changes in the world outside the center." The ESL program director is professionally involved and active. This means taking an active part in organizations such as the National Association for Foreign Student Affairs (NAFSA), Teachers of English to Speakers of Other Languages (TESOL), and the International Association of Teachers of English as a Foreign Language (IATEFL) that are closely related to the mission of the program, as well as organizations such as the National Council of Teachers of English (NCTE), the American Association of Applied Linguistics (AAAL), and the International Reading Association (IRA), which have broader missions that can contribute to the success of the ESL program. The director also meets periodically with colleagues to discuss developments in their programs and in the field at large. In addition to keeping abreast of relevant trends in the field, the director also keeps in touch with teachers, students, and their sponsors to determine their needs and desires. Continually gathering information, the director must pause from time to time to reassess the program in terms of all this new information and to determine the degree to which the program is meeting its objectives and the objectives of its clientele.

5. "The well director focuses her attention on areas where superior performance on her part will have the most important impact." Here the ESL program director determines what the most pressing tasks are and how to distribute the time available among them. The tasks the director takes on should be those that can gain the greatest benefits for the program for the time that will be spent on them. Time management is thus an essential skill for the ESL program director.

6. "The well director is continually working to develop an effective management team." The ESL program director, like any other

230

administrator, cannot do everything alone. To run an efficient program, the director develops an effective team and delegates responsibility. The administrative team for an ESL program might consist of any of the following positions, depending on size: a curriculum coordinator responsible for the oversight of the academic program and teachers; level coordinators responsible for the curriculum and teachers at each level—for example, beginning, intermediate, and advanced; and skill-area coordinators who are responsible for the curriculum and teachers of each of the skill areas, such as reading, writing, speaking, and listening. To develop an effective team, the director must consider the strengths and weaknesses of the staff and carefully select those members who will be most effective in the desired position according to the requirements of the job. Here, as in the other aspects of the administration of the program, the lines of communication must be kept open between the team and the director and between the team and the rest of the staff.

7. "The well director doesn't work to make people love her, but makes people love to work for her." The ESL program director involves the staff in the program's goals and curriculum and makes them feel that they are an integral part of the program and have a vested interest in it (see Chapter Four, this volume). The director maintains a professional attitude and does not use friendship as either a club or a carrot. This may mean striking a delicate balance at times between showing a personal care or concern and a respect for individual privacy. If a staff member should have a crisis, the director is there to offer assistance and show concern, but not to force advice or assistance on the staff member.

8. "The well director constructs a stimulating, yet secure, working environment for staff members." This is perhaps the most important of Neugebauer's attributes, and is one of the ESL program director's most important concerns, since a challenged and secure staff will be a happy and cooperative staff. Here the ESL program director has a number of responsibilities, perhaps the most important of which is the status of the staff. The director works to secure permanent status for the staff within the bounds set by the larger organization of which the program is a part. The director strives to gain status for the staff equal to that of their colleagues in other departments—that is, faculty status, either tenured or nontenured, which will give the staff the same privileges and responsibilities as their colleagues. Once this has been accomplished, a stimulating environment will be easier to establish, since the staff will be expected to perform at a high level. The director has the right and, indeed, the responsibility—to the students and to the program as a whole—to demand that the staff perform at a high level and to provide opportunities for staff members to show their ability. The director also

has the responsibility to be a problem solver when the staff cannot resolve a problem at hand.

The "well" ESL program director respects the autonomy of a staff member who has been given a task to do and does not establish a "big brother" atmosphere of surveillance. When a staff member does a good job, then recognition is given. If the task is not done well, then gentle, constructive guidance is called for to help the staff member improve performance. Professional opportunities are also provided. Staff members can be given the opportunity to grow professionally through attending conferences and workshops or visiting other programs to gain a broader perspective. The director attempts to provide at least partial funds for these activities. The staff can be given the opportunity and encouragement to be creative through developing new courses or materials or writing articles and books. Again, the director supports these creative activities by providing clerical assistance and release time insofar as possible.

9. "The well director is an effective decision maker." The ESL program director does not make decisions in a vacuum, but gives range to the considerations of staff, budget, and program goals and solicits the opinions of the staff and others before making a decision. The final decision rests with the director, but "effective" should mean "democratic," not "dictatorial."

10. "The well director keeps her work life in its proper perspective." The "well" ESL program director does not become so involved in the job that the job equals life. The director leaves "work life" at the office and returns to "social life" at the end of the day. The director's personal life, family, and friends are beyond the reach of the work life, and the balance between the two must be maintained. The director takes allocated vacation time without the fear that the program will collapse, but with the knowledge that the staff will provide for the smooth operation of the program.

## Skills of an Effective ESL Program Director

The "ten vital attributes" identified by Neugebauer fall essentially into the areas of what Katz (cited in Pennington 1985) calls "human" and "conceptual" skills, with a lesser emphasis on "technical" skills. Individual technical skills are of two types: professional, such as a knowledge of English phonology, morphology, syntax, teaching methodology, curriculum design, and second language acquisition theory for the ESL professional; and administrative, such as personnel matters, recordkeeping, budgeting, scheduling, and program promotion. However, technical skills do not seem to be as important in the minds of faculty and higher level administrators as do the human and conceptual skills. In reviewing a recent evaluation of a department head at my institution, I was surprised to find that only one of the ten questions asked by the evaluation team might have been interpreted as dealing with technical skills (though it could also be seen as involving conceptual and human skill), and that question concerned "enhancing the Department's image and reputation." There were no questions relating to any of the other administrative or professional technical skills; perhaps it is only faculty members who are evaluated for their technical expertise by their students and by their supervisors in hiring and promotion decisions.

That technical skills seem to rate last should not be surprising. Cowden (1984) surveyed 42 music faculty at 14 institutions and discovered that "personal relationships will make or break you" (p. 47). What characteristics were these faculty members looking for in an administrator? When asked what the music executive did that was most successful, the six most common responses were:

- He listens
- He is accessible
- He can make decisions
- He shows a great understanding of the issues
- He is honest in his dealings
- He handles money well.[2]

Only the last is a technical skill. When asked to think in ideal rather than real terms, the number one response was vision—the person should be able to see into and project the future. "We need to know where we are going and how we're going to get there" (p. 47).

The development of a unique vision is certainly a conceptual skill. Obviously, then, for the music faculty in question, human and conceptual skills are far more important than technical skills, although professional technical skills would seem to be a prerequisite for "vision." Though the professional technical skills seem to be implied, the administrative technical skills do not. It is clear in the minds of these faculty members that the institution and program come first and that the administrator's career comes second. As a result of this kind of attitude among faculty members, an educator's professional technical skills may suffer over the course of an administrative career.

The ESL program administrator must combine the professional technical skills of the field with those of a business manager. The director must be conversant with the various aspects of the English language and how to apply this knowledge in the classroom. The director should have had several years of practical experience in the classroom and have worked through a series of progressively more challenging situations to prepare for the position of director.

Once appointed as director, the administrator's responsibility is total, as is the power to enhance or destroy the program and its reputation. How the director handles this power and responsibility involves human and conceptual skill. Total responsibility places a heavy burden on the director to ensure that the program is run well and grows within the constraints established by the institution. The director must become financially adept to assure that the budget is sufficient and is distributed properly across the essential line items. Then the director must approve and account for expenditures. The director also has to be familiar with immigration rules and regulations, with affirmative action regulations in personnel matters, and with the minimal professional requirements established by professional associations, and assure that they are applied. The ESL program director's technical skills, then, are both those required to be a member of the profession and those required to be an effective administrator: they embrace matters relating to finances, personnel, recordkeeping, INS (Immigration and Naturalization Service) regulations, and so on.

To summarize, three types of skills are required for the ESL program director:

1. Human: how the director relates to others
2. Conceptual: a vision of where the program is going and how to get there
3. Technical: a knowledge of the professional content area of ESL and administrative skills

The why and the how of evaluating the ESL program administrator, to which I now turn, must be considered in the light of the characteristics and skills that have been identified above for effectiveness in directing an ESL program.

## The Rationale for Evaluating the ESL Program Director

Why evaluate the ESL program director? There are various reasons for doing this, chief among them accountability. Gunn (1986, 10) states, "A primary reason for the poor quality of university management is that administrators, as a rule, have not been held strictly accountable for their performance." This notion of accountability is recurrent in the literature and forms the basis of most approaches to evaluation. Baum (1983, 183) proposes two reasons for performance evaluations: one is to focus "on past performance to improve future performance by changing behavior through the reward system"; the second is "development with a view to preparation for future performance improvement through self-learning and professional growth." Baum, drawing on the work of Charles Fisher, also lists various reasons for establishing a formal evaluation process. Among them are the following:

- To define, through evaluation feedback, need [sic] areas of individual professional development and personal growth
- To improve individual administrative performance
- To help define more clearly individual objectives consistent with institutional missions and goals
- To reward outstanding administrative performance
- To enlighten all audiences regarding the [program's] integrity and worth. (Baum 1983, 184)

It should be noted again that none of the reasons given in the literature cite dismissal or punishment as a reason for evaluation. The reasons given all stress the concept of accountability through performance evaluation, professional development and personal growth, and reward for outstanding performance. For these same reasons, the ESL program director should be evaluated in order to become aware of strengths and weaknesses and to develop a program for improvement in the areas of weakness.

## Conducting the Evaluation of the ESL Program Director

How should the evaluation be conducted, and who should conduct it? Before these "how" and "who" questions can be considered, the ESL program director must know exactly what is expected of the position, based on a position description and what the goals of the ESL program as established by the institution are. The evaluation then is predicated on how successfully the director is doing the job in terms of what is expected and how successfully the established goals are being met. Since job descriptions and goals are subject to change and modification over time as circumstances change, the evaluation instrument must be revised each time it is administered. There does not seem to be any agreed-upon length of time between evaluations, but since a formal evaluation can be very time consuming, it would seem that a formal evaluation conducted every three years with informal evaluations in the intervening years should be sufficient to determine that satisfactory progress is being made in remedying identified problem areas.

The development of the evaluation instrument and the conduct of the actual evaluation are participatory by nature. According to Featherstone and Romano (1983, 217), those persons who are involved in the development of the procedures and criteria for the performance evaluation are:

1. Those who have legal responsibility to appraise—in the case of the ESL program director, this would be the administration of the institution: the immediate dean, vice-provost, and so on.

2. Those who will be appraised and have knowledge of the competencies needed to perform the tasks of administration —in this case the ESL program director.

3. Those who are affected by leadership and management and are in the position to appraise—in this case, the ESL program faculty, staff, and students, and possibly sponsors.

Establishing a committee composed of members of each of the above groups will assume that the "evaluation criteria and norms [are] agreed on in advance" (Baum 1983, 193). Following the approach adopted by McCleary (1983), the committee can choose to evaluate "being," "doing," or "consequences." That is, the ESL program director can be evaluated for personal characteristics, for administrative style, or for what has been achieved in terms of the goals and objectives established for the program. A review of the literature shows a growing tendency to base evaluations on "consequences," which can only be accomplished when the goals and objectives are clearly stated and achievable. If the goals and objectives are poorly stated and vague, then an evaluation of "consequences" or outcomes is practically impossible.

The development of an effective evaluation instrument is difficult, since there seem to be few criteria established for selecting ESL program directors. Most of the training of the prospective ESL program director is done on the job, with only a handful of academic programs offering any type of ESL administrative courses. This difficulty is not peculiar to ESL, however. In 1977, after a number of years of effort, the National Association of Secondary School Principals (NASSP) developed a list of 12 areas of competence needed by secondary school principals, and proposed that these competencies be incorporated into the curriculum of Educational Administration programs so that future principals would be prepared to do the job effectively from the beginning. The 12 areas of competence were used by Redfern (1983, 271) to develop a set of performance criteria for evaluating middle-management personnel. The 12 criteria are the following:

1. Problem analysis
2. Judgment
3. Organizational ability
4. Decisiveness
5. Leadership
6. Sensitivity

7. Range of interests
8. Personal motivation
9. Educational
10. Stress
11. Oral communication skills
12. Written communication skills

Most of the criteria are obvious and need no explanation. However, "range of interests" is taken to mean the competence to discuss a variety of issues, which for the ESL program director might include immigration issues, political issues involving international students, and problems international students have adjusting to the American educational system, as well as a competence in the technical areas of the field. "Personal motivation" means that the ESL program director is the director because personal satisfaction and a sense of achievement are important to him or her. "Educational Values" means that the ESL program director is committed to the concept of international education and that the ESL program plays a vital part in achieving the goals of international education.

Whatever criteria are developed for the evaluation instrument, they must be agreed on by all parties and be impartial and fair. With the criteria selected, the committee now has the task of developing the instrument itself. Again, the idea that the evaluation is not punitive must be recognized and provision made for developing a "professional improvement plan" (Schiller and McGarry 1986, 31) to assist the ESL program director in further professional growth. There is no agreed-upon form for the evaluation, but a number of authors seem to prefer a tripartite form that includes a statement of the goal, objective, or task being evaluated, a space for written commentary, and a rating scale such as "accomplished role expectation," "partially accomplished role expectation," and "needs performance improvement" (Schiller and McGarry 1986, 31) or "fully achieved," "partially achieved," and "not achieved" (Redfern 1983, 270). Such a rating scale avoids the absolute extremes of a two-point scale, such as "satisfactory" and "unsatisfactory," and permits recognition that a task may have been partially accomplished or accomplished at a lesser level of performance than desired.

Once the evaluation instrument is completed, the committee might send it to a variety of people, not just to the faculty, staff, and students of the ESL program and higher level administrators, but to selected faculty, staff, and administrators in the areas that the ESL program director interacts with and to selected off-campus offices such as sponsors, other ESL programs in the area, and so on, that have a knowledge of the ESL program and its director. As with any type of questionnaire,

237

the committee cannot expect a one hundred percent response, but it should expect and require all members of the ESL program faculty and staff to respond. Evaluation forms should be signed and the confidentiality of the respondent guaranteed. Unsigned evaluations, whether positive or negative, are to be considered invalid.

Once the data have been collected, the committee has the responsibility of developing a narrative report addressing each point in turn. Care is taken to assure that the report is descriptive rather than judgmental and that areas that need improvement are noted, with possible courses of action indicated for improvement in those areas where a rating of "not achieved" is given. The results of the evaluation need wide dissemination in full form to the faculty and staff of the ESL program and in summarized form to others, after the ESL program director has had the opportunity to see them and respond, if that is appropriate.

One of the most important results of the evaluation is the development of an improvement plan by the ESL program director, which should form the basis of interim informal evaluations. The ESL program director can be evaluated on how successfully the development plan is being implemented, so that on the next formal evaluation a rating of "fully achieved" can be expected. It is also important to show the ESL program faculty, staff, and others that the evaluation process was not a futile effort on their part, but that the results are being taken seriously and that steps are being taken to strengthen identified areas of weakness. Finally, the ESL program director should be rewarded for making efforts and attempts to improve, so that the whole process will not be just an opportunity for the administration to punish the director for falling short of perfection.

## Conclusion

The time has come for the regular, formal evaluation of the ESL program director. The director, like any other administrator, is accountable for demonstrating that the goals and objectives of the ESL program, as established by the institution, are being met in an effective and timely manner. The director cannot be evaluated in isolation, but has to be evaluated by his or her superiors, peers, and the faculty and staff. An impartial committee representing all groups is responsible for selecting the evaluation criteria, designing (as far as possible) an objective evaluation instrument, and reporting the results. Based on the results of the evaluation, the director develops an improvement program and is rewarded for accomplishments. The task is clear, but the means to accomplish it are difficult, especially since there are no explicit guidelines for such an evaluation. It is not only time to evaluate the ESL program director, but also for the ESL program community to determine the competencies that are essential for the director to have. Further, it is time for the ESL program community and the ESL community as a whole to insist that training programs offer courses to prepare future program administrators.

## Notes

1. Neugebauer uses female reference in the headings for his ten points. This usage is being maintained to remain faithful to the original, but the statements are taken to apply in a nongender-specific manner.

2. The masculine reference is retained from the original source.

## References

Barrett, R. P., ed. 1982. *The Administration of intensive English language programs.* Washington, D.C.: National Association for Foreign Student Affairs.

Baum, E. 1983. Evaluating the evaluation process for academic administrators. *College and University* 58(2):182–193.

Cowden, R. L. 1984. Administrator? *Music Educators Journal* 70(6):46–47.

Ediger, M. 1985. Issues in Educational Administration. ERIC Document Reproduction Service #ED 253974.

Featherstone, R. L. and L. Romano. 1983. Evaluation of administrative performance. In Zappulla, E., ed., *Evaluating administrative performance: current trends and techniques,* 215–220. Belmont, CA: Star Publishing Co.

Fox, R. P. 1988. ESL Program Administration in Higher Education. *ERIC Digest.* Washington, D.C.: Center for Applied Linguistics.

Gibbins, N. L. and M. M. Curnutte. 1987. Evaluating principals for your school district—20 questions. *NASSP Bulletin* 71(501): 113–118.

Gunn, B. 1986. The triadic format of administrative accountability. *Journal of the College and University Personnel Association* 37(4):10–17.

Howsam, R. B. 1983. Current issues in evaluation. In Zappulla, E., ed., *Evaluating Administrative Performance: Current Trends and Techniques,* 183–192. Belmont, CA: Star Publishing Co.

McCleary, L. E. 1983. Administrator evaluation: Concerns for the practitioner. In Zappulla, E., ed., *Evaluating administrative performance: current trends and techniques,* 174–181. Belmont, CA: Star Publishing Co.

Neugebauer, R. 1987. The Well Director. *Child Care Information Exchange* 54:3–6. Nickerson, N. 1986. Affecting Preservice, Inservice Programs at Universities. *NASSP Bulletin* 70(4):56–58.

Pennington, M. C. 1985. Effective administration of an ESL program. In Larson, P., E. Judd, and D. Messerschmitt, eds., *On TESOL '84: A brave new world for TESOL*. Washington, D.C.: Teachers of English to Speakers of Other Languages.

Redfern, G. B. 1983. Evaluating middle-management personnel. In Zappulla, E., ed., *Evaluating administrative performance: current trends and techniques*, 259–273. Belmont, CA: Star Publishing Co.

Schiller, R. E. and J. P. McGarry. 1986. Improving an administrator evaluation program: A case study. *ERS Spectrum* 4(2):26–31.

Zappulla, E., ed. 1983. *Evaluating administrative performance: current trends and techniques*. Belmont, CA: Star Publishing Co.

# 12
# Administrative Evaluation in ESL Programs: "How'm I Doin'?"

*Barbara F. Matthies*

## Introduction

Personal growth and professional development are two sides of the same valuable coin for any administrator, a coin to be invested so that it pays dividends in job satisfaction and effectiveness. Yet too often the busy directors of ESL (English as a Second Language) programs neglect to assess the rate of their own growth as professionals, perhaps preferring instead to focus evaluation on staff members, students, the curriculum, and the program's financial state. While those are certainly important matters, it behooves the administrator to undergo evaluation as well because, as Saltzer has pointed out, "it is inevitable that a program will take on the imprint of its director's personality, capability, and effectiveness in performing the needed functions; every program reflects its director" (1982, p. 92). For an ESL program to remain viable and up-to-date, therefore, its director should be perceived as a person who is growing in the job from year to year. What follows here is a rationale and framework for the ESL program administrator to employ in assessing his or her professional development and effectiveness.

## Why Evaluate?

Consider the case of university professors. At most schools, they are obliged to undergo peer review every few years to be tenured or promoted. The process requires them to gather information on all of their scholarly, teaching, and service activities in a form that colleagues can view and understand. Over the years they accumulate lesson plans, manuscripts, correspondence, reports, and so on; then for the review they must divide this material into coherent sections for others to evaluate against specific departmental and institutional standards for promotion and tenure decisions. In the process of doing all of that collecting and compiling, the individuals become acutely aware of which areas have been their strongest or most active since the last review period. Several months later, when the results of the review are presented, they can see clearly how others perceive their work and which areas need more attention for future professional development.

An ESL program administrator should benefit from a similar procedure. A periodic review allows the director and the staff to acknowledge their collective successes and growth over time as they gather and review curricula, annual reports, student test scores, records of individual professional activities, and other information. It also gives the staff an opportunity to comment on the director's effectiveness as an administrator who has guided the program to its present stage of development. The outcome of this review process should enable the director to calibrate the program's goals and practices with the guidelines established by NAFSA (National Association for Foreign Student Affairs) (1981, 1983) and TESOL (Teachers of English to Speakers of Other Languages) (1984) and highlight areas on which to focus strategies for future planning in both personal and programmatic development. Although the process is time-consuming, if it is not conducted systematically on a regular schedule, the beauty of the forest can get lost in a thicket of trees—everyone can lose sight of individual and programmatic goals while dealing with day-to-day challenges.

### What Approach?

There are three levels from which to evaluate the administration of an ESL program, ranging from the broadest perspective of national standards to the most narrow within the program itself (Figure 1). The approach at any level is usually that of self-study, although external review is, of course, another option, as discussed by Fox (see Chapter 11, this volume). It is not advisable to combine evaluations from all three levels; the preferred method is to adopt one as the main focus and mention the others in passing when reporting the findings.

The broadest approach is to compare the ESL program and its administration with professional guidelines and with other ESL programs of similar scope. In this case, the evaluator must be cognizant not only of models outside the institution but also of how they have been adapted to suit the program's specific location and clientele. A more limited

242

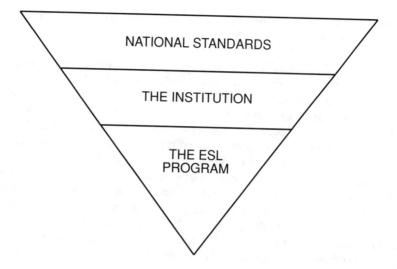

FIGURE 1. LEVELS OF EVALUATION FOCUS

NATIONAL STANDARDS

THE INSTITUTION

THE ESL PROGRAM

approach examines the ESL program administration within the context of a parent institution's mission statement and criteria for promotion. This might require the administrator to produce policy statements about the program's recruitment of students, entrance and exit criteria, the issue of offering credit for ESL courses, articulation with other institutions, services rendered to researchers and departments, and so on, and then to provide data and letters of support to show how effectively his or her implementation of these policies contributes to the overall mission of the institution.

The most narrowly focused approach to ESL administrative evaluation—and the one that is the main concern of this article—is to examine the director's effectiveness within the program itself. This is perhaps the most sensitive aspect to evaluate, but one that should not be neglected. After all, if students and teachers must undergo frequent evaluation, it is only fair that the program administrator's performance be judged objectively and periodically. As most professors do, the ESL director should find the process of gathering the supporting evidence to be salutary and enlightening, if not always enjoyable.

## What to Look For?

Let us assume, first of all, that the director is conducting the evaluation of his or her own administration. That may seem unwise or even suspect, but it is often the only approach to take unless a more formal review procedure is in place. Even those reviews, however, usually occur at such infrequent intervals that they may not be as helpful as responses to specific, immediate issues in guiding one's year-to-year planning and decision making.

**Administrative Style.** There are almost no suitable instruments designed to measure an ESL program administrator's effectiveness in any standardized way. Those that have been developed for the corporate world (e.g., the Leader Behavior Description Questionnaire[1] or the Myers-Briggs Type Indicator[2]) are not well suited to the context of higher education, much less to the specialized nature of an ESL program. Those instruments that have been validated for assessing the performance of academic deans or department chairpersons are closer to the mark, and the ESL director might benefit from an analysis of his or her administrative style using a self-administered inventory designed for that purpose. For example, Reasor (1981) used the Educational Administrative Style Diagnosis Test in a study of ESL directors; however, the outcomes of his survey proved to be difficult to interpret.

**Job Skills.** One study (Matthies 1983, 1984) designed a survey instrument specifically to ascertain which job skills the directors of intensive English programs (IEPs) in the United States thought they had or needed. By using the major findings of that study, an ESL administrator in an IEP or comparable program might conduct a self-evaluation in the same categories of skills to establish a profile of his or her own strengths.

This inventory of skills was designed and validated by experienced English language program administrators. Six general areas of desirable job skills had been identified from the literature on educational administration and ESL program development:

- Communicating
- Planning
- Educating
- Organizing
- Evaluating
- Negotiating

Each of those areas was then assigned several skill descriptors. These were further divided according to whether they represented behaviors associated with the role of manager or of educator, the two identities that most ESL directors share. The whole set was then randomly ordered in a questionnaire and sent to 335 IEP administrators, from whom 177 usable responses were received.

In brief, the respondents rated as "most important" those skills that could be associated more with the role of manager than with the role of educator, even though many English language program directors also teach and very few have had any formal training in management. In descending order, the following skills were rated most important for the administrator of an English language program:

1. Communicating effectively across cultures
2. Maintaining an environment conducive to learning
3. Developing a staff "team" (hiring, orienting, assigning, and so on)
4. Managing available time efficiently
5. Evaluating the program's needs
6. Effectively anticipating problems, changes, conflicts
7. Keeping adequate records
8. Maintaining enrollments; recruiting new students
9. Formulating long-range plans for the program
10. Managing crises (equipment failures, illnesses, and so on) effectively

However, when asked which of the 29 skills listed in the questionnaire were among their best, the respondents rated themselves highest on a somewhat different set:

1. Teaching courses within the ESL program
*2. Communicating effectively across cultures
3. Preparing program schedule
4. Explaining basic operating procedures
5. Overseeing testing and placement of students
*6. Managing crises effectively
*7. Evaluating the program's needs
8. Interpreting program policies to others
*9. Developing a staff "team"
*10. Keeping adequate records

Only the five starred items appeared in the other list of "most important" skills, so it would seem that the respondents' actual job skills did not match their ideals. In fact, most of their self-perceived "best" skills were related to the educator's role, not the manager's. Discovering such disparities might motivate the person who completes a self-evaluation to seek further training or to read on those topics where self-improvement is needed. After some time, a reassessment should be undertaken so that real professional growth can be documented.

**Effectiveness.** Of course, evaluating one's own perceived skills or administrative style does not necessarily provide a measure of one's effectiveness on the job. That can only be assessed by others and reported

FIGURE 2. THE PROGRAM DIRECTOR'S WORLD

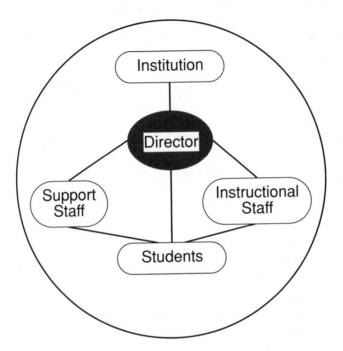

to the administrator in ways that vary greatly in terms of formality and validity, some of which will be discussed below. It is important for these to be elicited from representatives of every major constituency in the ESL director's "world" (see Figure 2).

One of the informal measures of effectiveness that the director can use is to look at the state of his or her desk top at the end of each week. If any crucial requests from teachers or students are left unresolved, if correspondence or phone calls are left unanswered, that can be taken as a sign of ineffectiveness during the week. It is advisable to try to catch up on Friday afternoon or Monday morning, then to take a few minutes to reflect on how some time could have been reallocated during the past week. That serves as a reminder to delegate some responsibilities and to prioritize responses to the many demands on administrative time. Another important source of evaluation of administrative effectiveness is the feedback received from staff members, supervisors, and—directly or indirectly—students. Much of this feedback is informal, picked up in conversations or verbal reports of classroom comments. Thus, it tends to reflect both the climate that pervades the entire program and the perceptions of the staff and students. Administrators cannot expect to be effective if they ignore these signals, whether positive or negative, which are indicative either of trends that should be encouraged or of potential problems that should be confronted before they grow out of proportion to their real seriousness. One extreme result of ignoring or discouraging informal feedback could be that the director becomes increasingly isolated from both students and staff, even to the extent of seeming to hide behind a closed office door or finding frequent excuses to be away from the office altogether and thus unapproachable. The person in this situation should seek advice or training in dealing more effectively with stress and in improving lines of communication within the program.

Of course, the size of the program will determine how many layers of bureaucratic insulation there are between the director and the teachers and students, and in a large organization somewhat more formal means of obtaining useful feedback may have to be devised. The regular staff meeting is not the best forum for seeking evaluative comments, but individual or small group conversations can be informative, as can a day-long staff retreat held in a location away from telephones and other distractions. There the director can set the tone by encouraging staff members to bring up questions of policy or curriculum for deliberation by the whole group, then suspending judgment or a decision until all aspects of the question under discussion have been explored. While specific comments on administrative effectiveness will rarely be made in such a setting, enough hints are usually given to indicate either that the director is considered to be on top of the situation or that there is a need for more decisive leadership in some areas.

To follow up on signals like these, the director should attempt to get some feedback in written form. An effective way to achieve a good return is to send out a response memo that requests some specific information or a straw vote by a certain stated deadline. At the bottom of the memo is a simple form to be filled in, torn off, and returned to the director's mailbox. Use of this technique allows the staff to share decision-making responsibility with the director as well as to communicate their reactions to, or suggestions about, policies that affect them.

A variation of the response memo is the more detailed checklist. (See Appendix A for an example.) Here the staff and/or students are provided with a number of very specific aspects of the director's performance to evaluate using a scale of responses ranging from very positive to very negative. If all respondents are instructed to return their completed checklists on the same designated day to a collection box, no one's list will be identifiable by how promptly or to whom it was returned. Either the director or someone neutral tallies the responses and reports them in summary form to the staff and to any supervisor who is evaluating administrative performance. This not only provides information on the director's strengths and shortcomings as an administrator but also gives the staff—including secretaries and other assistants—an opportunity to express their opinions anonymously with the assurance that they will be reported fairly.

While the immediate outcomes of such techniques as these are perhaps too ephemeral for a formal evaluation of administrative effectiveness, their cumulative effect can be to guide the director into formulating better strategies for communication and leadership. Thus, they can contribute subtly yet effectively to long-term professional development.

The conscientious administrator of an ESL program will also seek objective evaluation from students. A good way of eliciting their opinions is through open-ended questions. (See Appendix B for an example.) Even though their command of English may be weak, they can usually list by the end of the term those aspects of the program—including its staff—that are its strengths and its weaknesses. To ignore students' perceptions of the way the program is run is to disenfranchise them and to overlook perhaps the most valid judgments of all, surely a sign of either arrogance or insecurity about one's professional competence. Students, like others in the director's "world," may not have total appreciation of all the constraints operating on the program, but their view of things must be given due consideration (see Chapter One, this volume).

To complement these evaluations by others, as well as to put them in some perspective, the ESL director should ponder the characteristics and limitations of administering his or her particular type of ESL program in its unique setting. (See articles by Barrett and Daesch in Barrett 1982 for an outline of many of those variables.) The small private or university-affiliated English language program with few "frills" may be just as demanding of administrative skills as the large, multilevel program with numbers of core teachers, part-time instructors and/or graduate assistants, and support personnel. Each presents unique challenges to the director's creativity and tolerance of stress. If such factors are not acknowledged in the process of evaluation, the extent of congruence between the director's policies or behaviors and the program's needs or outcomes may well be misconstrued. The findings of a self-study or external evaluation can be truly useful only to the extent that the bases for judgment are trustworthy and realistic.

The outcome of any evaluation should help the administrator and the whole organization "work smarter" (Honda 1987). In order to move the developmental process along, then, the director needs to inform everyone up and down the line that evaluation has occurred (and will continue) and that there is a plan of action to follow up on the findings.

Because the TESOL organization advocates periodic self-study by all ESL programs, some good examples for reporting a program evaluation have appeared in the *TESOL Newsletter* (e.g., in "The Standard Bearer" section of the August 1988 issue, p. 7ff.), and sample reports can be obtained from the TESOL Central Office. A thorough program evaluation should be summarized and filed in the offices of the ESL program director, his or her supervisor, TESOL, and NAFSA. Besides making a written report, there are other steps to be taken after evaluating any program and/or its administration.

Planning to receive some training is one logical way to follow up an evaluation that has pointed out skills that need strengthening. On a university campus or at a nearby community college, one can usually find professional development workshops and short courses that deliver a great deal of useful information at a very low cost. Some last only half a day; others may meet one evening a week for a semester, covering such topics as how to conduct effective meetings, manage time, maintain an adequate budget, deal with interpersonal conflicts, and so on. Because most ESL program directors have been trained as academics and not as business managers, they may find courses in accounting, personnel management, and computer use to be especially useful. The program's budget might contain a small fund to support this kind of professional development.

Ochsner (1980) reported that 81 percent of the graduates of an M.A. program in TESL (Teaching English as a Second Language) felt that they "knew little or nothing" about administrative work, and 25 percent thought the subject should be added to the M.A. program. Since the time that article was written, several universities have added coursework in ESL program administration (e.g., American University, Florida State University, University of Hawaii at Manoa, and the University of Southern California). Additional training of a sort is offered during national and regional conferences of NAFSA and TESOL in the form of workshops, panel presentations, and formal papers on topics related to ESL administration. Both organizations also have publications and interest sections with ESL administration as a focus.

A different outcome of the evaluation process might be to call in a consultant to give a fresh perspective on the ESL administrator's situaation. This could be someone from the larger institution within which the program might be housed, such as a psychologist or foreign student adviser with expertise in cross-cultural communication, or an outside expert on marketing, ethical recruitment of foreign students, or curriculum design.

For many years NAFSA's Field Service has provided trained consultants on a cost-sharing basis to educational institutions of all sizes that enroll, or are planning to attract, foreign students. These consultants are either generalists in all aspects of international educational exchange or specialists in ESL, admissions, advising, and so on. A typical ESL consultation begins with the consultant reviewing all available documentation relevant to the development and current state of the ESL program and its administrative structure. The on-site visit may last two or three days, during which time the consultant meets individually and collectively with people at all levels of the program and (where relevant) the larger institution in which it is housed, gathering information and impressions about its mission and operation. These meetings tend to give visibility to the ESL program's serious purpose and to build a support group for implementing and monitoring subsequent developmental changes. The visit is followed by a lengthy written report to all concerned in which the consultant outlines the structure and needs of the ESL program, then specifies one or more courses of action that should lead to its improvement according to nationally promulgated guidelines. (For more discussion of the NAFSA Field Service Consultation service, see Chapter Two, this volume.)

Another aspect of professional development that NAFSA's Field Service supports is in-service training. This NAFSA initiative enables the administrator to observe the operation of similar programs elsewhere in the geographic region for a few days. Such firsthand experiences can be very enlightening in terms of alternative structures, physical facilities, policies, record-keeping practices, and so on. Back at the home institution, the director can decide which of the observed practices and policies might be adapted to the local situation. The support group mentioned above can also be involved in this decision-making process and in future evaluations of its implementation.

### Conclusion

The ESL program director can and should continue to grow in practical expertise as well as theoretical competence throughout his or her career. By taking time to ask oneself and others, "How'm I doin'?" one can discover both strengths to build on and shortcomings to work on. Colleagues and professional organizations stand ready to lend support if asked, because they too will benefit from participating in the process. Evaluation need not be dreaded; it should be a natural part of personal and program development.

# Notes

1. For a discussion of the LDBQ, see Charters (1964).
2. See Myers-Briggs (1980).

# References

Barrett, R. P. 1982. Introduction. In Barrett, R. P., ed., *The administration of intensive English language programs*, 1–5. Washington, D.C.: National Association for Foreign Student Affairs.

Charters, W. W., Jr. 1964. *Teacher perceptions of administrator behavior.* Cooperative Research Project, no. 929. U.S. Office of Education, 176–189. St. Louis, MO, January.

Daesch, R. L. 1982. The general administration of the IEP. In Barrett, R. P., ed., *The administration of intensive English language programs*, 7–9. Washington, D.C.: National Association for Foreign Student Affairs.

Honda, G. 1987. ESL administration: Working smarter NOT harder. Workshop presented at the Annual Conference of the National Association for Foreign Student Affairs, Long Beach, May–June.

Matthies, B. F. 1983. *A study of the characteristics, qualifications, and perceived roles of the directors of intensive ESL programs.* Ph.D. diss. University of Illinois, Urbana.

_____. 1984. The intensive English program director'sjob skills. *The American Language Journal* 2(1):5–16.

Myers-Briggs, I. 1980. *Gifts differing.* Palo Alto, CA: onsulting Psychologist Press.

National Association for Foreign Student Affairs Task Force on Standards and Responsibilities. 1981, 1983. *NAFSA principles for international educational exchange.* Washington, D.C.: NAFSA.

Ochsner, R. 1980. Job-related aspects of the M.A. in TESOL degree. *TESOL Quarterly* 14(2):199–207.

Reasor, A. W. 1981. *Administrative styles of English-as-a-second-language administrators.* Ph.D. diss. The American University, Washington, D.C.

Saltzer, M. G. 1982. The evaluation of an intensive English program. In Barrett, R. P., ed., *The administration of intensive English language programs*, 89–97. Washington, D.C.: National Association for Foreign Student Affairs.

Teachers of English to Speakers of Other Languages Committee on Professional Standards. 1984. *TESOL's statement of standards for language and professional preparation programs with checklists for self-evaluation.* Washington, D.C.: TESOL.

# Appendix A

Checklist for Evaluating the ESL Program Director (p. 1)

TO:      All Staff

FROM:    The Director

Now that mid-semester evaluations are behind you once again, I'd like you to turn your attention to my position. It's good to get feedback periodically in a form that pinpoints strengths and weaknesses in my job performance so that I can try to improve and so that I can have something on file for my supervisors to see.
Attached is a checklist that shouldn't take long to fill out. To maintain your confidentiality, here are the rules:

1. Everybody should **turn the forms in on the same day,** [insert date], so that customary early birds and procrastinators will not be identifiable.
2. All comments should be **typewritten.**
3. The only identification requested is whether your status is "permanent" within the program or a one-semester appointment.
4. The results will be tabulated (probably by me and/or my research assistant) and reported in summary form. This summary will be available to you if you want to see it, and I will submit it if requested during a future review by my supervisors.

Thanks for your honest responses!

# Checklist for Evaluating the ESL Program Director (p. 2)

[Date]

Evaluation of English Program Director
[Insert Name of Director here]

This form has been completed by: ☐ a member of the "permanent"
Program staff
☐ a one-semester appointee

An X or ✓ under one of these letters indicates your response:

U=Unsatisfactory
N=Needs improvement
S=Satisfactory
E=Excellent

Add comments at the end to clarify any response, as desired.

## GENERAL IMPRESSIONS

|  | U | N | S | E |
|---|---|---|---|---|
| 1. overall effectiveness as an administrator |  |  |  |  |
|    a. of staff | — | — | — | — |
|    b. of students | — | — | — | — |
|    c. of curriculum/program | — | — | — | — |
| 2. overall ability to demonstrate leadership | — | — | — | — |
| 3. knowledge of the TESL field | — | — | — | — |
| 4. general level of attention to the Program's needs | — | — | — | — |
| 5. overall ability to make sound judgements | — | — | — | — |

## SPECIFIC SKILLS

| Communication | U | N | S | E |
|---|---|---|---|---|
| 6. level of informative communication (as far as you know) |  |  |  |  |
|    a. to the Program's staff | — | — | — | — |
|    b. to the Program's students | — | — | — | — |
|    c. to relevant persons outside of the Program | — | — | — | — |
| 7. effectiveness/impact of written communications | — | — | — | — |
| 8. effectiveness/impact of spoken communications | — | — | — | — |
| 9. availability when you need to communicate with her | — | — | — | — |

# Checklist for Evaluating the ESL Program Director (p. 3)

| Decisiveness | U | N | S | E |
|---|---|---|---|---|
| 10. ability to reach a well-reasoned action | — | — | — | — |
| 11. consideration of/respect for other points of view | — | — | — | — |
| 12. ability to act upon a decision effectively | — | — | — | — |
| 13. ability to adapt existing policies to changing circumstances | — | — | — | — |
| 14. consistency in setting/implementing policies | — | — | — | — |

| Staffing | U | N | S | E |
|---|---|---|---|---|
| 15. process of hiring teachers for the Program (within the institution's constraints) | — | — | — | — |
| 16. supervision/guidance of staff members' work | — | — | — | — |
| 17. support of the staff's professional development | — | — | — | — |
| 18. ability to balance individuals' preferences and strengths in planning schedules | — | — | — | — |

| Management | U | N | S | E |
|---|---|---|---|---|
| 19. ability to provide a satisfactory workplace | — | — | — | — |
| 20. efforts to improve working conditions | — | — | — | — |
| 21. use of funds for reasonable expenses | — | — | — | — |
| 22. ability to distribute tasks fairly | — | — | — | — |
| 23. ability to devote sufficient time to the program's operations | — | — | — | — |
| 24. ability to plan ahead effectively | — | — | — | — |
| 25. effectiveness in running meetings | — | — | — | — |

| Interpersonal skills | U | N | S | E |
|---|---|---|---|---|
| 26. general attitude toward: | | | | |
| a. you personally | — | — | — | — |
| b. other staff members | — | — | — | — |
| c. the Program's students | — | — | — | — |
| d. positions in relation to others | — | — | — | — |
| 27. crosscultural effectiveness (avoidance of stereotypes, communicating) | — | — | — | — |

(Attach paper for comments on the above or other relevant points.)

# Appendix B

## Evaluation Form for Students

Please give us your opinion of the program this semester. You may want to mention the teachers, the directors, the textbooks, the weekend activities, or other important things. We will use your ideas when we plan for the next semester.


Your grammar class at this time is at the — <u>Beginning Level</u>


— <u>Intermediate Level</u>


— <u>Advanced Level</u>


In my opinion, these are the **strengths** of the program:


In my opinion, these things **should be improved** in the program:


THANK YOU VERY MUCH FOR YOUR OPINIONS!

# Contributors

JAMES D. BROWN holds a Ph.D. in applied linguistics from the University of California at Los Angeles. He is associate professor of English as a second language and director of the English Language Institute at the University of Hawaii at Manoa.

PATRICIA BYRD holds a Ph.D. in English from the University of Florida. She is associate professor and chair of the Department of Applied Linguistics and ESL at Georgia State University. Within NAFSA, she has served as chair of the ATESL section and member of the board of directors and of the nominations and elections committee. She is currently a Field Service consultant and the ATESL representative to the Field Service Steering Committee.

JANET CONSTANTINIDES holds an M.A. in English from the University of Oklahoma. She is associate professor and assistant chair in the Department of English at the University of Wyoming. Within NAFSA, she has served as a regional chair, a member of the national ATESL team, chair of the Field Service Steering Committee, a member of the board of directors, and a Field Service consultant.

DAVID E. ESKEY holds a Ph.D. in English from the University of Pittsburgh. He is associate professor of education and former director of the American Language Institute at the University of Southern California. He has served as chair of the ATESL section of NAFSA and is currently a Field Service consultant.

ROBERT P. FOX holds a Ph.D. in linguistics from the University of Illinois at Urbana-Champaign. He is professor of linguistics at The American University. He has twice served as chair of the ATESL section of NAFSA and has been a member of the NAFSA Board of Directors and a number of NAFSA committees.

FREDERICK JENKS holds a Ph.D. in education from Wayne State University. He is professor and program coordinator of Multilingual/Multicultural Education at Florida State University and has served NAFSA as a member of the national ATESL team.

CHERYL A. KRAFT holds an M.A. in teaching English as a second language from the University of Illinois. She is a full-time instructor and a level supervisor in the American Language Institute at the University of Southern California.

RICHARD LACY is a Ph.D. candidate in linguistics at the University of California at San Diego. He is director for International Students and coordinator of Computing Facilities in the Freshman Writing Program at the University of Southern California.

BARBARA F. MATTHIES holds a Ph.D. in education from the University of Illinois. She is associate professor of English at Iowa State University, where she also serves as director of the Intensive English and Orientation Program. Within NAFSA, she has been a regional chair, a member of the national ATESL team, and a Field Service consultant.

GEOFFREY C. MIDDLEBROOK holds an M.A. in English as a second language from the University of Hawaii at Manoa and is pursuing a doctoral degree in American studies at that university, where he is employed in the Office of International Programs and Services.

MARTHA C. PENNINGTON holds a Ph.D. in linguistics from the University of Pennsylvania. She is now reader in English at the City Polytechnic of Hong Kong. She was formerly assistant professor of English as a second language and director of the English for International Managers program in the College of Business at the University of Hawaii at Manoa. She has served within NAFSA as chair of the ATESL section and of the ATESL Nominations and Elections.

ROGER PONDER holds a Ph.D. in multilingual/multicultural education from Florida State University, where he is assistant in English in the Department of English.

BILL POWELL holds a Ph.D. in multilingual/multicultural education from Florida State University, where he is assistant director of the Center for Intensive English Studies and visiting assistant professor in the Department of Curriculum and Instruction.

258

Louis J. Spaventa holds a Ph.D. in education policy studies from The Pennsylvania State University, an M.A. in linguistics from The State University of New York at Buffalo, and an M.A.T. in English as a second language from the School for International Training. He is assistant professor in the Department of Education at Guilford College.

Janis S. Williamson holds a Ph.D. in linguistics from the University of California at San Diego. She is academic supervisor of the English Language Program at the University of California Extension at Santa Barbara.

Christine Winskowski-Jackson holds a Ph.D. in psychology and an M.A. in English as a second language from the University of Hawaii at Manoa. She is assistant professor of English at Hawaii Loa College.

Aileen L. Young holds an M.A. in English as a second language from the University of Hawaii at Manoa. Formerly a teacher in the Hawaii public school system and at Hawaiian Mission Academy, she is now retired.